BULLETIN
of the
Virginia State Library
(Issued quarterly)

| Vol. 9. | JANUARY, APRIL, JULY, 1916. | Nos. 1, 2 and 3. |

Virginia Counties:
Those Resulting from Virginia Legislation.

By MORGAN POITIAUX ROBINSON
Archivist.

JANAWAY PUBLISHING, INC.

Notice

In many older books, foxing (or discoloration) occurs and, in some instances, print lightens with wear and age. Reprinted books, such as this, often duplicate these flaws, notwithstanding efforts to reduce or eliminate them. The pages of this reprint have been digitally enhanced and, where possible, the flaws eliminated in order to provide clarity of content and a pleasant reading experience.

Originally published as:

Bulletin of the Virginia State Library
Vol. 9, January, April, July, 1916, Nos. 1, 2 and 3.

Reprinted:

Janaway Publishing, Inc.
732 Kelsey Ct.
Santa Maria, California 93454
(805) 925-1038
www.JanawayGenealogy.com

2013

ISBN: 978-1-59641-296-5

Made in the United States of America

State Library Board of Virginia

Armistead C. Gordon, Chairman............................*Staunton, Va.*
R. T. W. Duke, Jr...*Charlottesville, Va.*
Egbert G. Leigh, Jr. ....*Richmond, Va.*
Edmund Pendleton ....*Richmond, Va.*
Lyon G. Tyler ....*Williamsburg, Va.*

H. R. McILWAINE, Librarian,
Ex officio Secretary of the Board.

State Library Staff

H. R. McIlwaine ....*Librarian*
Earl G. Swem ....*Assistant Librarian*
J. R. C. Brown ....*Head of Traveling Library Department*
Morgan P. Robinson ....*Archivist*
Miss Coralie H. Johnston ....*Reference Librarian*
Miss Elise T. Clark ....*In Charge of Periodicals*
F. H. Moore ....*Cataloguer*
Miss Ethel I. Nolin.....................................*Assistant Cataloguer*
Miss Rose Goode ....*Stenographer*
Miss Virginia Jones ....*Copyist*

John D. Snyder ....*Janitor*
S. T. Taylor ....*Assistant Janitor*

CONTENTS

Frontispiece (map).
Preface, ... 5
      General section, ... 6
      Alphabetical section, ... 14
      Chronological section, ... 14
      Geographical section, ... 15
      "Genealogical" section, ... 16
      Origin of County Names section, ... 18
      Texts of Acts of Assembly section, ... 18
      Bibliographical section, ... 19
      Acknowledgments, ... 20
Introductory, ... 23
Part I, Alphabetical Arrangement, ... 41
Part II, Chronological Arrangement, ... 89
Part III, Geographical Arrangement (with maps), ... 123
Part IV, "Genealogical" Arrangement (with charts and index), ... 161
Part V, Origin of County Names, ... 173
Part VI, Texts of Acts of Assembly (concerning counties) not in Hening, 197
Part VII, Bibliography, ... 209
General Index, ... 277

BULLETIN
of the
Virginia State Library
(Issued quarterly.)

No. 9.   JANUARY, APRIL, JULY, 1916.   Nos. 1, 2 and 3.

Virginia Counties:
Those Resulting from Virginia Legislation

By MORGAN P. ROBINSON

PREFACE

The compiler of this BULLETIN will be glad to have his attention called to such errors and omissions as almost necessarily occur in a compilation of this character,—and the more especially to any sources which may have escaped him,—while the student is warned that this does not claim to be an absolutely final list of the Virginia Counties, but only such as the compiler has been able to identify.

Although these pages will doubtless be of convenience to title examiners, as well as to genealogists and to students of Virginia history, there are several items of particular historical value to which attention should be called,—in the order in which they occur:

FIRST: an attempt has been made to print in full the proceedings of the first court of each of the counties, the exact date of the actual origin of which is unavailable, as in the cases of Lancaster and Stafford (see also the captions of the first courts of Accomack and Middlesex)—these proceedings giving the earliest positive dates for these counties which we have been able to ascertain,—while a copy of the proceedings of the first court of Brunswick is quoted in full, not only because the original has been destroyed, but also because it shows that the county was not organized until 1732,—nearly twelve years after the passage of the act authorizing its formation.

SECOND: there appear under several counties statements of efforts made to save their records from fire, accident, and the public enemy,—an especially interesting one narrating the part played by a masonic flag in saving the records of Brunswick, during the War between the States.

THIRD: there is a set of unpublished maps, which has been inserted in Part III, the Geographical Arrangement, which maps,—prepared under the direction of Dr. Lyon G. Tyler, of Williamsburg, Va., and delineated in the United States Geological Survey,—were a part of the Library's exhibit at the Jamestown Exposition in 1907, and now hang in the Library.

FOURTH: Part VI contains the full texts of two Acts of Assembly (concerning counties), of 1639 and 1643-1646, respectively, and of nine Acts of Assembly (forming counties), none of which appears in Hening,—five of them not even being mentioned in Hening by title. Copies of the original manuscripts of the last nine texts were recently secured by the Library from the Public Record Office in London, for use in this connection.

This Preface, in addition to the foregoing, is composed of a "general" section and of seven sub-sections, which might be called "departmental" sections for want of a better term,—these "departmental" sections dealing individually with the seven parts of the text, while the "general" section deals with those phases which concern the BULLETIN as a whole; and since this compilation has been prepared for ready reference and for convenience, it has been thought better to re-print at the beginning of each Part the section of the Preface which deals with that portion of the text individually, appending thereto a list of the abbreviations which appear in that particular Part.

GENERAL

From February 7 to December 31, 1914, the undersigned (before assuming the duties of Archivist of the Virginia State Library) was stationed at this Library in the capacity of "Historian for the War and Navy Departments", under authority of an Act of Congress of March 2, 1913, "authorizing the Collection of the Military and Naval Records of the Revolutionary War, with a view to Publication" (United States Statutes at Large, vol. 37, pt. 1, 728); and during that tenure he made to the Director of Publication of Revolutionary War Records, Washington, D. C., a report upon the "Development of Virginia Counties",—of which the alphabetical portion of this text is substantially a copy.

One of the most constant sources of annoyance to title examiners and to workers in genealogy and in Virginia history is the absence of some handy reference volume which gives in concise form reliable data concerning the dates of formation, the territory from which formed, and the origin of the names, of the counties which have resulted from Virginia legislation,—with references to the sources upon which these data are based.

With this phase of the situation in mind, application was made for permission to print the material of the above-mentioned report as a number of the BULLETIN of the Virginia State Library; and it is to the courtesy of Captain Hollis C. Clark, Director of Publication of Revolutionary Military Records, No. 259½ War Department Building, Washington, D. C., that the Virginia State Library owes this privilege.

Permission having been obtained in May, 1915, it appeared desirable to re-arrange the same data in chronological form, in geographical form (in which part of the work are inserted eleven unpublished maps), and in what is called "genealogical" form (with an index),—to which are appended an alphabetical list of the counties, giving the source of the name of each one, and the full text of eleven Acts of Assembly (concerning counties) which do not appear in Hening. There is also a bibliography and, of course, a general index.

It is of more than ordinary interest to cite the fact that while there are at present only one hundred counties in the State of Virginia, yet at least one hundred and seventy-two counties have resulted from Virginia legislation. Naturally one asks, "What has become of the other seventy-two?" This question is answered in the following table.

Of the one hundred and seventy-two counties here listed as resulting from Virginia legislation, the following are the ones which are at present extinct,* and which are in Kentucky, and are in West Virginia,—the remaining one hundred being still in Virginia:

---

* A county is classified as "extinct", when it ceases to exist, either by a change of name or by a division of its area into new counties of different names.

EXTINCT,—†
Accawmack,
  (1634-1642/3);
Charles River,
  (1634-1642/3);
Dunmore,
  (1772-1778);
Fincastle,
  (1772-1777);
Illinois,
  (1778-1784);
Kentucky,
  (1777-1780);
Lower Norfolk,
  (1637-1691);
New Norfolk,
  (1636-1637);
Rappahannock,
  (1656-1692);
Upper Norfolk,
  (1637-1642);
Warrosquyoake,
  (1634-1637);
Warwick River,
  (1634-1642/3);
Yohogania,
  (1776-1786),——13.

KENTUCKY,—‡
Bourbon,
Fayette,
Jefferson,
Lincoln,
Madison,
Mason,
Mercer,
Nelson,
Woodford,——9.

WEST VIRGINIA,—||
Barbour,
Berkeley,
Boone,
Braxton,
Brooke,
Cabell,
Calhoun,
Clay,
Doddridge,
Fayette,
Gilmer,
Greenbrier,
Hampshire,
Hancock,
Hardy,
Harrison,
Jackson,
Jefferson,
Kanawha,
Lewis,
Logan,
McDowell,
Marion,
Marshall,
Mason,
Mercer,
Monongalia,
Monroe,
Morgan,
Nicholas,
Ohio,
Pendleton,
Pleasants,
Pocahontas,
Preston,
Putnam,
Raleigh,
Randolph,
Ritchie,
Roane,
Taylor.
Tucker,
Tyler,
Upshur,
Webster,
Wetzel,
Wirt,
Wood,
Woodford,——50.

† Each marked with a superior "E": ᵉ.
‡ Each marked with a superior "K": ᵏ.
|| Each marked with a superior "W": ʷ.

Counties listed in this BULLETIN as resulting from Virginia legislation...172
Counties here listed as resulting from Virginia legislation, but now extinct:
  Extinct (area now in Virginia),..........................10
  Extinct (area now "on western side of the Ohio river [Illinois]") 1
  Extinct (area now in State of Kentucky (Kentucky))........ 1
  Extinct (area now in western Pennsylvania (Yohogania)).... 1—13
Counties here listed as resulting from Virginia legislation, but now in Kentucky 9
Counties here listed as resulting from Virginia legislation, but now in West Virginia...50— 72

Counties in Virginia, Census of 1910............................... 100

    Each of the extinct counties shows the limiting dates of its existence in the parentheses immediately under the name, while these limiting dates are explained in the notes given under the Alphabetical Arrangement, Part I.

    No account is taken of the "County of Denbigh" (Denby), the only mention of which we have observed being in Hening i, 148, 179, 203, and in the "Virginia Magazine of History and Biography", ii, 68-9; iii, 177, 279; iv, 81, 83, 202; and xx, 34,—in which former its burgesses are noted, though at that time it was but a plantation: or of "James County" ("Journals of the House of Burgesses" (Virginia State Library) 1659/60—1693, 32), which is obviously a transcriber's error for "James City County".

    "Chickacoan" ("Chickawane", "Chickcoun": H. i, 337, 352) is covered by Northumberland; while "West Augusta District" and "Kentucky District" find their places in the notes under Augusta and Kentucky Counties, respectively.

    In the selection of a proper caption for the date-columns, there were available the words, "create", "erect", "establish" and "form". An historical study of the use of these words in the titles and the texts of the Acts of Assembly providing for new counties, and in the editors' marginal notes referring to these texts, shows that their usage was substantially as follows:

	Acts forming Counties.	Word in title of Act.	Word in text of Act.	Word in marginal note.
Hening i............	23	23 no title.	23 no text.	23 no note.
ii............	3	3 no title.	3 no text.	3 no note.
iii............	7	7 "dividing".*	7 "called".	7 "formed".
iv............	9	5 "dividing".	4 "called".	7 "formed".
		4 "erecting".	4 "become";	1 "established";
			2 "erected";	1 no note.
			1 "made".	
v............	6	4 "dividing";	4 "erected".	4 "formed";
		2 "erecting".	1 "shall be";†	2 no note.
			1 "made".	
Not in Hening; see Part				
v............	4	4 "dividing".	3 "shall be";	4 no note.
			1 "erected".	
vi............	6	6 "dividing".	5 "shall be";	6 "formed".
			1 "be".	
vii............	4	4 "dividing";	4 "shall be called".	4 "formed";
viii............	7	7 "dividing".	6 "shall be";	7 "formed".
			1 "shall be established".	
ix............	14	9 "dividing";	13 "shall be";	13 "formed";
		4 "forming";	1 "shall be established".	1 "established".
		1 "establishing".		
x............	5	3 "establishing";	3 "shall be";	5 "formed".
		2 "dividing".	2 "called".	
xi............	2	2 "dividing".	2 "called".	2 "formed".
xii............	12	10 "dividing";	8 "shall be";	12 "formed".
		2 "forming".	3 "shall form";‡	
			1 "called".	
xiii............	7	6 "dividing";	5 "shall form";	7 "formed".
		4 "forming";	2 "shall be".	
		1 "forming".		
Shepherd ii............	5	4 "dividing";	5 "shall form".	2 no note;
		1 "forming".		2 "name of new county";
				1 "formed".
iii............	3	2 "dividing";	2 "shall form";	2 "established";
		1 "forming".	1 "called".	1 "called".

	Acts forming Counties.	Word in title of Act.	Word in text of Act.	Word in marginal note.
Acts of Assembly, 1808-9 to 1829-0......	10	5 "forming"; 4 "dividing"; 1 "establishing".	10 "shall form".	5 "formed"; 3 "named"; 1 "called"; 1 "denominated".
1830-1 to 1836-7......	11	10 "forming"; 1 "creating".	11 "shall form".	11 "create".
1838 to 1845-6......	13	12 "establishing"; 1 "forming".	13 "shall form".	13 "create".
1846-7 to 1855-6......	15	8 "establishing"; 5 "forming"; 1 "erecting"; 1 "extend jurisdiction".	12 "shall form"; 1 "established"; 1 "constitute"; 1 "called".	10 "create"; 4 "boundaries of"; 1 "formed".
1857-8 to 1879-0......	6	4 "forming"; 2 "establishing".	2 "shall form"; 4 "established".	6 "boundaries of".
	172	172	172	172

* "dividing" [the parent county].
† "shall be" [one distinct county].
‡ "shall form" [one distinct county].

A re-capitulation, omitting the twenty-six counties in Hening i and ii, shows the following situation:

	Acts forming Counties.	Word in title of Act.	Word in text of Act.	Word in marginal note.
Hening iii to Acts of Assembly, 1857-8 to 1879-0......	146	76 "dividing"; 34 "forming"; 27 "establishing"; 7 "erecting"; 1 "creating"; 1 "extend jurisdiction".	63 "shall form"; 41 "shall be"; 18 "called"; 7 "erected"; 5 "established"; 4 "shall be called"; 2 "become"; 2 "made"; 2 "shall be established"; 1 "be"; 1 "constitute".	81 "formed"; 34 "created"; 10 "boundaries of"; 9 no note; 4 "established"; 3 "named"; 2 "called"; 2 "name of new county"; 1 "denominated".
	146	146	146	146

Disregarding the seventy-six instances of the use of the word "dividing" in the title of the Acts, since the word refers only to the parent-county (as the "Act for dividing the County of Goochland" (H. v, 266), resulted in the formation of Albemarle County, although the name of the child-county does not appear in the title of the Act), we find that the word "forming" first appeared in 1778 (H. ix, 420) and appears with approximate uniformity until the early part of 1860 (A (1859-0), 151).

In the texts of the Acts, it seems that the phrase "shall form" [one distinct county] is in a large majority, while the next closest competitor is almost a synonym,—"shall be" [one distinct county].

In the marginal notes, it appears that Hening and Shepherd almost uniformly used the word "form", while the editors of the following Acts of Assembly were even more uniform in the use of the word "create", which first appeared in 1831 (A (1830-1), 134),—though it seems to have disappeared after 1856.

These facts, in addition to the further fact that it seems to be less technical than the other words,—although one of the others seems to be etymologically more in harmony with the English Common and Statute Law,—have resulted in the choice of the word "form" as the caption for the date-columns.

In all the arrangements, the date of the origin of the county, as given in black-faced type, is the year when the county came into actual existence,—when it became a place of record,—reference to the text of the Act giving the month and the day. The date of the final passage of the Act forming the county follows each of these dates in parentheses, the letter "J"* in these parentheses referring to the "Journal of the House" (Burgesses, or Delegates, as the case may be) of the date indicated: nor does this close discrimination seem unwarranted, when one recalls the fact that forty-seven† of the counties came into actual existence during the year following the passage of the Acts authorizing the formation of these counties, while Augusta

---

* This "J", from 1619 to 1775, refers to the "Journals of the House of Burgesses", published by the Virginia State Library, 1905-1915; from 1776 to 1790, to the 1828 re-prints of the Journals of those sessions, and from 1791 to 1879-80, to the Journals as printed after the close of each session of the General Assembly.

†Amelia,
Bath,
Bedford,
Botetourt,
Bourbon,
Brooke,
Campbell,
Caroline,
Charlotte,
Culpeper,
Cumberland,
Franklin,
Goochland,
Grayson,
Greensville,
Hampshire,
Hanover,
Hardy,
Henry,
Kanawha,
Kentucky,
King George,
King William,
Lee,
Madison (1786),
Madison (1793),
Mason (1789),
Mathews,
Mecklenburg,
Mercer (1786),
Montgomery,
Nelson (1875),
Nelson (1808),
Nottoway,
Patrick,
Pendleton,
Pittsylvania,
Prince Edward,
Prince George,
Prince William,
Randolph,
Spotsylvania,
Sussex,
Tazewell,
Washington,
Woodford,
Wythe.

and Frederick, authorized in 1738, were not organized until 1745 and 1743 respectively; and Brunswick, although authorized in 1720, was not finally organized until 1732,—nearly twelve years later.

Thus, following the precedents of Hening (from p. 412 of vol. xii), Shepherd and the Acts of Assembly, the date of the signing of the bill has been disregarded as perfunctory and formal routine: and so it is that the investigator has the year from which he can expect to find records at any county seat,—fire, accident and the public enemy excepted,—while those tracing the course of legislation are afforded a starting-point.

Each county is set forth as formed from some named area, while the authority on which the statement is based is to be found in the column to the extreme right; and, if any more territory has been added to the county, the addition is noted and the source of information given. If references intervene, or have no statements for which they seem to stand sponsor, it shows that some portion of that county has been cut off and added to another county, under which other county will be found a statement as to the item added, with the same authority cited; or the reference may be to an Act which defines, establishes, adjusts, confirms, marks, or otherwise involves the boundaries, and therefore the tertorial area of the county under consideration,—in which latter case, the same reference, of course, appears under all the counties affected by this Act relating to the boundaries. All references under each county are in chronological order.

Thus, Albemarle is formed from Goochland (H. v, 266); then comes the reference, H. vi, 441, which takes "parts of Albemarle and Lunenburg" and adds them to Bedford, and this same reference, of course, appears under Lunenburg in its proper chronological order while Bedford shows the additions and the reference; next we see that a "part of Louisa" is added to Albemarle by H. vii, 419, with the same reference appearing in its proper sequence under Louisa, from which the area was taken.

In this way there are under each county references to every piece of legislation which we have been able to locate, which in any wise involves the territorial area of that county, with the result that the references under each county are as near as may be a complete compendium of references to the legislation upon which that county bases its claim to its present metes and bounds.

All dates are those of the English calendar of the date cited, unless otherwise stated; and an attempt has been made to preserve the then current orthography, but no effort has been made to set forth the promoting causes which resulted in the formation of the various counties, for the reason that the necessary data are not at present available.

Where a county has been initially formed from parts of several different counties, the order in which the names of the parent-counties are mentioned in the title of the Act has been most scrupulously preserved throughout the BULLETIN, for the reasons set forth in the "Genealogical" portion of this Preface.

The notes are serial throughout the whole of the BULLETIN, (except in several cases, where an asterisk seems to simplify matters), but are assembled in full-text form at the end of Part I, the Alphabetical Arrangement; while under each recurring appearance of the same county a note refers back to the full-text note under the Alphabetical Arrangement. Thus there is but one presentation of the text of the notes, some of which are quite lengthy and cumbersome, as is the case with those under Accomack, Brunswick, Augusta and Kentucky. And we count ourselves particularly lucky in that we have secured for these notes reliable statements setting forth the efforts which have been made,—especially during the War between the States,—to save the records of Albemarle, Brunswick, Elizabeth City, Hanover, Henrico, Louisa and Middlesex; but have been no little disappointed that we were unable to secure similar data concerning such efforts as may have been made in other counties.

ALPHABETICAL

The Alphabetical Arrangement needs no comment other than the statement that in the several instances in which there are two counties of the same name (Accomack, Fayette, Jefferson, Madison, Mason, Mercer, Nelson and Rappahannock) the arrangement is chronological under each of these pairs of names. Of course, no two counties of the same name existed in Virginia at the same time, as will be seen below:

> Accawmack of 1634 having been changed to Northampton in 1642/3, Accomack of the present day was formed in 1663.
> Rappahannock of 1656 having become extinct in 1692, when its territory was formed into Essex and Richmond, Rappahannock of the present day was formed in 1833.
> Fayette of 1780, Jefferson of 1780, Nelson of 1785, Madison of 1786, Mercer of 1786, and Mason of 1789, all passed into the new State, when Kentucky was admitted to the Union in 1792.
> Virginia, ever-mindful of her ideals, again formed Madison of 1793, Jefferson of 1801, Mason of 1804, Nelson of 1808, Fayette of 1831, and Mercer of 1837; but the formation of West Virginia in 1863 carried all of these out of the jurisdiction of Virginia, except Madison and Nelson,—and thus it happens that, after twice honoring Jefferson, La Fayette, Mason and Mercer in this manner, the Old Dominion has at the present time no county of one of these names within her borders.

CHRONOLOGICAL

In the Chronological Arrangement, the date of the operation of the Act of Assembly has, of course, been the guide, but when several Acts became operative in the same year, the dates of the final passage of these Acts decide the chronology; while resort has been had to alphabetizing the names where two or more counties came into actual existence in the same year as the result of Acts finally passed on the same date. Striking illustrations of this appear under the years 1777, 1778 and 1786. Kentucky, Montgomery and Washington came into actual existence in 1777 as the result of an Act passed Dec. 7, 1776. Hence these counties appear under this date in the order named. Fluvanna and Powhatan came into actual existence in 1777 as the result of two acts finally passed on June 3, 1777, and therefore appear in alphabetical order under the latter date. Henry, however, is the first of those listed under 1777, because it came into actual existence that year, and the Act forming it was passed earlier than the other three.

GEOGRAPHICAL

As the rivers, streams, mountain barriers and natural defences influenced the routes of migration into the wilderness more than anything else, it seems appropriate to base the geographical treatment of the counties upon the grand geological divisions of the State,—the counties in each of these geological divisions being arranged chronologically in accordance with the plan used in Part II,—as the best manner in which to show the gradual development of population in each of these sections, and how the ever-restless settler pushed on into the wilderness, as each section of the colony was securely peopled.

Disregarding the popular interpretation of "Southside" and "Southwest" and following the geological divisions of the State in a general, though not in a technical, sense, the counties fall into the following groups:

(For map illustrating these geological divisions, see frontispiece.)

Tidewater (Coastal Plain), extending from the ocean to the fall-line, containing counties to the number of.................. 39
Piedmont, extending from the fall-line to the crest of the Blue Ridge Mountains, containing counties to the number of...... 41
Valley, extending from the crest of the Blue Ridge to the crest of the Alleghanies, containing counties to the number of...... 17
Trans-Alleghany, extending from the crest of the Alleghanies, westward to the limits of Virginia jurisdiction, containing counties to the number of 75

Counties here listed................................ 172

The popular interpretations having been disregarded, it will doubtless not seem so odd to have Hanover and Henrico classified as Tidewater Counties, and to find that Chesterfield, Grayson, Floyd and Carroll have been assigned to the Piedmont section. We believe that an examination of the geology of the State will justify this rather unusual classification. One should not omit to note that the "Southside" has fallen mostly in the geological Piedmont Plateau, while the "Southwest" is given its natural geological position as a portion of the Valley and Trans-Alleghany areas.

The maps (# 1 to 9) show the settlement of the Coastal Plain up to 1702; and # 10 shows the drift of population on through the Piedmont Plateau to the Blue Ridge Mountains up to 1729, except that Brunswick and Caroline are not indicated; while # 11 completes the occupation of the present limits of Virginia by county formations up to 1775, except that the following are not indicated: Amherst, Bedford, Botetourt, Buckingham, Charlotte, Dinwiddie, Dunmore, Fauquier, Fincastle, Halifax, Loudoun, Mecklenburg, Pittsylvania, Prince Edward, Prince William and Sussex.

The text varies from the maps in the following instances:

(a) In names, on map # 6 (1634), York appears instead of Charles River, and Warwick appears instead of Warwick River.
(b) In dates, reference to the name of any particular county in Part I, Alphabetical Arrangement, will show why the dates in the text vary from those on the maps,—the fact that the maps obviously deal with the counties as of the date of the passage of the Acts authorizing them, while the text deals with them as of

the date of actual existence, and the further fact that the full-text copies of Acts of Assembly in Part VI furnish data which were not available at the time the maps were delineated. The following variations of dates cover the whole series of maps, the black-faced dates following the text, while the dates in parentheses are those which appear on the maps,—the figures following these dates being the numbers of the individual maps on which the variations appear,—

*Amelia, 1735 (1734),—# 11.
*Brunswick, 1732 (1720),—# 11.
**Caroline, 1728 (no date on map),—# 11.
**Chesterfield, 1749 (1748),—# 11.
**Culpeper, 1749 (1748),—# 11.
**Cumberland, 1749 (1748),—# 11.
**Goochland, 1728 (1727),—# 10, 11.
**Hanover, 1721 (1720),—# 10, 11.
  Isle of Wight, 1637 (1634),—# 7, 8, 9, 10, 11.
**King George, 1721 (1720),—# 10, 11.
*King William, 1702 (1701),—# 9, 10, 11.
  Lancaster, 1651 (1652),—# 7, 8, 9, 10, 11.
**Nansemond, 1642 (1637),—# 9, 10.
**Nansemond, 1642 (1640),—# 7, 8, 11.
  Norfolk, 1691 (1637),—# 9, 10, 11.
  Northampton, 1642/3 (1634),—# 9, 10, 11.
**Prince George, 1703 (1702),—# 10, 11.
*Prince William, 1731 (1730),—# 11.
**Southampton, 1749 (1748),—# 11.
*Spotsylvania, 1721 (1720),—# 10, 11.
**Stafford, 1664 (1666),—# 8, 9, 10, 11.
  Warwick, 1642/3 (1634),—# 7, 8, 9, 10, 11.
  York, 1642/3 (1634),—# 7, 8, 9, 10, 11.

GENEALOGICAL

It is but natural that the eight original shires (or counties: Hening i, 224) and the "original county" of Northumberland (Hening i, 337-8) should be selected as the "immigrant ancestors" of the counties which have resulted from Virginia legislation, with the result that the charts which compose this part of the BULLETIN are numbered 1 to 9,—# 9 having four supplemental charts on account of the large number of counties descended through this line. In preparing these "family trees", it soon developed that the lines often crossed from one chart to another, as in the case of Louisa, which came through the Charles River line and appears on chart # 3, a portion of which was added to Albemarle (Hening vii, 419),— a county which came through the Henrico line and appears on chart # 5. Thus, it was obviously difficult to present clearly the data for all the counties on one chart, and show lines connecting every pair of counties which are territorially related. The complexity of such a task will be recognized

---

* As stated, the black-faced date is based upon the date of the actual existence of this county, as used in the text, while the date in parentheses is based upon the passage of the Act of Assembly forming this county, as used on the maps.

** The black-faced date is based upon the full-text copies of recently discovered Acts of Assembly, which were not available at the time the maps were delineated, which Acts appear in Part VI, below, and are cited in the notes under Part I.

more clearly when one considers the fact that Appomattox, Craig, Doddridge, Fayette and Logan were each initially formed from portions of four counties, one of them (Craig) having as many as five additions to its area, while twenty-six were initially formed from portions of three counties,—to one of which (Giles) there were added six territorial increments.

For these reasons, it was decided to give to each of the "immigrant ancestors" a chart of its own, and to have an individual index for this Part of the BULLETIN,—chart 9 having four supplemental charts on account of the large number of counties which descend through the Northumberland line,—one hundred and sixteen in number.

The number of counties "descended" from each of the "immigrant ancestors" is as follows:

```
1634,—Accawmack, .................................................. 3;
       Charles City, .............................................. 18;
       Charles River, ............................................. 9;
       Elizabeth City, ............................................ 7;
       Henrico, ................................................... 11;
       James City, ................................................ 3;
       Warrosquyoake, ............................................. 3;
       Warwick River, ............................................. 2;
1648,—Northumberland, .....................................30;
                         Augusta,....................20;
                              Monongalia,...........18;
                              Botetourt,............39;
                                   Kentucky,....... 9;   116;
                                                        ———
                         Counties here listed.............172.
```

The horizontal lines on the charts have no significance other than the adjustment and balance of each individual chart, except, of course, that the earliest county from each parent-county appears at the left, while the vertical lines indicate in an approximately correct degree the chronological descent,—the "scale" being uniform on each chart, but not the same for all,—and where two or more counties on any chart come into existence in the same year, they appear at the same distance below the parent-county, or,—if formed from different parent-counties,—at the same distance below the "immigrant ancestor". If they be from the same parent-county, they are in alphabetical order from left to right, as can be seen by reference to chart 9, where it appears that Essex and Richmond were formed from Rappahannock in 1692; that Berkeley and Dunmore were formed from Frederick in 1772; and that Warren and Clarke, formed from different parent-counties in 1836, are on the same chronological line, though not in alphabetical order, for reasons which have been given.

In naming the parent-county in cases where portions of several counties were initially utilized to form the new county, only the name of the first county mentioned in the title of the Act has been used, as where Appomattox was formed from Buckingham, Prince Edward, Charlotte and Campbell, in which case the chart (# 5) shows only that Appomattox was formed from Buckingham; but in each of these cases an asterisk refers to a note which says, "Initially formed from portions of more than one county,—the parent-county here shown being the first one mentioned in the title of the Act of Assembly forming this county: for other counties, portions of which were utilized in the formation of this county, see Part I, Alphabetical Arrangement". Some such arbitrary treatment was necessary in order to evade the alternative of a confused tangle of crossing lines; and the plan adopted gives a direct and unconfused "line of descent" for each of the one hundred and twenty-three counties which were initially formed from but one county (which include the eight original shires; Northumberland, an "original county", which was formed from an indeterminate area called "Chickacoan"; Brunswick, which was formed from an area not named [Prince George]; and Illinois, which was formed from territory "on the western side of the Ohio river" [Augusta], while the twenty-one which were initially formed from portions of two counties, the twenty-three which were initially formed from portions of three counties, and the five which were initially formed from portions of four counties are just as clearly set forth, with an asterisk and the corresponding note which explains that there was more than one parent-county and refers to direct data as to these additional parent-counties.

It is a source of the greatest regret to the compiler that the financial condition of the Library prevented the adoption of his suggestion that all these charts be assembled on one chart originating from "Virginia (1607)", which presentation he considered as necessary to a proper exhibition of the relativity of the counties, as is a map of the United States to the same status concerning the several States.

ORIGIN OF COUNTY NAMES

In the preparation of Part V no account has been taken of conflicting county traditions, nor has any attempt been made to harmonize such traditions with apparently correct interpretations, but an effort has been made to assemble, under an alphabetical arrangement of the county names, the most reliable and concise quotations bearing upon this phase of the subject.

Each quotation is immediately followed by a citation of the authority quoted, while additional references,—in alphabetical order,—furnish corroborative and cumulative evidence in support of the quotation actually offered.

In cases of widely varying interpretations, these several interpretations have been given,—each with its own citation,—with a view to offering the student the greater scope in connection with this phase of the matter; but where the Acts of Assembly are quoted as to the origin of the name, no corroborative evidence is offered, as there is no appeal from such authority.

TEXTS OF ACTS OF ASSEMBLY (CONCERNING COUNTIES) WHICH DO NOT APPEAR IN HENING.

On April 20, 1916, Mr. Earl G. Swem, Assistant State Librarian, discovered in the Library a full-text copy of the Acts passed "at a Grand Assembly summoned the 6th Jany. 1639", which Acts appear in Hening (i, 224) only in the most abridged form,—one of which (see chap. i, below) defines the bounds of Isle of Wight, Upper Norfolk and Lower Norfolk counties; while an Act [concerning the bounds of the counties of Nansemond and Isle of Wight], "passed at the sessions of 1643-1646", is quoted from the "Virginia Magazine of History and Biography", xxiii (July, 1915), 254-5.

The Library had before been fortunate enough to locate in the Public Record Office in London original manuscript copies of nine Acts of Assembly (forming counties) which do not appear in Hening, copies of which are here printed in full (Chaps. iii to xi, below) for the first time, so far as we have been able to ascertain. Certain it is that those forming the following counties appear in Hening by title only, under the references cited:

> Prince George, passed August 25, 1702 (Hening iii, 223);
> King George, passed November 24, 1720 (Hening iv, 95);
> Hanover, passed November 26, 1720 (Hening iv, 95);
> Goochland, passed March 6, 1727 (Hening iv, 240);
> Caroline, passed March 15, 1727 (Hening iv, 240);

while the following are not even mentioned by title in Hening (vols. 5 and 6):

> Culpeper, passed March 23, 1748;
> Cumberland, passed March 23, 1748;
> Southampton, passed April 30, 1749;
> Chesterfield, passed May 1, 1749.

The notes appended to the titles of these Acts (Chaps. iii to xi) carry the references current in the Public Record Office in London.

It is hoped that these full-text copies will be of interest to those who are preparing histories of the counties referred to.

BIBLIOGRAPHY

This bibliography in a way follows the plan of the preface as a whole, in that there is a "general" group, which contains the various official collections of information touching all the counties in a greater or less degree, while there are grouped under the name of each of the counties such additional titles as the Library contains (as of October 1, 1915) which relate to that particular county,—these county groups being based directly upon Assistant State Librarian Earl G. Swem's "Bibliography of Virginia, Part I" (Virginia State Library Bulletin, vol. 8, # 2-3-4, April-July-October, 1915), to which acknowledgment is hereby gratefully made, and to which the student is referred for fuller and more detailed data than are here given. As the Library does not contain separate histories of all the counties resulting from Virginia legislation which are now in other jurisdictions, there have been utilized in those cases such available histories of Kentucky and West Virginia as seem to contain the desired information, although bearing the titles of state histories; and in the case of Yohogania County recourse has been had to a history of Westmoreland County in western Pennsylvania.

One cannot but be struck by the fact that there are at least fourteen counties* in the present State of Virginia of which not a single separate title is now available in the Library; and it is hoped that this presentation of the paucity of such material will stimulate others to add to this all-too-meagre collection.

Such a compilation,—based, as it is, upon data collected from scattered sources and from various localities,—would, of course, have been an impossibility in so short a time were it not for the liberal assistance of those who were in a position to aid. Hence it is pleasing to make grateful acknowledgment to Dr. H. R. McIlwaine, State Librarian, for generous co-operation (and especially in connection with the maps), and for helpful criticisms: to Assistant State Librarian, Earl G. Swem, for his kindly encouragement, ever-constant co-operation, and unstinted suggestions of guidance and value: to Mr. W. W. Scott, State Law Librarian; Mr. William G. Stanard, Secretary of the Virginia Historical Society; Mr. William Clayton Torrence, Secretary of the Valentine Museum, and to Dr. Lyon G. Tyler, President of the College of William and Mary and Editor of the "William and Mary Quarterly", for critical examinations of Part V (Origin of County Names) and for adopted suggestions in connection therewith and to the last of these for generous aid in connection with the introduction: to Dr. Thomas L. Watson, State Geologist, for geological data: to the Hon. John W. Williams, Clerk of the House of Delegates, for correct interpretations of Acts of Assembly forming counties, and the more especially for the assistance afforded by his "Index to Enrolled Bills", without which the completeness of this BULLETIN would have been well-nigh impossible: to Mr. David I. Bushnell, jr., of the U. S. Bureau of Ethnology, for data concerning the county names of Indian origin: to the following persons and officials for extracts from and data concerning the records of their several counties, as stated in the respective notes,—Hon. W. C. Burnham, Clerk of Warwick; Hon. M. E. Bristow of Gloucester, for data concerning the records of Middlesex; Mr. James H. Corbitt, of Nansemond; Judge R. T. W. Duke, jr., and Mr. Allan W. Perkins, of Albemarle; Hon. C. W. Eastman, Clerk of Middlesex; Hon. John D. Grant, jr., Clerk of Accomack; Hon. Henry S. Green, State Historian and Archivist of West Virginia, for data concerning the Virginia counties which are now in West Virginia; Hon. George P. Haw, Commonwealth's Attorney of Hanover; Hon. George W. Herring, Clerk of Stafford; the late Mr. William H. Hill and the Hon. Robert Turnbull, of Brunswick; Hon. H. H. Holt, Clerk of Elizabeth City; Hon. T. T. Hudgins, Clerk of York; Miss Sally Jackson, Librarian of the Kentucky State Historical Society, for data concerning the Virginia counties which are now in Kentucky; Hon. B. O. James, Secretary of the Commonwealth, for data concerning the records of Norfolk County; Mrs. J. O. James, of Petersburg, for a copy of the proceedings of the first court of Brunswick; Hon. A. S. Johnson, Clerk of Isle of Wight; Hon. H. B. McLemore, Clerk of Southampton; Hon. Alvah H. Martin, Clerk of Norfolk County; Mr. Oren F. Morton, of Union, W. Va., for data concerning Virginia counties which are now in West Virginia; Hon. J. B. Raines, Clerk of Rich-

---

*Bland, Buchanan, Carroll, Craig, Dickenson, Floyd, Giles, Greene, Lee, Nelson, Patrick, Pulaski, Rappahannock (1833) and Russell.

mond County; Hon. Thomas B. Robertson, of Northampton, for data concerning the records of Accomack; Judge Frederick W. Sims, of Louisa; Hon. Harrison Southworth, Clerk of Essex; Hon. W. D. Temple, Clerk of Prince George; Mr. William Clayton Torrence, of Richmond City, for data concerning the origin of Brunswick; Dr. Lyon G. Tyler, of Williamsburg, for data concerning the origin of eight of the earlier counties*; Hon. A. T. Wiatt, Clerk of Gloucester; Hon. W. W. Woodward, of Elizabeth City, for data concerning the records of Middlesex: to Miss Virginia E. Jones, of the Library Staff, for general assistance, and the more especially for the preparation of the Texts (Part VI) and the Bibliography (Part VII): and to Miss Anna M. Bolton and Miss Lucy T. Throckmorton, of the Apprentice Class of the Library, for verifying the references. And, by no means least, to the Hon. Armistead C. Gordon, Chairman, and the gentlemen of the Library Board, for furthering the suggestion that the data in the original report to the War Department be used as the basis for a BULLETIN of the Library.

The following abbreviations appear in the text:

A.: Acts of the General Assembly of Virginia for the session indicated.
Brock: R. A. Brock's "Virginia and Virginians".
Collins: Collins's "History of Kentucky" (1878).
E (superior): resulted from Virginia legislation, but now extinct, as shown by accompanying dates.
Green: Green's "Word Book of Virginia Folk Speech" (1912).
H.: Hening's "Statutes at Large".
H. A. I.: "Handbook of American Indians" (Bureau of Ethnology Bulletin 30: 1907).
H. B.: "Journals of the House of Burgesses, 1619-1776 (Virginia State Library: 1905-1915).
J.: "Journal of the House" (Burgesses or Delegates, as the case may be, as interpreted in the note on the subject in the "General" section of the Preface, p. 12).
K (superior): resulted from Virginia legislation, but now in Kentucky.
Lewis: Virgil A. Lewis's "History of West Virginia" (1889).
Long: Charles M. Long's "Virginia County Names" (1908).
S.: Shepherd's "Statutes at Large" (continuation of Hening).
U. S.: United States Geological Survey, Bulletin 258 (1905).
U. S. Stats.: "United States Statutes at Large".
W (superior): resulted from Virginia legislation, but now in West Virginia.

MORGAN POITIAUX ROBINSON,
Virginia State Library, Richmond, Va.,
July 1, 1916.

---

* Charles City, Gloucester, Lancaster, Middlesex, Northumberland, Rappahannock, Surry, and Westmoreland.

INTRODUCTORY:

BEING A RUNNING SKETCH, SETTING FORTH HOW SUNDRY ENGLISHMEN,—TRANSPLANTED INTO THE WILDERNESS OF VIRGINIA AND BRINGING WITH THEM THEIR LAWS, RELIGION, USAGES, CUSTOMS AND TRADITIONS,—GRADUALLY EVOLVED CERTAIN POLITICAL AND CIVIL UNITS, WHICH IN TURN BECAME THE BASES OF THE COUNTIES OF THE PRESENT DAY, AS THE POPULATION INCREASED FROM DECADE TO DECADE. IT IS BASED DIRECTLY UPON THE DETAILED ACCOUNT IN STITH'S "HISTORY OF VIRGINIA", SUPPLEMENTED BY THE SOURCES CITED IN THE BIBLIOGRAPHY AT THE END OF THIS INTRODUCTION.

On May 13, 1607,—after a voyage of something over four months and a sojourn of several days at Cape Henry after the landing there on April 26,—the one hundred and five colonists*, who were to found the first permanent English settlement in North America, cast anchor off Jamestown Island, Virginia, in their three vessels,—the ship, Sarah Constant† (one hundred tons), Captain Christopher Newport; the ship, Goodspeed† (forty tons), Captain Bartholomew Gosnold; and the pinnace, Discovery† (twenty tons), Captain John Ratcliffe.

After disembarkation (on the 14th), the first thoughts of the colonists were of gratitude for a safe passage through the terrors of the uncharted ocean, which the witch-craft imagination of the period filled with squirming masses of indescribable monsters; and for this purpose, there was hung from the trees an old sail-cloth, under which the Rev. Robert Hunt led in prayer, and so the thanks of our forefathers at Jamestown first went up to God:

> "the awning made of an old sail hung to three or four trees; the seats from unhewn trees; the bar of wood between two of them for a pulpit; later the old rotten tent; and then later still 'a homely thing like a barn, set with crotchetts, covered with rafts, sedge and earth', and 'yet we had daily common prayer, morning and evening, every Sunday two sermons, and every three months the holy communion, till our minister (the Rev. Mr. [Robert] Hunt) died; but our prayers daily, with homily on Sundays, we continued two or three years, till more preachers came' all make a graphic picture of the first religious exercises in the wilderness".‡

---

* Arber's "Travels and Works of Captain John Smith", pp. lxx, cxxix.

† While Purchas' "Pilgrims", ed. 1705, iv, p. 1625, gives the names as Susan Constant and Godspeed, with no name for the pinnace, to which the name "Discoverer" is often attributed, yet we find that Brown and Neill quote the original official documents which carry the names "Sarah Constant", "Goodspeed" and for the pinnace, "Discovery" (Brown's "Genesis", i, pp. 76, 85; "First Republic", p. 22; Neill's "History of the Virginia Company of London", p. 5), though it must be confessed that Neill's own text (p. 15) follows Purchas, except that he gives the name "Discovery" to the pinnace in spite of the fact that the quotation on p. 5 has it otherwise. See also Tyler's "Cradle of the Republic" (1906), pp. 8-9.

‡ Barton's "Virginia Colonial Decisions", i, p. 77.

Amongst the "Instructions by way of Advice for the intended Voyage to Virginia", were these:*

"When it shall please God to send you to the coast of Virginia, you shall do your best endeavour to find out a safe port in the entrance of some navigable river, making choice of such a one as runneth farthest into the land, and if you happen to discover divers portable rivers, and amongst them any one that hath two main branches, make choice of that which bendeth most toward the sea.
When you have made choice of the river on which you mean to settle, be not hasty in landing your victuals and munitions; but first let Captain Newport discover how far that river may be found navigable, * * * .
You must observe if you can, whether the river on which you plant doth spring out of the mountains or out of lakes. If it be out of any lake, the passage to the other sea will be more easy, and [it] is like enough, that out of the same lake you shall find some spring which run[s] the contrary way towards the East India Sea; for the great and famous rivers of Volga, Tan[a]is and Dwina have three heads near joyn[e]d; and yet one falleth into the Caspian Sea, the other into the Euxine Sea, and the third into the Paelonian Sea".

Immediately the work of home and defense were organized, and, in accordance with these instructions, Captain Newport set out from Jamestown on a voyage of discovery on May the 21st, accompanied by five gentlemen,† four mariners,‡ and fourteen sailors,‖ explored the Powhatan (James) River to the Falls (14th Street and Mayo's Bridge in the present City of Richmond) and on Whit Sunday, May the 24th (June the 3rd, N. S.)¶ "upon one of the little Islets at the mouth of the falls he sett up a Crosse with the inscription 'Iacobus Rex 1607' and his owne name below";†† on which occasion they named the stream "King's River". Then they started the return trip to Jamestown, rather than displease Powhatan by making an exploration into the country of his enemies, the Monacans

---

* Arber's "Travels and Works of Captain John Smith", i, pp. xxxiii-xxxv.

† George Percy, esq. Captaine Gabriel Archer, Captaine Ihon Smyth, Master Ihon Brookes, Master Thomas Wotton. (Arber's "John Smith", i, xli).

‡ ffrancys Nellson, John Collson, Robert Tyndall, Mathew ffytch. (*Ibid.*)

‖ Ionas Poole, Robert Markham, Iohn Crookdeck, Olyver Browne, Beniamyn White, Rychard Genoway, Thomas Turnbrydge, Thomas Godword, Robert Iackson, Charles Clarke, Stephen, Thomas Skynner, Iremy Deale Danyell. (*Ibid.*)

¶ Charles Campbell's "History of the Colony and Ancient Dominion of Virginia", 1860, p. 42, erroneously says, "On the day of their arrival, the tenth of June, the party visited the falls, * * * " which probably accounts for the fact that this erroneous date of the tenth of June is the more generally accepted one.
This error on the part of Campbell seems to have resulted in a queer custom; for, while we celebrate May the 13th (an *old* Style date) as the anniversary of the landing at Jamestown, yet we also celebrate June the 10th (a *new* Style date) as the anniversary of the first visit of white men to the Falls of James River,—thus putting these anniversaries twenty-eight days apart, though the actual events were only eleven days apart. This discrepancy of seventeen days is accounted for by Campbell's error of seven days and by the difference of ten days between the Old and the New Style.

†† Arber's "John Smith", i, xlvi, lxix.

(Manakins, etc.), and arrived on the 27th, after which all energies were set to strengthening the fortifications until June 22, on which date Captain Newport set sail for England, leaving one hundred and four persons and provisions for thirteen or fourteen weeks.* He promised to return within twenty weeks.

In view of their "Instructions", in view of the fact that the general flow of the rivers of the Atlantic seaboard is from northwest to southeast, and in view of the immediate contact of the colonists with the Werowance of Paspihae and those living along the Chickahominy River,† it was no mere accident that Newport's expedition, which planted the cross at the Falls of the Powhatan River, kept straight up the river instead of turning into the present Appomattox and reaching the falls of that river at the site of the present City of Petersburg.

During the summer of 1607, Smith explored down the river to Kiccoughtan, and across to Waroskoyack (now Isle of Wight) on the south side of the river, while there were several journeys to Paspahegh; and in the fall of that year, he started on his discovery of the Chickahominy country and,—after several digressions,—explored the river of that name as far as it was navigable in a canoe.‖

On September 17, 1607, and again in November of that year, there were trials by jury at Jamestown, and so this English custom was inaugurated at once.‡

On January 8, 1608, the first ship of the First Supply arrived some ten weeks overdue, while the second (and final) ship arrived on the 20th of April, following,—the two together bringing one hundred and twenty colonists, which gave a total of one hundred and fifty-eight, after allowing for sixty-seven deaths.§

In June of that year, Captain Smith explored as far as Cape Charles and discovered Smith's Islands, which were named after Sir Thomas Smith,% then explored up the bay to the Patuxent River, now in Maryland, later discovered the Patomack to its falls and the Rappahannock to its falls, and still later explored the Appomattox River.

On the 6th of October, Captain Newport had arrived with the Second Supply, which brought seventy more colonists, thus making a total of two hundred, after allowing for twenty-eight other deaths.§

These additional colonists gave a firmer and broader working basis, and Newport had brought back with him with the Second Supply express orders to explore the country of the Monacans (the area immediately west of the Falls), with a view to the discovery of the South Sea, which objective was sought with greater or less persistency certainly until 1621,

---

* Arber's "John Smith", i, pp. lxx, 8.

§ *Ibid.*, i, cxxix.

† *Ibid.*, i, pp. lxvi-lxvii. The Chickahominy River flows into the James from the northwest at Dancing Point, some seven and a half miles above Jamestown Island.

‡ *Ibid.*, i, pp. lxxxiii, 12.

‖ Stith's "History of Virginia", pp. 50-1.

% Brown's "First Republic", p. 173.

when Powhatan entered into a league of friendship, which it was supposed would greatly further that much-sought-after object.‡

But Smith firmly held that Jamestown should be made secure before any effort was made to explore the wilderness west of the Falls, while it was charged that he only wished to delay Newport's efforts in order that he might later do the same thing under more auspicious circumstances and thus gain the credit of having discovered the South Sea. This charge received countenance from Smith's own activities the December before, while exploring the Chickahominy River.

However, Newport,—who had brought with him a boat built in five parts, so that it might be carried around the falls and rapids in the rivers and would be more convenient in case of portage*,—did actually explore the Monacan country to the extent of some forty miles above the Falls (approximately the western boundary of the present County of Goochland)†; and so acquired a knowledge of this area as early as 1608, though he secured no information as to the South Sea.

In December, 1608, Smith again explored to Warrosqueake and sent Sicklemore to the country of the Chowanocks to the south, "chiefly to look for Silkgrass, and to enquire after Sir Walter Raleigh's lost Colony"** and then made an exploration up the present York River, in search of corn, information and the friendship of the Indians.

Under date of May 23, 1609, His Majesty issued the Second Charter, "which finally afforded Sir Edwin Sandys and other progressive thinkers the opportunity for developing their liberal ideas of government in a new nation in the new world",‖ and gave enlarged powers to the Company, but expressly abrogated the powers of the President and Council in Virginia; and in that same year Lieutenant Percy was sent with twenty men to establish an outpost at Point Comfort, in order to help ward off starvation at Jamestown,§ and to guard against any surprise attack by the Spaniards.

Then came a few months of relief and prosperity, during which the population of the colony reached as many as four hundred and ninety,†† followed by the horrors of "Starvation Time" in 1610, during which year "of near five hundred Persons left by Captain Smith at his Departure, within

---

‡ Bruce's "Economic History of Virginia", i, p. 38.

"In May, 1669", says the said authority (p. 39), "sixty years after the memorable expedition of Newport into the Monacan country, Berkeley, at that time Governor of the Colony, wrote to the authorities in England that two hundred gentlemen had agreed to accompany him in an expedition to the west, which he had arranged for the discovery of the East India Sea, but that unusually heavy and prolonged rains had for that season disconcerted his plans. He petitioned that a commission should be sent to him, which would empower him to undertake the expedition the following spring".

* Stith's "History of Virginia", p. 77.

† Ibid., p. 79.

** Ibid., p. 85.

‖ Brown's "First Republic", p. 650.

§ Stith's "History of Virginia", pp. 97-8.

†† Yonge's "Site of Old James Towne", p. 43.

six Months, there remained not above sixty, Men, Women, and Children"†;
but on the 10th of June, Lord Delawarr, with a fleet which brought the
population of Virginia up to some three hundred and fifty souls, arrived
as Captain-General of Virginia, took charge with a firm hand, began to
set things in order, and later built two forts (Fort Charles and Fort
Henry) at Kiccoughtan (Hampton), where was to be developed a plantation
for acclimating the colonists as they arrived,—where "those, who came
from England,‡ should be quartered at their first Landing, that the Weari-
someness and Nausea of the Sea might be refreshed, in this pleasant Situation, and wholesome Air". ‖

Sir Thomas Dale arrived on the 10th of May, 1611, with colonists and
provisions and at once began a personal exploration of the country by "view-
ing" the Nansemond River and later the James River, with the result
that "as early as 1611 a town named Henricopolis [at the present Dutch

---

† Stith's "History of Virginia", p. 117.

It was at this time that the life of the Colony hung on a gossamer-
like thread of Good Fortune, of which trying time, Tyler's "Cradle of the
Republic", p. 36, has the following to say:

"And it now appears, indeed, as if another sickening failure would
be added to the long list of fruitless endeavours to plant an English
colony in America. Sending ahead the pinnace VIRGINIA, built on the
coast of Maine in 1607, to Point Comfort to take on Captain Davis
and the guard there, the company at Jamestown made ready for their
own departure. June 7, 1610, Gates ordered all the small arms to be
carried aboard, buried the cannon at the fort gate, and commanded
every man to repair to the PATIENCE and DELIVERANCE at the beat-
ing of the drum; and while the men were going aboard, lest some one
might set fire to the buildings in the town which they were abandon-
ing, he caused his own company, under Captain George Yeardley, to
embark after the rest, and was himself the last to leave the shore.

It was in the evening that they left Jamestown, and they halted
that night at Hog Island about six miles below the fort. The next
morning, they resumed their voyage, and had reached Mulberry Island,
about eight miles further down, when they saw the white sails of
a little vessel coming to meet them. It was the pinnace VIRGINIA,
and never did vessel bring more important message. Edward Brewster,
its commander, informed Gates that Lord Delaware had arrived at
Point Comfort with 150 settlers; and, thereupon, the colonists were un-
willingly put back to Jamestown, and that evening took possession again
of their forlorn habitations. Sunday, June 10, Lord Delaware arrived
and went ashore in the afternoon with Sir Ferdinando Wainman. This
was a great occasion and one duly appreciated at the time. Sir Thomas
Gates caused his company to stand in arms, and William Strachey,
the secretary of state, acted as color bearer.

As soon as the Lord Delaware arrived near the south gate of the
fort opening towards the river, he fell upon his knees and made a
long and silent prayer to God. Then arising, he walked to the entrance
to the town, Strachey bowing before him with his colors, and letting
them fall in the gateway at his Lordship's feet, who passed on to
the church, where Rev. Richard Buck ("Sir Thomas Gates his preacher"),
delivered an impressive sermon."

‡ "Thus far [the Fall of 1610]", says Yonge's "Site", p. 43, "about 900
persons had been sent from England to Virginia, of whom about 700 had
perished."

‖ Stith's "History of Virginia", p. 120. It is of interest to note that
in 1610 Lord Delawarr thus established what was in substance more or less
of a quarantine station at a point only some thirty miles from the present
U. S. Quarantine Station on Fisherman's Island, at Cape Charles.

Gap] was built by Sir Thomas Dale 'with a good church'",¶ of which town Coxendale on the south side of the river was in substance a part.

In 1612, Captain Newport arrived with supplies and was sent to the Potomack River for corn and to explore; the next year Dale entered into an alliance with the Chickahominies by which they became "Tassautessus", or Englishmen, and accepted as their governor, Dale, whom they recognized as the deputy of the king;* and in this same year Bermuda Hundred, Charles City Hundred, Curls, Rocksdale Hundred and Shirley Hundred were located. Pocahontas, who was also called Matoax by the Indians, married John Rolfe in 1614 and was a short time thereafter baptized as Rebecca; and in this year a salt-works was located on Smith's Island.**

The Colony, however, did not prosper under the military rules established by Gates and Dale; and in England, for lack of subscriptions, the desperate expedient of a lottery was resorted to, but emigrants could not be had on any terms. The Colony was saved by the excitement created over the culture of tobacco introduced by John Rolfe. Gates and Dale tried to suppress it, but when Yeardley became deputy-governor a more liberal spirit prevailed and colonists flocked to the Colony in large numbers to plant tobacco. However, it should be stated that the Chickahominies refused to keep with Yeardley their agreement with Dale, and called him "only Sir Thomas Dale's Man",† after which there was bloodshed in which twelve Indians were killed and as many more captured, and eleven colonists drowned, at the very time that "Lady Rebecca," as Pocahontas was now called, was being much fêted in England; but in March, 1617, while on board ship at Gravesend waiting to sail for Virginia, she fell ill of small-pox and "it pleased God, at Gravesend, to take Pocahontas to his Mercy, in about the two and twentieth year of her Age".‡ At that time, there were, it is stated, four hundred persons‖ at James Towne, and in the same year there were located four more outlying plantations,§—Argall's Gift, (Martin's) Brandon and Smith's (afterwards Southampton) Hundred and Weyanoke.††

¶ Barton's "Virginia Colonial Decisions", i, p. 78.
* Stith's "History of Virginia", p. 130.
** Tyler's "Cradle of the Republic" (1906), opp. p. 201.
† Stith's "History of Virginia", p. 140.
‡ *Ibid.*, p. 146.
‖ Yonge's "Site of Old 'James Towne'", p. 43. Powhatan, ever solicitous of the fighting strength of England, sent his son-in-law, Tomocomo, so Stith says (p. 144), "to take the Number of the People in England, and to bring him a full and exact Account of their Strength and Condition. And, accordingly, being arrived at Plimouth, he got a long Stick, intending to cut a Notch, for every one, he saw. But he was soon tired with such an endless Work, and threw away his Stick; and being asked by the King, after his Return, how many People there were? it is said, that he replied: 'Count the Stars of the Sky, the Leaves of the Trees, and the Sand upon the Sea Shore; for such is the Number of the People in England'".
§ "He [Sir Edwin Sandys] therefore observed, that the Commodities of Virginia had three several sorts of Owners: First, the Company; secondly, particular Hundreds and Plantations, belonging to private adventurers in England, as Southampton Hundred, Martin's Hundred, and the like; and thirdly, Planters inhabiting and residing in Virginia, whose Part he conceived to be far the largest and most considerable."
†† Tyler's "Cradle of the Republic", pp. 232, 209, 217, respectively.

Yeardley, upon becoming acting-governor in 1616, had encouraged the raising of tobacco; with the result that, when Argall arrived as governor, he found some of the necessary works neglected, and every available space in Jamestown,—the margin of the streets and the market-place,—occupied by the plant. Argall appears to have restrained the people and to have required a due proportion of corn to be planted, but he was himself accused of money-lust, and he engaged surreptitiously in the tobacco trade to a very considerable extent. Many charges of what are nowadays called "graft" were brought against him, but he was saved from final prosecutions by the Earl of Warwick.*

Brown's "First Republic", p. 254 (see also p. 313) says, under date prior to June 17, 1617,—"It seems certain, however, that he (Argall) located the then bounds of the four great 'Incorporations and Parishes of James Citty, Charles Citty, the citty of Henricus and Kiccowtan'" "(which hereafter [in reply to the 6th petition of their General Assembly of August, 1619] shall be called Elizabeth City, by the name of his Majesties most vertuous and renowned Daughter)",† while the four outlying plantations already mentioned were located.

In many respects the year 1618 was an unfortunate one for the Colony, in that Lord Delawarr, Powhatan and Sir Walter Raleigh died, and there was much quarreling amongst the members of the London Company. We find, however, that there were at that time "about six hundred Persons, Men, Women, and Children in Virginia",‡ and that to the plantations previously established, several new ones were added,—Flower de Hundred, Martin's Hundred and Maycock's Hundred.¶

A new era began with the resignation, on April 28, 1619, of Sir Thomas Smith, who had held the post of treasurer of the Colony for twelve years. The results of his long administration were stated to be that, after "fourscore thousand Pounds Expense and twelve Years Labour, the Colony consisted of about six hundred Persons, Men, Women and Children. And they had about three hundred Head of Cattle, and an infinite Number of Hogs, wild and tame".§

Sir Edwin Sandys and the Earl of Southampton now assumed control of affairs. In the spring of 1619 Sir George Yeardley arrived as governor, bringing various grants and Orders of Government, amongst which were instructions to issue writs for a General Assembly, "with two Burgesses from each Plantation [of the then eleven] freely to be elected by the inhabitants thereof",**—"a Privilege", says Stith (p. 182), "granted immediately upon the Disgust taken, by the worthier Part of the Company,

---

* Stith's "History of Virginia", pp. 149-157.
† Brown's "First Republic", p. 377.
‡ Stith's "History of Virginia", p. 281.
¶ Tyler's "Cradle of the Republic", pp. 211, 236, 212, respectively.
§ "But all the Company's Lands and Plantations were utterly ruined and depopulated by Captain Argall, there being only three Tenants left thereon, and six Men of what he called his Guard. And notwithstanding Sir Thomas Smith's boast that he had left six thousand Pounds, for the new Treasurer to proceed upon, it was found, upon Examination, that the Company was above that Sum in Debt" (Stith, pp. 159-160).
** Brown's "First Republic", p. 312.

at Sir Thomas Smith's ill Government, and the insufferable Tyranny and Iniquity of Captain Argall",—whereupon the new governor soon afterwards published his intention to assemble such a body;† and this prospect of a representative legislature evidently stimulated the proprietors of land, for we find that there were located in that year at least the eight following plantations,—Archer's Hope, Berkeley, Chaplin's Choice, Jordan's Journey, Lawne's Plantation, Savage's Neck, Warde's Plantation, and Westover.‡

This, the first popular representative legislative assembly of America, met in the little wooden church at Jamestown on July 30, 1619, with twenty-two representatives present,* who, in imitation of the House of Commons and conscious of their importance, "sat in the choir with their hats on, but after prayer had been said and the oath of supremacy taken, took their seats in the body of the church fronting the governor and council [in the same house, after the manner of the Scotch Parlia-

---

† Stith says (p. 160),—"And about the latter End of June, he called the first General Assembly, that was ever held in Virginia. Counties were not yet laid off, but they elected their Representatives by Townships. So that the Burroughs of James Town, Henrico, Bermuda Hundred, and the rest, each sent their Members to the Assembly. And hence it is that our Lower House of Assembly is called the House of Burgesses, a Name proper to the Representatives of Burroughs or Towns; and it hath, by Custom, ever since retained that Appellation altho' the Burgesses, or Members for Towns and Corporations, are very few and inconsiderable at present [1747] in Comparison of the Representatives for Counties".

‡ Tyler's "Cradle of the Republic" (1906), pp. 234, 225, 213, 214, 205, 254, 210, 227, respectively.

* "Of the twenty-two members thus elected [whose names and plantations are given below] two of them were denied their seats because the patents of the land they represented exempted their owners from obedience to the law and authority of the colony, except in matters of defense" (Barton's "Virginia Colonial Decisions", i, p. 34, n); and so we see that the "Credentials Committee" of the first Assembly was active and alert.

(From "Journals of the House of Burgesses", 1619-1658/9, vii).

ARGALL'S GIFT:
    Thomas Pawlett
    Edward Gourgaing

CHARLES CITY:
    Samuel Sharpe
    Samuel Jordan

FLOWERDIEU HUNDRED:
    Edmund Rossingham
    John Jefferson

HENRICUS:
    Thomas Dowse
    John Polentine [probably Pollongton]

JAMES CITY:
    William Powell
    William Spense (Spence)

LAWNE'S PLANTATION:
    Christopher Lawne
    Ensign Washer

MARTIN'S BRANDON:
    Thomas Davis
    Robert Stacy

MARTIN'S HUNDRED:
    John Boys
    John Jackson

CAPTAIN WARD'S PLANTATION:
    John Warde
    John Gibbes

SMYTHES HUNDRED:
    Thomas Graves
    Walter Shelley

KICCOWTAN:
    William Tucker
    William Capp

ment]";† and proceeded to the consideration of the business which was "divided into fower severall objects" (as set forth in Brown's "First Republic", pp. 317-8).

This election of representatives naturally required definite bounds and limitations for each of the plantations represented, which bounds were, of course, the forerunners of the metes and bounds of the shires and counties which were at a later date to include the areas of these early plantations.*

---

† Barton's "Virginia Colonial Decisions", 1, p. 61.

* The location and bounds of these plantations were as follows:

* ARGALL'S GIFT: located in 1619, was just above Jamestown Island on the north side of the river, situated between the Chickahominy River and Powhatan Creek, and was a portion of the three thousand acres appointed by the Company for the Governor's Land.

** CHARLES CITY: located in 1613, "extended from the said pale [run by Dale between the James River and the Appomattox River], included the neck of land now known as Jones Neck, eastward, down James River, on both sides, to the mouth of the Chickahominy River."

* FLOWER DEW HUNDRED: located in 1618, situated on the south side of the river and just opposite Weyanoke, was a grant of one thousand acres.

** HENRICUS: located in 1611, "included Henrico (Farrar's Island), extending thence on both sides of James River to the westward, the pale run by Dale between the said River and the Appomattox River being the line on the south side."

** JAMES CITY: located in 1617, "extended down on both sides of the river, with the same bounds near the river as the present [1898] James City and Warwick counties on the north side, and as the present Surry and Isle of Wight counties, or it may have extended to the Elizabeth River on the south side, as the southern bounds are not definitely stated."

** KICCOWTAN: located in 1610, "extended from James City corporation to the bay."

* LAWNE'S PLANTATION: located in 1619, was situated on the south side of the river, on the east side of Lawne's Creek.

* MARTIN'S BRANDON: located in 1617 (the present Lower Brandon), was on the south side of the river, on the west side of Upper Chippokes Creek.

* MARTIN'S HUNDRED: located in 1618, consisted of some eighty thousand acres and was situated "in the east end of James City county on the west side of Skiffes (Keith's) Creek.

* SMITH'S (SOUTHAMPTON) HUNDRED: located in 1617, contained eighty thousand acres and was situated on the north side of the river, and "ran from 'Tanks Weyanoke' to the Chickahominy River".

* CAPTAIN WARDE'S PLANTATION: located in 1619, contained twelve hundred acres, situated on the south side of the river, on the east side of Warde's Creek.

The items marked thus: (*) are from Tyler's "Cradle of the Republic", 1906, chap. xiv.

The items marked thus: (**) are from Brown's "First Republic", pp. 313-14.

Owing to the great mortality which prevailed in the Colony by reason of the climate, the population suffered serious fluctuations,* but in 1620, it was estimated that there were two thousand, four hundred persons in Virginia**; for "by Captain Smith's Account, there were twenty-one Sail of Ships sent this Year, with thirteen hundred, Men, Women, and Children".†

The next year the "Fourth Charter", of June 24, confirmed former grants and privileges and "provided that the Governor should call together the General Assembly once a year, and not oftener, unless on very extraordinary and important occasions‡ and should "imitate the policy of the form of government, laws, customs, manner of tryal, and other administration of justice used in England, * * *"; while the Instructions to Governor Wyatt at the same time ordered him to provide for "dividing the colony into cities, boroughs, &c, * * *, and to appoint proper times for administration * * *, and law suits".‖

"Inferior Courts were therefore, in the Beginning of the Year 1622 appointed in convenient Places, to relieve the Governor and Council of the vast Burthen of Business, and to render justice more cheap and accessible. This was the Original and Foundation of our County Courts; altho' the Country was not yet laid off in Counties,¶ but still continued in Townships and particular Plantations, as they called those settlements, which were not considerable enough, to have the Title and Priviledges of Burroughs".††

---

* Of the striking fluctuations in population, Tyler's "Cradle of the Republic", 1906, pp. 183-4, has this to say:

"The following figures may be taken as approximately representing the population of the colony at different times from 1607 to 1776. The number of emigrants brought over to June 10, 1610, inclusive of Lord Delaware's company, was about 800. Between this time and December, 1618, 1,000 arrived, making a total of 1,800 persons, and of this number 1,200 died, leaving 600 survivors. Then in the interval between December, 1618, and November, 1619, 840 emigrants arrived, who made with the survivors 1,440 persons, of whom 540 died, leaving about 900 survivors. There were sent to Virginia between November, 1619, and February, 1625, 4,749 emigrants, who with the 900 of November, 1619, make a total of 5,649, of whom only 1,095 were living in Virginia February 20, 1625; showing a total mortality in about eighteen years of 6,294 persons out of 7,389 imported. After this time, the violent fluctuations of the early years ceased, and there was a slow but steady increase. In 1629, the population of Virginia was about 3,000; in 1634, 5,000; in 1649, 15,000 (of whom 500 were negroes); in 1654, 21,600; in 1665, 40,000 (of whom 2,000 were negroes); in 1681, 70,000 or 80,000; in 1715, 95,000 (of whom 23,000 were negroes); in 1755, 295,672 (of whom 120,156 were negroes); in 1776, 567,614 (of whom 270,762 were negroes)."

** U. S. Census, 1910, Abstract, p. 567, n.
† Stith's "History of Virginia", pp. 203-4.
‡ Barton's "Virginia Colonial Decisions", i, p. 62.
‖ Hening, i, pp. 113, 115, 116.
¶ Although Hening i, p. 224, quotes the word "shires" for the original divisions of the colony, yet on p. 223 of the same volume, we find quoted from "Roll No. 11,—1634", "Pa. 174,—Sheriffs appointed for the several counties", which is the earliest use of the word "county" officially used that we have been able to locate. Page 228, of this same volume gives an abstract (very brief) of an Act (XXII) of 1639-'40, a copy of the full text of which will be found in Part VI, chap. i, below, wherein the word "countye" is used as many as five times; again, we find the word used in this volume of Hening, p. 247, and again on p. 272-3, for designating the "countie courts", for the first time.
†† Stith's "History of Virginia", p. 207-8.

On March 22, 1622, occurred the Great Massacre, in which, "in one Hour, and almost at the same Instant, fell three hundred and forty-seven, Men, Women, and Children [of the twelve hundred and forty English living in Virginia]".*

The news of this was received by the Company with "inexpressible Grief" and was a sincere shock to the adventurers and to the English generally. The disaster discouraged colonization and greatly dampened the ardour of those who wished to settle new plantations on the outskirts of civilization, though the whole affair was largely attributed to the negligence of the governor and the colonists, who had not heeded such warnings as the attempt of Opechancanough to poison the whole Colony, and the death of Nemattenow. But a re-action set in almost at once, and there was a patriotic, though more or less non-effectual, effort to assist and re-inforce such as had escaped the tragic affair, with the result that the king gave "for immediate Dispatch" twenty barrels of powder, but only "upon the Security of the Company's Seal, afterwards to repay it", Lord St. John of Basing gave sixty coats of mail; and there were many other offers of assistance, for it was felt that the Colony, settled at so great expense and at the cost of so many lives,* should be saved and perpetuated; while the colonists, after formally rejecting a proposal to abandon James Towne, at once began a concentration of all resources at the most easily defended plantations† and especially those in the neighborhood of Jamestown Island.

Right on top of this disaster, the king laid oppressive imposts on tobacco, while the Company quarrelled violently amongst themselves and thus re-

---

* Brown's "First Republic", p. 464; wherein it is said, "In March, 1621, there were 843 English in Virginia, of whom about 750 were acclimated. Between that date and March, 1622, seventeen ships arrived in Virginia, which left England with 1,580 persons. In March, 1622, there were by the census 1,240 English living in Virginia. Of 2,423 people (about 750 acclimated and 1,673 newcomers) 1,183 had died en route and in Virginia, showing that the death rate among the newcomers had been almost as great in the summer of 1621 as in that of 1620, probably equally as great, because of the 1,240 living, about four hundred had recently arrived and had not yet gone through the seasoning".

Stith (p. 281), quoting from the Company's "Declaration", says "there were still (Christmas, 1622) remaining (as was computed) above five and twenty Persons, sent over at the Expense only of thirty thousand Pounds of the public Stock, * * *". Yonge's "Site", p. 43, says, "A census taken in 1623 gives the population of the town (James Towne) at 183. It also shows that during the preceding year, eighty-nine people had died in the town".

Yonge's "Site" (p. 44) says, "Captain Nathaniel Butler represented that up to the winter of 1622, the mortality was 8,000 out of 10,000, while the resident colonists declared that up to the winter of 1622 not over 6,000 were sent to Virginia, of whom 2,500 were living. Captain John Smith says that 'neere 7,000 people out of 8,500 had died to 1627'".

† Flower dew Hundred, Kiccoughtan, Paspahey, Shirley Hundred, Southampton Hundred, Jordan's Point and Newport News,—the latter two having been successfully defended by their respective owners, who refused to obey the orders to concentrate at the other points,—to say nothing of "Mrs. Proctor, a proper, civil, and modest Gentlewoman, who, with an heroic spirit, defended her Estate for a Month, till she, with all with her, were obliged, by the English Officers, to go with them and leave their substance to the Havock and Spoil of the Enemy" (Stith, pp. 235-6).

tarded development just at the time when it was most needed; for, "according to John Wroth, a member of the Warwick faction, up to 1623, 3,570 out of 5,720 colonists died in the four years ending 1622".‡

The Assembly of 1623/4 provided "that there shall be courts kept once a month in the corporations of Charles City and Elizabeth Citty for the decyding of suits and controversies not exceeding the value of one hundred pounds of tobacco and for punishing of petty offences, * * *";|| and so for the first time undoubtedly came up the question of the territorial jurisdiction of these several courts,—the question of over what area, to what extent and within what metes and bounds each of the now three courts had jurisdiction,—the forerunner of the question of county boundaries, for "this was the first step taken 'by law' for the establishment of the Monthly Courts which were afterwards given the English name of County Courts".* The "Humble Petition" and Butler's "Unmasked Face", with their charges and counter-charges, brought on more violent quarrels within the Company, as well as between the Company and His Majesty, with the result that the year 1623 saw a demand from the king forced upon the Company to state whether they would surrender their old charters and accept a new one with certain suggested amendments; to which the Company replied in the negative, whereupon His Majesty appointed Commissioners "to make particular and vigilent Enquiry, touching divers Matters, which concerned the State of the Colony of Virginia",† after which the king forced various irregular rulings against the Company.

"However, at the time, [the dissolution of the Company] was by no means the wish of the colonists, for the good things that had come to them had come through the Company, while the evil ones had been chiefly of the King's making". The end of the Company came, however, from several influences, but more immediately from James's jealousy of the freedom of discussion in the meetings of the council of the London Company, * * *". Factions in the Company itself hastened its downfall, and finally, in October, 1623, about seventeen years after it came into existence, its charter was revoked by an Act of the Privy Council, and its delegated powers of sovereignty were resumed by the King,§ after "they had also expended largely above an hundred thousand Pounds, out of their own private Fortunes",** and although "between November, 1619, and February, 1625, 4,749 came to Virginia and 4,400 died, thus making a total mortality in about nineteen years of 6,040, out of 7,289".¶

At the time the Colony was turned over to the Crown in February, 1625, the population was one thousand, two hundred and twenty-seven, which number included twenty-three negroes and two Indians,†† while the General

---

‡ Yonge's "Site", p. 43-4.
|| Hening, i, p. 125.
* Barton's "Virginia Colonial Decisions", i, p. 194.
† Stith's "History of Virginia" p. 299.
§ Barton's "Virginia Colonial Decisions", i, p. 65.
** Stith's "History of Virginia", p. 340.
¶ Yonge's "Site", p. 43.
†† Brown's "First Republic", p. 627.

Assembly of that year contained twenty-three burgesses,† representing without doubt the sixteen political units, which had sent burgesses to the Assembly of 1623/4,—one of which was the Eastern Shore.†

The Company defunct, James fortunately appointed good governors to look after his interests in the colony, and Sir Francis Wyatt at once took severe measures against the Indians. However, James soon died, but King Charles continued the policy of his father and gave further good government to the colony by sending as Governor, our old friend, Sir George Yeardley, who unfortunately died the following year; and in November, 1627, Captain Francis West was appointed to fill the vacancy.

The general good government of these men is reflected in the fact that many grants issued and the population of the Colony in 1628 was estimated to be three thousand souls;‡ while the business of the courts had increased to such an extent that the next year the Commissioners of the Monthly Courts were substituted for the Commanders of Plantations as judges, and in February 1631/2, it was "ordered that the mounthlie corts be held and kept in remote parts of this colony: vizt.

ffor the upper parts; for Warwick River;
ffor Warrosquyoake; for Elizabeth Citty;
ffor Accawmacke",‖—

and it was also provided that "fowre quarter corts shall be held at JamesCitty yearlie";* from all of which it would seem that the population was fast scattering along the outlying water-fronts, as is further evidenced by the fact that the Assembly of September, 1632, included in its membership thirty-nine burgesses, representing twenty-five political units,§ which units must, of course, have had approximately definite metes and bounds and were so inadvertently determining the boundaries of the counties which were later to embrace their respective areas.

"In 1619, these scattered settlements [see note, above] were gathered into four large corporations with a capital city in each. * * *

Each corporation contained one or more boroughs, and each borough was represented by two burgesses in the general assembly, for the first time called in 1619.

This system of corporations did not continue long, because the wealth of water-courses and the cultivation of tobacco provoked separation and isolation, and society became very soon distinctly agricultural and rural. As a consequence, after fifteen years, borough representation was abandoned, and the whole colony was divided into eight counties or shires." (Tyler's "Cradle of the Republic", 1906, p. 197).

Up to 1634, the political units were called hundreds and plantations,— of which twenty-one were represented by thirty-two burgesses in the Assembly of February 1632-3,—no list of the burgesses attending the Assembly of August, 1633, being available at present.**

† Ibid., pp. 579-80; "Journals of the House of Burgesses" 1619—1658/59.
‡ U. S. Census, 1910, Abstract, p. 567, n.
‖ Hening, i, p. 168.
* Hening, i, p. 174.
§ Ibid., pp. 178-9.
** "Journals of the House of Burgesses of Virginia", 1619-1658/9, pp. xiv, xv, xvi.

"In 1634 [see Hening, i, p. 224]. The country divided into 8 shires,† which are to be governed as shires in England.

The names of these shires are‡

James City	Warwick River
Henrico	Warrosquyoake
Charles City	Charles River
Elizabeth Citty	Accawmack"

ACCAWMACK, "on the Eastern Shore, over the bay" [the present Counties of Accomac and Northampton] had a population of three hundred and ninety-six persons.

CHARLES CITY, "extending on both sides of the river,—on the south side from Upper Chippokes Creek to Appomattox River, and on the north side from Sandy Point to Turkey Island Creek", was inhabited by five hundred and eleven persons.

CHARLES RIVER, composed of the plantations lying on the modern York River, and subsequently York County, had a population of five hundred and ten.

ELIZABETH CITTY, "extending on both sides of Hampton Roads,—on the south side to Chuckatuck Creek, and on the north side of Newport News, and including a small part thereof", contained (with Warwick River) sixteen hundred and seventy people.

HENRICO, "extending from Charles City County indefinitely westward", contained four hundred and nineteen persons.

JAMES CITY, extending on both sides of the river,—on the south side from Lawne's Creek to Upper Chippokes, and on the north side from Skiffes Creek to above Sandy Point", was inhabited by eight hundred and eighty-six persons.

WARROSQUYOAKE, "subsequently, in 1637, Isle of Wight county, extending from Chuckatuck Creek to Lawne's Creek", contained five hundred and twenty-two inhabitants.

WARWICK RIVER, "extending, on the north side, from Elizabeth City county to Skiffes (Keith's) Creek", contained with Elizabeth City, a population, as stated above, of sixteen hundred and seventy.

It will be noted that three of these "original shires" were on both sides of the river; and it appears that the census of 1634 (Bruce's "Social Life", p. 18) credited the Colony with 4,914 persons, while the U. S. Census, 1910, Abstract, p. 567, n, gives the number as 5,119,—the difference being accounted for (in Bruce) by the fact that "after the census was taken a Dutch ship brought in one hundred and forty-five persons from the Bermudas, and an English ship sixty from England".

The colonists, as was most natural, gave to four of these shires the names by which these respective areas had been known from the time of the first General Assembly and for some while before,—thus attesting their loyalty to the house of Stuart,—while two were named after the Indian tribes to which the areas in those shires had belonged, one after Robert Rich, the Earl of Warwick,—and oddly enough, although Yorke was represented in the Assembly of 1632/3, yet we find that in 1634 the name Charles River was given to the area approximately embracing the former political unit called Yorke, and later again named York in 1642/3.

---

† The only place we find this use of the word.

‡ Tyler's "Cradle of the Republic", 1906, p. 198, gives the bounds and Bruce's "Economic History of Virginia", i, pp. 319-20, gives the population (Bruce's "Social History", p. 18, says, "In 1634 alone twelve hundred [colonists] arrived") of these shires as follows:

The year 1636 gave us New Norfolk, probably named after Norfolk County in England, which was formed from that portion of Elizabeth City Shire which was on the southern side of the river; and the following year there were formed Lower Norfolk and Upper Norfolk,—from the lower and upper portions of New Norfolk, respectively,—and Isle of Wight,—another English name substituting the original Indian name.

The estimated population had increased to 7,466 in 1640,¶ at which time there were ten counties, after allowing for New Norfolk and Warrosquyoake which had become extinct; and the next few years brought an adjustment in the names of four other counties, when Upper Norfolk became Nansemond, Accawmack became Northampton, Charles River became York and Warwick River became Warwick, although in 1648 there were only eleven actually existing counties of the seventeen which had been formed and named, at which time the population was estimated at 15,000,* not including three hundred slaves then owned in the Colony. The formation of Rappahannock, half a century after the settlement at Jamestown, gave the Colony a total of seventeen existing counties,—seven of which originally had other names,—and an estimated population of 30,000, in 1659.*

As the rivers had naturally influenced the drift of the population more than anything else, it was but natural that all these counties should fall well within the Tidewater Section of the colony, 'though one is rather startled when he is brought to a realization of the fact that as early as 1664, the hardy colonists had established and formally organized the County of Stafford,—approximately two hundred miles by water from the seat of government and actually falling within the geological Piedmont Plateau.

With a population estimated at 40,000 in 1671,* and at 50,000 in 1675,† the colony in 1673 formed its twenty-sixth county, of which six had at that time ceased to exist under their original names; while the close of the 17th Century credited the colony with a population of about 80,000,‡ distributed through twenty-three existing counties, of which eight had originally been formed under other names. There was now a lull in countyforming for something like two decades, during which interim Spotswood and his "Knights of the Horseshoe"‖ crossed the mountains and visited the Valley in 1716. This was the first trip ever made to that region in the one hundred and nine years of the Colony, although Smith in his trip to the Falls of the Patomack in 1608 was within some fifty miles of the crest of the Blue Ridge. The object of this trip, as Spotswood states, was to pre-émpt the title to the West against the menace of French colonization,

---

¶ U. S. Census, 1910, Abstract, p. 567, n; Bruce's "Social Life", p. 18.

* U. S. Census, 1910, Abstract, p. 567, n.

† Bruce' "Social Life of Virginia", p. 20.

‡ *Ibid.*, pp. 20-1.

‖ The popular and unquestionably erroneous "Knights of the GOLDEN Horseshoe" seems to have arisen from the fact that each of the members of the party received as a souvenir of the trip a small golden horseshoe, which was engraved "Sic Juvat [not 'Jurat'] transcendere Montes": "So it delights one [not 'they swore'] to cross the mountains",—and this in spite of Dr. W. A. Caruthers' "Knights of the Horseshoe", 1845; and of chap. xii of W. W. Scott's "History of Orange County, Virginia", 1907, which bears the same title.

though it is evident that the estimated population of 100,000* in 1717 also demanded expansion in that direction. But whatever the cause, we know that there followed a period of county-forming, with the result that in 1754 an estimated population of 284,000* was living in fifty existing counties, eight of which were formed under other names, while all the Tidewater units, except Greensville and Mathews, had been formed; the Piedmont Plateau was getting pretty well filled by county organizations, the Valley contained at least two organized counties, and the Trans-Alleghany Section had one.

The Piedmont Plateau securely peopled, the ever-restless settlers now rapidly pushed the van of civilization over the Blue Ridge into the Valley, only to ascend the higher ridges of the Alleghanies and penetrate deeper into the wilderness; while, with an estimated population of 550,000 in 1775,* the opening year of the Revolution found Virginia with sixty-one existing counties, of which eight had been formed under other names: and thus at the time of the Declaration of Independence, we find that the loyalty of the colonists to the Mother Country is strikingly reflected by the fact that of these seventy-two counties, the sources of their names seem to have been (for names of the counties in each group, see Part V, "Origin of County Names"):

Reigning houses of England, and members thereof................ 25;
Localities,—former English homes of the colonists,............... 19;
Governors appointed by the Crown,............................. 12;
Englishmen of prominence, who had befriended the Colony........ 8;
Indian tribes which had owned the areas of these counties........ 8;

                            Counties named by the Colony,............... 72.

The close of the 18th Century credited Virginia with a population of 880,200,† and ninety-nine actually existing counties, although thirteen had become extinct through changes of names and nine had passed into Kentucky, when that State was admitted to the Union in 1792.

In 1860, a population of 1,596,318† was distributed through the one hundred and forty-eight then Virginia counties, while Bland, formed in 1861, was named after Richard Bland, of Revolutionary fame: but the admission of West Virginia to the Union in 1863 left but ninety-nine counties in the Old Dominion, and the last county resulting from Virginia legislation was Dickenson, formed in 1880 and named after the Hon. William J. Dickenson, of Russell County, a prominent member of the Re-adjuster Legislature which passed the Act of Assembly forming this county, and thus rounded off the one hundred counties which are to-day in the State.

---

* U. S. Census, 1910, Abstract, p. 567, n.
† U. S. Census.

Of these one hundred counties, the sources of their names seem to have been,—(for names of counties in each group, see Part V, below, "Origin of County Names")—

      Soldiers (chiefly Revolutionary), ... 23.
      Governors, ... 19.
      Revolutionary patriots, statesmen, etc., ... 14.
      Indian tribes and personages, ... 14.
      Virginians of prominence (jurists, senators, officials, etc.),. 11.
      Presidents of the United States, ... 5.
      Natural features .... 3.
      American statesmen, ... 3.
      Frontiersmen and hunters, ... 2.
      Englishmen of prominence, once connected with colonial affairs,. 2.
      English queen, ... 1.
      Land-owner's family .... 1.
      Re-adjuster legislator, ... 1.
      Royal family of France .... 1.

            Counties named by the State,..................... 100.

BIBLIOGRAPHY
(of Introduction).

Arber, Edward. Travels and Works of Captain John Smith. 2 vols. London, 1910.

Barton, R. T. Virginia Colonial Decisions. 2 vols. Boston, Mass., 1909.

Brown, Alexander. The First Republic in America. Boston and New York, 1898.

Brown, Alexander. The Genesis of the United States. 2 vols. Boston and New York, 1890.

Bruce, Philip Alexander. The Social Life of Virginia in the Seventeenth Century. Richmond, Va., 1907.

Bruce, Philip Alexander. Economic History of Virginia in the Seventeenth Century. 2 vols. New York and London, 1896.

Hening, William Waller. Statutes at Large of Virginia. 13 vols. Second edition. New York, 1823.

Long, Charles M. Virginia County Names. New York and Washington, 1908.

Stith, William. The History of Virginia. Sabin Reprint, New York, 1865.

Tyler, Lyon Gardiner. The Cradle of the Republic. Second edition. Richmond, Va., 1906.

Yonge, Samuel H. The Site of Old "James Towne". Tercentenary Edition. Richmond, Va., 1907.

U. S. Census Reports.

PART I.

ALPHABETICAL ARRANGEMENT

The Notes in full text are assembled in series at the end of this Part.

The Alphabetical Arrangement needs no comment other than the statement that, in the several instances in which there are two counties of the same name (Accomack, Fayette, Jefferson, Madison, Mason, Mercer, Nelson and Rappahannock), the arrangement is chronological under each of these pairs of names. Of course, no two counties of the same name existed in Virginia at the same time, as will be seen below:

> Accawmack of 1634 having been changed to Northampton in 1642/3, Accomack of the present day was formed in 1663.*
>
> Rappahannock of 1656** having become extinct in 1692, when its territory was formed into Essex and Richmond, Rappahannock of the present day was formed in 1833.
>
> Fayette of 1780, Jefferson of 1780, Nelson of 1785, Madison of 1786, Mercer of 1786 and Mason of 1789, all passed into the new State, when Kentucky was admitted to the Union in 1792.
> Virginia, ever-mindful of her ideals, again formed Madison of 1793, Jefferson of 1801, Mason of 1804, Nelson of 1808, Fayette of 1831 and Mercer of 1837; but the formation of West Virginia in 1863 carried all of these out of the jurisdiction of Virginia, except Madison and Nelson,—and thus it happens that, after twice honouring Jefferson, La Fayette, Mason and Mercer in this manner, the Old Dominion has at the present time no county of one of these names within her borders.

The following abbreviations are used in this Part:

A.: Acts of the General Assembly of Virginia, for the session indicated.

E. (superior): resulted from Virginia legislation, but now extinct, as shown by accompanying limiting dates.

H.: Hening's "Statutes at Large".

H. B.: "Journals of the House of Burgesses", 1619 to 1776 (Virginia State Library: 1905-1915).

J.: "Journal of the House" (Burgesses or Delegates, as the case may be) as interpreted in the note on the subject under the "General" section of the Preface.

K. (superior): resulted from Virginia legislation, but now in Kentucky.

S.: Shepherd's "Statutes at Large" (continuation of Hening).

U. S.: "United States Statutes at Large".

W. (superior): resulted from Virginia legislation, but now in West Virginia.

---

* See note 3.

** See note 65.

County	Formed	Land formed from	References
*Accawmack; (1634-1642/3)[3]	1634 (See note 1.);	Original Shire;	H. i, 224; H. i, 249.
Accomack;	1663 (See note 3.);	Northampton;	H. ii, 122, 186.
Albemarle;[4]	1744 (J. Oct. 16, 1744);	Goochland; and part of Louisa; "and certain islands in the Fluvanna River."	H. v, 266; H. vi, 441; H. vii, 419; H. viii, 395; H. ix, 325; A (1836-7), 38; A (1838), 57; A (1855-6), 99; A (1861), 151; A (1871-2), 342; A (1876-7), 21; A (1876-7), 228;
Alexandria;[5]	1847 (J. Mar. 13, 1847);	District of Columbia; (that portion of it which was formerly a part of Fairfax County);	U. S. Stats. i, 130, 214; U. S. Stats. ii, 103, 115; A (1845-6), 50; A (1846-7), 41; A (1846-7), 48.
Alleghany;	1822 (J. Jan. 5, 1822);	Bath, Botetourt and Monroe;	A (1821-2), 28;

Amelia;	1735 (J. Sep. 30, 1734);	and part of Monroe; and part of Bath;	A (1822-3), 88; A (1842-3), 40; A (1846-7), 57; A (1855-6), 97; A (1885-6), 383.
Amherst;	1761 (J. Apl. 7, 1761);	Prince George and Brunswick;	H. iv, 467; H. vi, 379; H. xii, 723; H. xii, 596;
Appomattox;	1845 (J. Feb. 8, 1845);	Albemarle; "and certain islands in the Fluvanna River."	H. vii, 419; H. viii, 395. S. iii, 378.
		Buckingham, Prince Edward, Charlotte and Campbell; and part of Campbell;	A (1844-5), 38; A (1847-8), 41; A (1859-0), 151.
Augusta;⁶	1745 (J. Dec. 15, 1738);	Orange;	H. v, 78; H. vi, 376; H. viii, 395; H. ix, 262; H. ix, 420; H. x, 114; H. x, 351; H. xii, 637; H. xiii, 165.

County	Formed	Land formed from	References
w Barbour;	1843 (J. Mar. 3, 1843);	Harrison, Lewis and Randolph;	A (1842-3), 37; A (1843-4), 34; A (1850-1), 23.
Bath;	1791 (J. Dec. 14, 1790);	Augusta, Botetourt and Greenbrier;	H. xiii, 165; S. ii, 53; A. (1821-2), 27; A (1821-2), 28; A (1822-3), 88; A (1846-7), 52; A (1846-7), 57.
Bedford;r	1754 (J. Dec. 13, 1753);	Lunenburg; and parts of Albemarle and Lunenburg;	H. vi, 381; H. vi, 441; H. x, 447; H. xii, 70.
w Berkeley;	1772 (J. Mar. 24, 1772);	Frederick;	H. viii, 597; S. ii, 271; A (1819-0), 27; A (1862, Wheeling), 3; A (1865-6), 194; A (1865-6), 195.

Virginia Counties

Bland;	1861 (J. Mar. 30, 1861);[9]	Giles, Wythe and Tazewell; and part of Giles;	A (1861), 45; A (1899-0), 665.
w Boone;	1847 (J. Mar. 11, 1847);	Kanawha, Cabell and Logan;	A (1846-7), 49.
Botetourt;[19]	1770 (J. Nov. 28, 1769);	Augusta; and part of Rockbridge;	H. viii, 395; H. viii, 600; H. ix, 420; H. xii, 74; H. xiii, 76; H. xiii, 165; S. i, 406; S. ii, 64; S. ii, 345; A (1821-2), 28; A (1838), 54; A (1850-1), 21; A (1887-8), 556.
k Bourbon;	1786 (J. Dec. 29, 1785);	Fayette;	H. xii, 89; H. xii, 658.
w Braxton;	1836 (J. Jan. 15, 1836);	Lewis, Kanawha and Nicholas; and part of Randolph;	A (1835-6), 18; A (1843-4), 37; A (1848-9), 30; A (1857-8), 111; A (1859-0), 151.
w Brooke;	1797 (J. Nov. 30, 1796);[10]	Ohio;	S. ii, 54; A (1847-8), 30.

County	Formed	Land formed from	References
Brunswick;[11]	1732 (J. Dec. 17, 1720);	Area not named [Prince George];[11,a] and parts of Surry and Isle of Wight;	H. iv, 77; H. ix, 355; H. iv, 467; H. v, 383; H. x, 363; H. xli, 596.
Buchanan;	1858 (J. Feb. 16, 1858);[12]	Tazewell and Russell;	A (1857-8), 108; A (1879-0), 125.
Buckingham;	1761 (J. Apl. 7, 1761);	Albemarle;	H. vii, 419; H. ix, 559;
w Cabell;	1809 (J. Jan. 2, 1809);	and part of Appomattox; Kanawha;	A (1844-5), 38; A (1859-0), 171. A (1808-9), 44; A (1817-8), 185; A (1823-4), 20; A (1829-0), 117; A (1841-2), 36; A (1846-7), 49; A (1847-8), 34; A (1849-0), 24.
w Calhoun;	1856 (J. Mar. 5, 1856);	Gilmer;	A (1855-6), 90.

Virginia Counties 47

Campbell;	1782 (J. Dec. 15, 1781);	Bedford;	H. x, 447; A (1844-5), 38; A (1847-8), 41.
Caroline;[13]	1728 (J. Mar. 15, 1727);	Essex, King and Queen and King William; and part of King and Queen; and part of King and Queen;	H. B. (1727-40), 39; H. iv, 420; H. v, 185; H. vii, 620.
Carroll;	1842 (J. Jan. 17, 1842);	Grayson; and part of Patrick;	A (1841-2), 32; A (1855-6), 98.
Charles City;	1634 (See note 1.);	Original Shire;	H. i, 224;[14] H. iii, 233; H. iv, 94,14,a
*Charles River; (1634-1642/3)[15]	1634 (See note 1.);	and enlarged, but no metes or bounds given; Original Shire;	H. i, 224; H. i, 249;
Charlotte;	1765 (J. Nov. 27, 1764);	Lunenburg;	H. viii, 41; H. ix, 327; A (1844-5), 38.
Chesterfield;[16]	1749 (J. May 1, 1749);	Henrico;	H. B. (1742-9), 384. A (1849-0), 26;
Clarke;	1836 (J. Mar. 8, 1836);	Frederick; and part of Warren;	A (1835-6), 20; A (1859-0), 496;

County	Formed	Land formed from	References
w Clay;	1858 (J. Mar. 29, 1858);	Braxton and Nicholas;	A (1857-8), 111.
Craig;	1851 (J. Mar. 21, 1851);	Botetourt, Roanoke, Giles and Monroe;[17] and part of Monroe; and part of Montgomery; and part of Alleghany; and part of Monroe; and part of Giles;	A (1850-1), 21; A (1852-3), 130; A (1852-3), 130; A (1855-6), 97; A (1855-6), 97; A (1857-8), 114; A (1879-0), 183.
Culpeper;[18]	1749 (J. Mar. 23, 1748);	Orange;	H. B. (1742-9), 346; H. xiii, 558; A (1832-3), 44.
Cumberland;[19]	1749 (J. Mar. 23, 1748);	Goochland; and part of Buckingham;	H. B. (1742-9), 346; H. ix, 322; H. ix, 559.
Dickenson;	1880 (J. Feb. 27, 1880);[20]	Russell, Wise and Buchanan;	A (1879-0), 125.
Dinwiddie;	1752 (J. Mar. 9, 1752);	Prince George;	H. vi, 254.
w Doddridge;	1845 (J. Feb. 4, 1845);	Harrison, Tyler, Ritchie and Lewis;	A (1844-5), 42; A (1849-0), 33.

Virginia Counties

• Dunmore; (1772-1778);[21]	1772 (J. Mar. 24, 1772);	Frederick;	H. viii, 597; H. ix, 424.
Elizabeth City;[22]	1634 (See note 1.);	Original Shire;	H. i, 224; A. (1881-2), 43.
Essex;	1692 (J. Apl. 26, 1692);	Rappahannock;	H. iii, 104; H. iv, 77; H. iv, 240,[23]
Fairfax;	1742 (J. May 27, 1742);	Prince William; and part of Loudoun;	H. v, 207; H. vii, 148; S. ii, 107; U. S. Stats. i, 130, 214; U. S. Stats. ii, 103, 115. A. (1845-6), 50; A. (1846-7), 41; A. (1846-7), 48.
Fauquier;[24]	1759 (J. Apl. 5, 1759);	Prince William;	H. vii, 311. A. (1823-4), 82.
κ Fayette;	1780 (J. June 30, 1780);	Kentucky;	H. x, 315; H. xii, 89; H. xii, 663.
w Fayette;	1831 (J. Feb. 28, 1831);	Logan, Greenbrier, Nicholas and Kanawha; and part of Kanawha;	A. (1830-1), 134; A. (1830-1), 136; A. (1832-3), 47; A. (1839), 33; A. (1849-0), 19. A. (1849-0), 25; A. (1850-1), 26.

County	Formed	Land formed from	References
*Fincastle; (1772-1777);[26]	1772 (J. Apl. 8, 1772);	Botetourt;	H. viii, 600; H. ix, 257.
Floyd;	1831 (J. Jan. 15, 1831);	Montgomery; and part of Franklin;	A (1830-1), 137; A (1872-3), 85.
Fluvanna;	1777 (J. June 3, 1777);	Albemarle;	H. ix, 325; H. xii, 71; A (1836-7), 33; A (1838), 57; A (1855-6), 99; A (1861), 151; A (1871-2), 342; A (1876-7), 20; A (1876-7), 228.
Franklin;	1786 (J. Nov. 29, 1785);	Bedford and Henry; and part of Patrick;	H. xii, 70; A (1847-8), 42; A (1872-3), 85.
Frederick;[26]	1743 (J. Dec. 15, 1738);	Orange; and part of Augusta;	H. v, 78; H. vi, 376; H. viii, 597; A (1827-8), 51; A (1835-6), 20; A (1835-6), 22;

Virginia Counties

Giles;³⁷	1806 (J. Jan. 16, 1806); Montgomery, Monroe and Tazewell; and part of Wythe;	S. iii, 244;
		S. iii, 389;
	and part of Tazewell;	A (1823-4), 20;
		A (1825-6), 39;
		A (1826-7), 42;
		A (1827-8), 52;
	and part of Monroe;	A (1828-9), 119;
	and part of Tazewell;	A (1835-6), 24;
		A (1836-7), 31;
	and part of Mercer;	A (1840-1), 61;
		A (1850-1), 21;
		A (1857-8), 114;
		A (1861), 45;
	and part of Craig;	A (1879-0), 183;
		A (1899-0), 665.
w Gilmer;	1845 (J. Feb. 3, 1845); Lewis and Kanawha;	A (1844-5), 45;
		A (1846-7), 58;
		A (1855-6), 90;
		A (1855-6), 91.
Gloucester;	1651 (See note 28.); York;	H. i, 374;
		H. xiii, 162.

A (1847-8), 43;
A (1862, Wheeling), 3;
A (1865-6), 194;
A (1865-6), 195.

County	Formed	Land formed from	References
Goochland;[29]	1728 (J. Mar. 6, 1727);	Henrico;	H. B. (1727-40), 83; H. iv, 240; H. v, 266; (See note 19.) H. xii, 71;
Grayson;	1793 (J. Nov. 7, 1792);	Wythe; and part of Patrick;	H. xiii, 559; S. i, 315; A (1809-0), 58; A (1817-8), 185; A (1824-5), 75; A (1840-1), 62; A (1841-2), 32; A (1874-5), 26; A (1874-5), 330.
w Greenbrier;	1778 (J. Jan. 12, 1778);	Botetourt and Montgomery; and part of Monroe; and part of Fayette; and part of Fayette;	H. ix, 420; H. xii, 670; H. xiii, 165; S. i, 388; S. ii, 168; A (1817-8), 34; A (1824-5), 73; A (1826-7), 41; A (1830-1), 134; A (1830-1), 136; A (1832-3), 47.

Greene;	1838 (J. Jan. 24, 1838);	Orange;	A (1838), 52.
Greensville;	1781 (J. Nov. 28, 1780);	Brunswick; and part of Brunswick; and part of Sussex;	H. x, 363; H. xii, 596; S. ii, 347.
Halifax;	1752 (J. Apl. 17, 1752);	Lunenburg;	H. vi, 252; H. viii, 205;
wHampshire;	1754 (J. Dec. 13, 1753);	Augusta and Frederick; and part of Augusta; and part of Hardy;	H. vi, 376; H. ix, 420; H. xii, 86; H. xii, 597; A (1819-0), 27; A (1820-1), 120; A (1823-4), 83.
wHancock;	1848 (J. Jan. 15, 1848);	Brooke;	A (1847-8), 30.
Hanover;⁹⁰	1721 (J. Nov. 20 [26], 1720);	New Kent;	H. B. (1712-26), 281; H. iv, 95; H. v, 208; H. xii, 620;
wHardy;	1786 (J. Dec. 10, 1785);	Hampshire;	H. xii, 86; H. xii, 597; H. xii, 637; A (1823-4), 83;

County	Formed	Land formed from	References
▼Harrison;	1784 (J. June 4, 1784);	Monongalia; and part of Monongalia; and part of Randolph; and part of Ohio;	H. xi, 366; H. xii, 393; S. ii, 170; S. ii, 203; S. ii, 345; S. iii, 174; A (1816-7), 152; A (1816-7), 154; A (1818-9), 142; A (1841-2), 34; A (1842-3), 36; A (1842-3), 37; A (1843-4), 34; A (1844-5), 42; A (1849-0), 33.
Henrico;[31]	1634 (See note 1.);	Original Shire;[31, a]	H. i, 224; (See note 31, b..) H. iv, 240; (See note 16); H. xii, 620.
Henry;	1777 (J. Oct. 23, 1776);	Pittsylvania; and part of Patrick;	H. ix, 241; H. xii, 70; H. xiii, 160; H. xiii, 290; A (1857-8), 113.

Virginia Counties

Highland;	1847 (J. Mar. 19, 1847);	Pendleton and Bath;	A (1846-7), 52.
e Illinois;[32] (1778-1784)[33]	1778 (J. Dec. 9, 1778);	"on the western side of the Ohio river [Augusta]"	H. ix, 552; H. x, 303.
Isle of Wight;	1637 (See note 34.);	Formerly Warrosquyoake; and part of Upper Norfolk; and part of Nansemond; and part of Nansemond;	H. i, 228;[34], a H. i, 247; H. i, 423; (See note 71.) H. viii, 405; H. viii, 602.
w Jackson;	1831 (J. Mar. 1, 1831);	Mason, Kanawha and Wood; and part of Wirt;	A (1830-1), 138; A (1847-8), 38; A (1852-3), 130; A (1855-6), 91.
James City;	1634 (See note 1.);	Original Shire; and part of New Kent; and part of York;	H. i, 224; H. iv, 95;[34], b H. viii, 208; H. viii, 405; H. viii, 419; A (1852), 31.
k Jefferson;	1780 (J. June 30, 1780);	Kentucky;	H. x, 315; H. xi, 469.
w Jefferson;	1801 (J. Jan. 8, 1801);	Berkeley;	S. ii, 271; A (1862, Wheeling), 3; A (1865-6), 194; A (1865-6), 195.

County	Formed	Land formed from	References
ᵂ Kanawha;³⁵	1789 (J. Nov. 14, 1788);	Greenbrier and Montgomery;	H. xii, 670; S. i, 388; S. ii, 263; S. iii, 77; A (1808-9), 44; A (1816-7), 157; A (1817-8), 34; A (1817-8), 185; A (1823-4), 20; A (1823-4), 80; A (1823-4), 81; A (1829-0), 117; A (1830-1), 134; A (1830-1), 138; A (1835-6), 18; A (1839), 83; A (1843-4), 37; A (1844-5), 45; A (1846-7), 49; A (1847-8), 34; A (1849-0), 24; A (1849-0), 25; A (1855-6), 91.
ˣ Kentucky;³⁶ (1777-1780)³⁷	1777 (J. Dec. 7, 1776);	Fincastle;	H. ix, 257; H. x, 315.

King and Queen	1691 (J. May 12, 1691);	New Kent;	H. iii, 94; H. iii, 211; H. iv, 77; H. iv, 240;38 H. v, 185; H. vii, 620.
King George;39	1721 (J. Nov. 24, 1720);	Richmond; and part of Westmoreland;	H. B. (1712-26), 279; H. iv, 95; H. iv, 303; H. ix, 244; H. ix, 432.
King William;	1702 (J. Sep. 12, 1701);	King and Queen;	H. iii, 211; H. iv, 77; H. iv, 240.40
Lancaster;	1651 (See note 41.);	Northumberland and York;	H. i, 374;
Lee;	1793 (J. Oct. 25, 1792);	Russell; and part of Scott;	H. xiii, 556; A (1812-3), 110; A (1814-5), 85; A (1814-5), 87; A (1822-3), 90; A (1836-7), 34; A (1855-6), 87.

County	Formed	Land formed from	References
w Lewis;	1816 (J. Dec. 18, 1816);	Harrison; and part of Randolph;	A (1816-7), 152; A (1817-8), 184; A (1818-9), 142; A (1835-6), 18; A (1842-3), 35; A (1843-4), 37; A (1844-5), 42; A (1844-5), 45; A (1846-7), 58; A (1849-0), 33; A (1850-1), 23.
k Lincoln;	1780 (J. June 30, 1780);	Kentucky;	H. x, 315; H. xii, 118.
w Logan;[42]	1824 (J. Jan. 12, 1824);	Giles, Cabell, Tazewell and Kanawha; and parts of Kanawha and Cabell;	A (1823-4), 20; A (1829-0), 117; A (1830-1), 134; A (1833-4), 33; A (1846-7), 49; A (1849-0), 21.
Loudoun;	1757 (J. May 17, 1757);	Fairfax;	H. vii, 148; S. ii, 107; A (1823-4), 82.

Louisa;[43]	1742 (J. June 2, 1742);	Hanover;	H. v, 208; H. vii, 419; A (1836-7), 33; A (1838), 57; A (1876-7), 20; A (1876-7), 21; A (1876-7), 228;
e Lower Norfolk; (1637-1691);[44]	1637 (See note 55.);	New Norfolk;	H. i, 228;[48], a H. i, 247. H. iii, 95.
Lunenburg;	1746 (J. Apl. 1, 1746);	Brunswick; and part of Charlotte;	H. v, 383; H. vi, 383; H. vi, 441; H. vi, 252; H. viii, 41; H. ix, 327.
w McDowell;	1858 (J. Feb. 20, 1858);	Tazewell;	A (1857-8), 106; A (1859-0), 169.
k Madison;	1786 (J. Dec. 15, 1785);	Lincoln;	H. xii, 118.
Madison;	1793 (J. Dec. 5, 1792);[45]	Culpeper;	H. xiii, 558.
w Marion;[46]	1842 (J. Jan. 14, 1842);	Monongalia and Harrison; and part of Monongalia;	A (1841-2), 34; A (1842-3), 40; A (1843-4), 34; A (1846-7), 57; A (1855-6), 98.

County	Formed	Land formed from	References
w Marshall;[47]	1835 (J. Mar. 12, 1835);	Ohio;	A (1834-5), 38.
k Mason;	1789 (J. Nov. 5, 1788);	Bourbon;	H. xii, 658.
w Mason;	1804 (J. Jan. 3, 1804);[48]	Kanawha;	S. iii, 77; A (1816-7), 157; A (1823-4), 81; A (1830-1), 133; A (1847-8), 34.
Mathews;	1791 (J. Dec. 16, 1790);	Gloucester;	H. xii, 162.
Mecklenburg;	1765 (J. Nov. 27, 1764);	Lunenburg;	H. viii, 41.
k Mercer;	1786 (J. Dec. 15, 1785);	Lincoln;	H. xii, 118.
w Mercer;	1837 (J. Mar. 17, 1837);	Giles and Tazewell;	A (1836-7), 81; A (1840-1), 61; A (1846-7), 57.
Middlesex;	1673 (See note 49.);	Lancaster;	H. ii, 327.
w Monongalia;	1776 (J. Nov. 6, 1776);	Augusta; and part of Augusta; and part of Augusta;	H. ix, 262; H. x, 114; H. x, 351; H. xi, 366; S. ii, 203; A (1817-8), 32; A (1818-9), 141;

Monroe (Munroe)[30] 1779 (J. Jan. 15, 1799);[31] and part of Preston;
A (1840-1), 61;
A (1841-2), 34;
A (1846-7), 57.

Greenbrier;
and part of Botetourt;
S. ii, 168;
S. ii, 345;
S. iii, 244;
A (1821-2), 28;
A (1826-7), 41;
A (1826-7), 42;
A (1828-9), 119;
A (1842-3), 40;
A (1850-1), 21;
A (1852-3), 130;
A (1855-6), 97;
A (1855-6), 383.

Montgomery; 1777 (J. Dec. 7, 1776); Fincastle;
H. ix, 257;
H. ix, 330;
H. ix, 420;
H. xii, 670;
H. xiii, 76;

and part of Botetourt;
S. i, 315;
S. i, 406;
S. ii, 64;
S. iii, 244;
A (1830-1), 137;
A (1839), 30;
A (1839-0), 35;
A (1841-2), 39;
A (1848-9), 28;
A (1852-3), 130.

and part of Pulaski;

County	Formed	Land formed from	References
wMorgan;	1820 (J. Feb. 9, 1820);	Berkeley and Hampshire;	A (1819-0), 27; A (1820-1), 120; A (1827-8), 51.
Nansemond;	1642 (See note 52);	Formerly Upper Norfolk;	H. i, 321; (Va. Mag. of Hist. and Biog., vol. xiii, 254.) H. viii, 405; H. viii, 602; H. xii, 69.
kNelson;	1785 (J. Nov. 29, 1784);	Jefferson;	H. xi, 469.
Nelson;	1808 (J. Dec. 23, 1807);⁵³	Amherst;	S. iii, 378;
New Kent;	1654 (————);	York; and part of James City;	H. i, 387-8; H. iv, 95,⁵⁴ H. viii, 208.
•New Norfolk; (1636-1637)⁵⁵	1636 (See note 55.);	Elizabeth City;	Norfolk Connty Records and Land Grants. See note 55.
wNicholas;	1818 (J. Jan. 30, 1818);	Greenbrier, Kanawha and Randolph;	A (1817-8), 34; A (1819-0), 72;

Norfolk;[37]	and part of Kanawha;	A (1819-0), 91; A (1823-4), 80; A (1830-1), 134; A (1835-6), 18; A (1843-4), 37; A (1857-8), 111; A (1859-0), 151.
Northampton;	Lower Norfolk;	H. iii, 95.
1691 (J. May 16, 1691);		
1642-3 (See note 58.);	Formerly Accawmack;	H. i, 249.
Northumberland;[39]	Chickacoun;	H. 4, 294, n; H. 1, 299; H. 1, 337-8; H. 1, 340; H. 1, 352; H. 1, 353; H. 1, 362.
1648 (See note 60.);		
Nottoway;	Amelia;	H. xii, 723; H. xiii, 561.
1789 (J. Dec. 23, 1788);[61]		
w Ohio;	Augusta; and part of Yohogania;	H. ix, 262; H. xii, 114; S. ii, 54; S. iii, 174; A (1814-5), 87; A (1832-3), 48; A (1834-5), 38.
1776 (J. Nov. 6, 1776);		

County	Formed	Land formed from	References
Orange;	1734 (J. Sep. 20, 1734);	Spotsylvania;	H. iv, 450. H. v, 78; (See note 18;; A (1838), 52.
Page;	1831 (J. Mar. 30, 1831);	Rockingham and Shenandoah;	A (1830-1), 140.
Patrick;	1791 (J. Nov. 26, 1790);	Henry; and part of Henry;	H. xiii, 160; H. xiii, 290; S. i, 315; A (1809-0), 58; A (1817-8), 185; A (1847-8), 42; A (1855-6), 98; A (1857-8), 113.
w Pendleton;	1788 (J. Dec. 4, 1787);	Augusta, Hardy and Rockingham; and part of Bath;	H. xii, 687; S. ii, 53; A (1821-2), 27; A (1846-7), 52.
Pittsylvania;	1767 (J. Dec. 15, 1766);	Halifax;	H. viii, 205; H. ix, 241;
w Pleasants;	1851 (J. Mar. 29, 1851);	Wood, Tyler and Ritchie;	A (1850-1), 25.

wPocahontas;	1821 (J. Dec. 21, 1821);	Bath, Pendleton and Randolph, and part of Greenbrier;	A (1821-2), 27; A (1824-5), 73.
Powhatan;	1777 (J. June 3, 1777);	Cumberland; and part of Chesterfield;	H. ix, 322; A (1849-0), 26.
wPreston;	1818 (J. Jan. 19, 1818);	Monongalia; and part of Randolph; and part of Randolph; and part of Monongalia;	A (1817-8), 32; A (1818-9), 141; A (1827-8), 53; A (1838), 57; A (1840-1), 61.
Prince Edward;	1754 (J. Nov. 17, 1753);	Amelia;	H. vi, 379; A (1844-5), 38.
Prince George;[63]	1703 (J. Aug. 25, 1702);	Charles City;	H. iii, 223; H. iv, 467; H. vi, 254.
Prince William;	1731 (J. June 19, 1730);	Stafford and King George;	H. iv, 303; H. v, 207; H. vii, 311.
Princess Anne;[63]	1691 (J. May 16, 1691);	Lower Norfolk;	H. iii, 95.
Pulaski;	1839 (J. Mar. 30, 1839);	Montgomery and Wythe;[64]	A (1839), 30; A (1839-0), 35; A (1841-2), 39; A (1861-2), 106.
wPutnam;	1848 (J. Mar. 11, 1848);	Kanawha, Cabell and Mason; and parts of Cabell and Kanawha;	A (1847-8), 34; A (1849-0), 24.

County	Formed	Land formed from	References
w Raleigh;	1850 (J. Jan. 23, 1850);	Fayette;	A (1849-0), 19; A (1850-1), 26.
w Randolph;	1787 (J. Nov. 29, 1786);	Harrison;	H. xii, 393; S. ii, 345; A (1817-8), 34; A (1817-8), 184; A (1821-2), 27; A (1827-8), 53; A (1838), 57; A (1842-3), 37; A (1848-9), 30; A (1850-1), 23; A (1855-6), 95; A (1859-0), 151.
• Rappahannock; (1656-1692)⁶⁶	1656 (See note 65.);	Lancaster;	H. i, 427; H. iii, 104.
Rappahannock;	1833 (J. Feb. 18, 1833);⁶⁷	Culpeper;	A (1832-3), 44.
Richmond;	1692 (J. Apl. 26, 1692);	Rappahannock;	H. iii, 104; H. iv, 95;⁶⁸
w Ritchie;	1843 (J. Feb. 18, 1843);	Harrison, Lewis and Wood;	A (1842-3), 35; A (1843-4), 24;

County		Formed from	References
Roanoke;[99]	1838 (J. Mar. 30, 1838);	Botetourt; and part of Montgomery;	A (1844-5), 42; A (1849-0), 33; A (1850-1), 25.
w Roane;	1856 (J. Mar. 11, 1856);	Kanawha, Jackson and Gilmer;	A (1838), 54; A (1848-9), 28; A (1850-1), 21.
Rockbridge;	1778 (J. Jan. 12, 1778);	Augusta and Botetourt; and part of Botetourt;	A (1855-6), 91. H. ix, 420; H. xii, 74; A (1887-8), 556.
Rockingham;	1778 (J. Jan. 12, 1778);	Augusta;	H. ix, 420; H. xii, 637; A (1830-1), 140.
Russell;	1786 (J. Jan. 6, 1786);	Washington;	H. xii, 110; H. xii, 556; S. ii, 217; S. iii, 310; A (1812-3), 110; A (1814-5), 85; A (1814-5), 87; A (1823-4), 83; A (1824-5), 76; A (1834-5), 40; A (1855-6), 87; A (1857-8), 108; A (1879-0), 125.

County	Formed	Land formed from	References
Scott;	1814 (J. Nov. 24, 1814);[70]	Lee, Russell and Washington;	A (1814-5), 85; A (1814-5), 87; A (1822-3), 90; A (1836-7), 34; A (1855-6), 87.
Shenando[ah];	1778 (J. Jan. 12, 1778);	Formerly Dunmore;	H. ix, 424; A (1830-1), 140; A (1835-6), 22; A (1847-8), 43.
Smyth;	1832 (J. Feb. 23, 1832);	Washington and Wythe;	A (1831-2), 47; A (1874-5), 830.
Southampton;[71]	1749 (J. Apl. 20, 1749);	Isle of Wight; and part of Nansemond;	H. B. (1742-9), 371; H. xii, 69.
Spotsylvania;	1721 (J. Dec. 17, 1720);	Essex, King William and King and Queen;	H. iv, 77; H. iv, 450.
Stafford;	1664 (See note 72.);	Westmoreland;	H. ii, 239; H. ii, 250; H. iv, 303; H. ix, 244.
Surry;	1652 (See note 73.);	James City;	H. i, 373; H. iv, 355.

Sussex;		Surry;	H. vi, 384; S. ii, 347.
wTaylor;[74]	1844 (J. Jan. 19, 1844);	Harrison, Barbour and Marion; and part of Marion;	A (1843-4), 34; A (1855-6), 98.
Tazewell;	1800 (J. Dec. 20, 1799);[75]	Wythe and Russell; and part of Russell; and parts of Washington and Wythe; and part of Logan; and part of Russell;	S. ii, 217; S. iii, 310; S. iii, 244; A (1823-4), 20; A (1825-6), 39; A (1825-6), 40; A (1827-8), 52; A (1833-4), 73; A (1834-5), 40; A (1835-6), 24; A (1836-7), 31; A (1857-8), 106; A (1857-8), 108; A (1859-0), 169; A (1861), 45.
wTucker;	1856 (J. Mar. 7, 1856);	Randolph;	A (1855-6), 95.
wTyler;	1814 (J. Dec. 3, 1814);[76]	Ohio;	A (1814-5), 87; A (1815-6), 154; A (1832-3), 48; A (1844-5), 42; A (1845-6), 51; A (1849-0), 33; A (1850-1), 25.

County	Formed	Land formed from	References
• Upper Norfolk; (1637-1642)[77]	1637 (See note 55.);	New Norfolk;	H. 1, 228;[76],a H. 1, 247; H. 1, 321; H. 1, 423.
w Upshur;	1851 (J. Mar. 27, 1851);[78]	Randolph, Barbour and Lewis;	A (1850-1), 23.
Warren;	1836 (J. Mar. 9, 1836);	Shenandoah and Fredericksburg;	A (1835-6), 22; A (1859-0), 496.
e Warrosquyoake; (1634-1637)[79]	1634 (See note 1.);	Original Shire;	H. 1, 224; H. 1, 249.
Warwick;	1642/3 (See note 80.);	Formerly Warwick River;	H. 1, 249; H. 1, 250; A (1881-2), 43.
• Warwick River; (1634-1642/3),[81]	1634 (See note 1.);	Original Shire;	H. 1, 224; H. 1, 249.
Washington;	1777 (J. Dec. 7, 1776);	Fincastle; and part of Montgomery;	H. 1x, 257; H. 1x, 330; H. xii, 110; S. 4, 315; A (1814-5), 85; A (1814-5), 87;

w Wayne;	1842 (J. Jan. 18, 1842);		A (1823-4), 83;
			A (1824-5), 76;
			A (1825-6), 40;
			A (1831-2), 47.
w Webster;	1860 (J. Jan. 10, 1860);		A (1841-2), 36.
Westmoreland;[33]	1653 (See note 83.);	Cabell;	A (1859-0), 151;
			A (1861), 50.
w Wetzel;[34]	1846 (J. Jan. 10, 1846);	Nicholas, Braxton and Randolph;	H. i, 321;
			H. ix, 432.
w Wirt;	1848 (J. Jan. 19, 1848);	Northumberland; and part of King George;	A (1845-6), 51.
Wise;	1856 (J. Feb. 16, 1856);	Tyler;	A (1847-8), 38;
			A (1852-3), 130.
w Wood;	1798 (J. Dec. 22, 1798);[35]	Wood and Jackson;	A (1855-6), 87;
			A (1879-0), 125.
		Lee, Scott and Russell;	S. ii, 170;
			S. ii, 263;
		Harrison; and part of Kanawha;	A (1830-1), 138;
			A (1842-3), 35;
			A (1843-4), 34;
			A (1847-8), 38;
			A (1850-1), 25.
k Woodford;	1789 (J. Nov. 12, 1788);	Fayette;	H. xii, 663.

County	Formed	Land formed from	References
w Wyoming;	1850 (J. Jan. 26, 1850);	Logan;	A (1849-0), 21.
Wythe;	1790 (J. Dec. 1, 1789);	Montgomery; and part of Grayson;	H. xiii, 76; H. xiii, 559; S. ii, 217; S. iii, 389; A (1824-5), 75; A (1825-6), 40; A (1831-2), 47; A (1839), 30; A (1839-0), 35; A (1840-1), 62; A (1861), 45; A (1861-2), 106; A (1874-5), 26.
• Yohogania;[86] (1776-1786)[87]	1776 (J. Nov. 6, 1776);	Augusta;	H. ix, 262; H. xii, 114.
York;	1642/3 (See note 88.);	Formerly Charles River;	H. i, 249; H. viii, 405; H. viii, 419; A (1852), 31.

Footnotes For Part I.

ALPHABETICAL ARRANGEMENT

[1] "In 1634. The country divided into 8 shires, which are to be governed as the shires in England.
The names of the shires are

James City	Warwick River
Henrico	Warrosquyoake
Charles City	Charles River
Elizabeth Citty	Accawmack

[Brown's "First Republic", p. 254 (see also p. 313), says under date prior to June 17, 1617, "It seems certain, however, that he (Argall) located definitely the then bounds of the four great 'Incorporations and Parishes of James Citty, Charles Citty, the city of Henricus and Kiccowtan'" (afterwards Elizabeth City County)]

And Lieuten'ts. to be appointed the same as in England, and in a more especial manner to take care of the warr against Indians. And as in England *sheriffs* shall be elected to have the same power as there; and *sergeants*, and *bailiffs* where need be.

Commissioners, instead of £5 causes, may determined £10 causes and one of the council to have notice to attend and assist in each court of shire."
(H. i, p. 224.)

[2] Accawmack was formed in 1634 (H. i, p. 224), but the name was changed to Northampton in 1642/3 (H. i, p. 249).

[3] The Accomack records begin April 21, 1663. The exact date of the formation of the county seems to be unavailable, but we know that the Act of March 1661/2 says (H. ii, p. 122) that "* * * the use of the mony raised this yeare out of the two shillings per hogshead in Northampton County [the name given to the whole of the Eastern Shore in 1642/3 (H. i, p. 249)], * * *" while the Act of September 1663—in referring to this Act of 1661/2,—says (H. ii, p. 186) "* * * prohibits the importation of any salt in the counties of Northampton and Accomack, * * * for the said counties, * * *",—specifying and twice referring to both counties, which must have been in existence at that time.

Also we are indebted to the Hon. John D. Grant, Jr., Clerk of Accomack, for the following caption of the first court of that county, as it appears in the earliest volume of records, (D. & W., 1663-1666):

"At a Court held in Accomack County ye 21st Aprill by his Majesty's justices of the Peace for ye said County in ye fifteenth year of the Raigne of our Sovreign Lord Charles ye Second by ye Grace of God of Great Britain, France, and Ireland,—King defender of ye faith, and in ye year of our Lord God 1663. Present, Anto. Hodgkins, Captain George Parker, Mr. Rev. Brown, Mr. West, Mr. John Wise." (See also Green's "Genesis of Counties" in Slaughter's "Brief Sketch of William Green, LL. D.", p. 101; and Wise's "Early History of the Eastern Shore of Virginia", p. 173).

[4] In regard to the lost and destroyed records of Albemarle County, Wood's "History of Albemarle County in Virginia", p. 25, says:

"Allusion has been made [p. 13] to the great misfortune sustained in the loss of the early records. The gap thus occasioned reaches from 1748 to 1783, a period of thirty-five years, and one intensely interesting in the history of the country at large. The loss was caused by the wanton ravages of the British troops near the close of the Revolutionary War [Tarleton's raid of June, 1781: see p. 44]. Many references to this event are met with in the subsequent proceedings of the County Court. In 1794 it recommended

John Key, * * * as 'Commissioners to reinstate such records as had been lost or destroyed'. These persons or others were certainly appointed for this purpose, as the Court in one place ordered the transactions of the Commissioners 'for reinstating the records destroyed by the enemy', to be recorded."

This entry of the 16th of June, 1794,—obviously in accordance with the Act of Assembly of 1787 (H. xii, p. 497),—is to be found in Order Book, County Court of Albemarle County, 1793-'95, p. 177, and is as follows:

"John Key, George Divers, Thomas Garth, Thomas W. Lewis, Garland Carr, Thomas Bell, Robert Jouett, W. W. Hening and Cornelius Schenk be nominated and recommended to the Governor and Council as proper persons to be Commissioners to reinstate such Records as have been lost or destroyed."

⁵ On Dec. 3, 1789, the Virginia Assembly passed "An Act for the cession of ten miles square, or any lesser quantity of territory within this State, to the United States, in Congress assembled, for the permanent seat of the general government" (H. xiii, p. 43). By Act of Congress of Feb. 27, 1801 (U. S. Stats. 2, pp. 103, 115), the United States took over exclusive jurisdiction of that portion of Fairfax County, therein named Alexandria County. By Act of Congress of July 9, 1846 (U. S. Stats. 9, p. 35), the United States retroceded to Virginia the territory comprising the County of Alexandria, and by Act of Assembly of Mar. 13, 1847 (Acts, 1846-7, pp. 41, 48), Virginia extended her jurisdiction over the retroceded territory.

⁶ "*Provided always*, That the said new counties [Augusta and Frederick] * * * shall remain part of the county of Orange, * * *, until it shall be made appear to the governor and council, for the time being, that there is a sufficient number of inhabitants for appointing justices of the peace, and other officers, and erecting courts therein, for the due administration of justice". (H. v, p. 79). But Augusta was "not fully organized until the 30th October, 1745". (Waddell's "Annals of Augusta County, Virginia, 1902, p. 52; "Virginia Magazine of History and Biography", ii, p. 426).

West Augusta District (17??-1776), says Waddell's "Annals of Augusta County, Virginia", 1902, p. 251, appears to have been evolved, rather than created by law. Its existence was first recognized by the Legislature during the session which began October 7, 1776, when an act was passed [H. ix, p. 262] "for ascertaining the boundary line between the county of Augusta and the district of West Augusta [and for dividing the said district into three distinct counties]".

An examination of the "Journals of the House of Burgesses" (Virginia State Library, 1905-1915),—all of which have appeared since Waddell's "Annals" was published,—does not throw any additional light upon the subject; but the 1828 re-print of the "Journal of the House of Delegates for 1776", p. 4,—in support of a petition of the inhabitants of the western parts of Fincastle county",—says, "* * *; that they consider themselves, and the said lands, to be within the State of Virginia, whose Legislature they acknowledge, and to which State they conceive they justly belong; that having assembled together, after due notice, they had elected two members to represent them in this House, and hoping that they may be received as their delegates; that they are ready and willing, to the utmost of their abilities, to assist in the support of the present laudable cause, by contributing their quota of men and money; and that, in order to preserve good order, they had, as was done in West Augusta, elected a committee of 21 members, * * *".

Obviously the result of the exigencies of frontier life, but without legislative or legal status, the District of West Augusta was, nevertheless, represented in the Convention of March, 1775 (Peyton's "Augusta County, Virginia", pp. 173, 176, 206), the "Journal" of which (1816 re-print) says, p. 4, "A Letter from the inhabitants of that part of Augusta county which lies to the westward of the Alleghany mountains, desiring that John Nevill and John Harvie, Esqrs. may be admitted into this Convention as their delegates, being read; upon a motion, *Resolved*, That the said John Nevill and John Harvie be admitted as delegates for the county of Augusta",.even though the same "Journal", p. 3, shows among the delegates listed, "Thomas Lewis, Samuel McDowell and John Harvie Esqrs. for Augusta", and Lewis's "Report of the Department of Archives and History of the State of West Virginia", 1908, p. 153, shows that Nevill and Harvie were delegates from the "District of West Augusta; and also (p. 154) that John Harvie and George Rootes were the delegates from the same district in the Convention of July, 1775, while the "Journal of the Convention of May, 1776" (1816 re-print), p. 3, contains this in the list of delegates,—"West Augusta, John Harvie and Charles Simms, Esquires".

There is every reason to believe that the District of West Augusta was represented in the House of Delegates of October, 1776, which session passed the act "for ascertaining the boundary, etc", as this bill was "committed to Mr. Treasurer, Mr. Simms, and the members for Augusta, Frederick, Dunmore, Hampshire, Botetourt and Fincastle, as can be seen by referring to pp. 31, 33, of the 1828 re-print of this "Journal",—Mr. Simms being the last delegate from the District of West Augusta whose name we have.

On the other hand, West Augusta does not seem to have been represented in the Convention of August, 1774, although after its abolition by the formation of Monongalia, Ohio and Yohogania in 1776 (H. ix, p. 262) it appears to have been represented in the Virginia Assemblies of May, 1777, May, 1778, October, 1778, May, 1779, and October, 1779, by David Rogers as Senator from the "District of West Augusta" (see Lewis, above, pp. 103-4),—though a careful analysis will show that this "District of West Augusta" was evidently the senatorial district composed of Monongalia, Ohio and Yohogania Counties, simply retaining its old and popular designation, for at the session of May, 1780, we find that the "District of West Augusta" has disappeared, while the senatorial district of "Monongalia, Yohogania and Ohio" appears for the first time,—such a district not appearing at the same time as the "District of West Augusta", although there were delegates from these individual counties.

[7] The title in Hening (vi, p. 381) is not the same as the title used in the "Journal of the House of Burgesses", under the date indicated.

[8] The "Journal of the House of Delegates", 1861, p. 252, carries these data under an obviously incorrect date-line of "1860".

[9] See note 17.

[10] The date of passage here given is taken from Shepherd, ii, p. 54, but has not been checked against the "Journal" of the date indicated, as we have been unable to locate a copy for the session of 1796-7.

[11] "which land from and after the time that it shall be laid off and bounded, shall become a county by the name of Brunswick county". '(H. iv, p. 77). And certain it is that the county was not fully organized until 1732 (see also note 11, a, below),—nearly twelve years after the passage of the Act of Assembly authorizing its formation, as will be seen by the following copy of the proceedings of the first court (now destroyed; formerly in Order Book 1, page 1),—this copy having been made "about four years" prior to May, 1916, and now generously contributed for use in this connection by Mrs. J. O. James, of Petersburg, Va.:

"Meeting of the Justices for Brunswick County at the Court House of the said County II [Second] day of May in the fifth year of the reign of our Sovereign Lord George II. by the grace of God of Great Britain France and Ireland King Defender of the faith in the year of our Lord Christ M. D. CC. XXXII,
Henry Fox
A Commission from the Honorable Gooch Esq. His Majestys said Gov and Commander in Chief of the Colony and Dominion of Va Directs to Henry Fox, Henry Embry, John Wall, John Irby George Walton, Richard Burth, Nathaniel Edwards Wm. Wyns, Charles, King & Wm. Marking,

Assigning the Kings Justices for the County of Brunswick, Situated [dated] at Williamsburg the twenty second day of April MD. CC. XXXII. being read as usual any one of you the said Justices pursuant to Henry Fox & Henry Embry, having first taken the oaths appointed to be taken by act of Parliament instead of the Oaths of Allegiance & Supremacy. The Oaths appointed to be taken by an act of Parliament, made in the ———— [5th] year of the Reign of his late Majesty King Geo 1st: Our Royal Father, Instituted [Intituled] An Act for the further, Security of his Majesty's Person and Government, and The. Succession of the Crown in the heirs of the late Princess Sophia, being Protestants and for extinguishing the Hopes of the pretended Prince of Wales & his open & secret abettors; & also the text together with the oaths appointed according to the act of the general assembly of the Colony of Va to be taken by the said Justices of the said County.

You the said Justices administer the same to George Walton & Wm. Marking who have also prescribed & taken their bench accordingly"

(Rest torn away)

Upon the suggestion of the late Mr. William H. Hill of Lawrenceville, Va., and through the generous co-operation of the Hon. Robert Turnbull, of the same address, we are able to offer the following letter in regard to the escape of the records of Brunswick County, during the War between the States:

Lawrenceville, Va.,
Oct. 16th, 1915.

"Mr. Morgan P. Robinson, Archivist,
Virginia State Library, Richmond, Va.
Dear Sir:

Mr. W. T. Sledge, who is at present Clerk of the County, has handed me your letter of the 15th inst. for reply.

My father, Edward Randolph Turnbull, was County Clerk at the time Kautz's [1864] raid came through this section. I was a small boy at the time, about twelve or thirteen years old, and was in the office of my father when he left it just before the raiders came into our town, and he took a Masonic flag that was in the office and spread it out on the office table before he left. I helped do this. About twenty minutes after the raiders came into town a guard was sent to my father's house, who gave him the flag. After the raiders left we went back to the office and it looked as if all the records were destroyed, or a great part of them, as the floor of the office was about a foot deep in papers, but upon careful examination we found nothing was injured that was of any value. We had a case in the office that was filled with old blanks and they threw these all over the floor. They tore the leaves out of the old register of births and deaths and the leaves out of a lot of blank books, and scattered these over the floor and then put ink over the top of this stuff they had thrown on the floor; otherwise nothing was injured, and the records are still intact beginning with 1732, and down to the present time.

With kind regards, I am,
Yours very truly,
R. Turnbull."

To Mr. William Clayton Torrence, Secretary of the Valentine Museum, Richmond, Va., we are indebted for the following invaluable note which establishes beyond question that the area of the initial Brunswick County was taken out of Prince George:

[11,a] The genesis of the County of Brunswick seems heretofore to have been enveloped in a maze of tradition. The statement made by Howe in his "Virginia", p. 205, that Brunswick was erected from Surry and Isle of Wight Counties has been accepted without critical examination. The statement by Howe is in all probability based on the fact that small portions of Surry and Isle of Wight were added to Brunswick in 1732 (Hening iv, p. 355). The following facts have been brought together to prove that Brunswick

County (while it unquestionably received later accessions of territory from Isle of Wight and Surry Counties) was in its original formation created from part of the territory of Prince George County.

By Act of Assembly, November 1720, the counties of Spotsylvania and Brunswick were created. "Brunswick County, begins on the south side the river Roanoke, at the place where the line lately run for ascertaining the uncontroverted bounds of this colony toward North Carolina, intersects the said River Roanoke, and to be bounded by the direction of the governour with consent of council, so as to include the southern pass; which land from and after the time that it shall be laid off and bounded shall become a county by the name of Brunswick county". (Hening, iv, p. 77, *et seq.*) After directing the erection of public buildings and the distribution of arms, reciting the privileges of inhabitants and declaring the jurisdiction for Spotsylvania County to reside in the justices of Essex, King and Queen and King William Counties, the act further recites, "And the court of Prince George county has the same power in Brunswick:"

It will be noticed that the act does not state from what counties Spotsylvania and Brunswick Counties were erected but the settling of jurisdiction in the magistracy of specifically named counties is very good circumstantial evidence that Spotsylvania and Brunswick were erected from parts of the territory of the counties whose magistrates were invested with jurisdiction until a final organization should be effected. Therefore from the provisional jurisdiction given the magistracy of Prince George County in the new county of Brunswick we infer that the first territory laid off into Brunswick was taken from Prince George.

The Land Patents seem, however, to settle definitely that Brunswick County was set off from Prince George. Reference to any map of Virginia will show that the dividing line between the present Dinwiddie County (which was until 1752 a part of Prince George) and the present counties of Greensville (which was until 1781 a part of Brunswick) and Brunswick is the Nottoway River. Now, in the year 1720, when the act establishing Brunswick County was passed, there were no Dinwiddie and Greensville Counties; therefore the Nottoway River was in Prince George County, as is also well established by the following patents: in August 1720 John King was granted 97 acres in Prince George County on south side of the Nottoway River beginning at the first falls above Sturgeon Run; at the same time John Wall was granted 185 acres in Prince George County on south side Nottoway River above the mouth of Waquiyoah (at present Waqua) Creek (Register of the Land Office, Patent Book, no. 11, pp. 39, 40). All maps show that the territory to the south of Nottoway River is in either Brunswick or Greensville County. The Sturgeon Run (now Creek) and Waquiyoah (now Waqua) Creek are today in the county of Brunswick.

Though the act creating Brunswick County was passed in 1720 there was apparently no court held for that county until 1732, when on May 2, 1732, by commission from the governor, dated April 22, 1732, a court met and organized. No records of proceedings in Brunswick County prior to this date have ever been found.

From the evidence adduced it seems quite clearly to have been the case that in 1720 Brunswick County was created from Prince George, and that on account of the sparseness of population no court was held until May 1732, and that at that time territory was added to Brunswick from the Counties of Isle of Wight and Surry, thereby adding more tithables and by the increase in population warranting the establishment of a regular court and forever removing jurisdiction over Brunswick affairs from the hands of the Prince George magistracy.

[12] The "Journal of the House of Delegates" (1857-8), p. 323, gives the date as Feb. 16, 1858, but A (1857-8), p. 108, gives the date as Feb. 13, 1858, the former, of course, being the correct one.

[13] The "Act for erecting a new County on the heads of Essex, King and Queen and King William Counties; and for calling the same Caroline County" appears in Hening (iv, p. 240) by title only; but reference to Part VI, chapter vii, below, will show the full text of this Act, a copy of which was recently

secured by the Library from the Public Record Office in London, for use in this connection. It will be noted that Caroline County,—although authorized by an Act passed in 1727,—came into actual existence in 1728,—the former date being the general and more popular interpretation of the earliest actual existence of this county.

[14] See note 62.

[14,a] "It took in the portion of Wallingford Parish west of the Chickahominy River (the Sandy Point region previously in James City County)"—Lyon G. Tyler.

[15] Charles River County was formed in 1634 (H. i, p. 224), but the name was changed to York in 1642/3 (H. i, pp. 224, 249).

[16] The "Act for dividing the County of Henrico into two distinct Counties" does not appear in Hening (1748,—vols 5 and 6) either by title or in full text; but reference to Part VI, chapter xi, below, will show the full text of this Act, a copy of which was recently secured by the Library from the Public Record Office in London, for use in this connection. It will be noted that Chesterfield County,—although authorized by an Act passed in 1749, and coming into actual existence in that year,— is usually credited to the year 1748,—this latter date being the general and more popular interpretation of the earliest actual existence of this county.

[17] The enrolled bills and the Acts (1850-1, p. 21) give this order as "Botetourt, Roanoke, Giles and Monroe", while a typographical error makes Williams's "Index to Enrolled Bills" (p. 104, l. 30), under the caption "Craig County", give the order as "Roanoke, Giles, Monroe and Botetourt".

[18] The "Act for dividing the County of Orange" does not appear in Hening (1748,—vols. 5 and 6) either by title or in full text; but reference to Part VI, chapter ix, below, will show the full text of this Act, a copy of which was recently secured by the Library from the Public Record Office in London, for use in this connection. It will be noted that Culpeper County,—although authorized by an Act passed in 1748,—came into actual existence in 1749,— the former date being the general and more popular interpretation of the earliest actual existence of this county.

[19] The "Act for dividing the County of Goochland" does not appear in Hening (1748,—vols. 5 and 6) either by title or in full text; but reference to Part VI, chapter viii, below, will show the full text of this Act, a copy of which was recently secured by the Library from the Public Record Office in London, for use in this connection. It will be noted that Cumberland County,—although authorized by an Act passed in 1748,—came into actual existence in 1749,—the former date being the general and more popular interpretation of the earliest actual existence of this county.

[20] The "Journal of the House of Delegates", 1879-80, p. 376, gives this date as February 27, 1880, while A (1879-'80), p. 125, gives the date as March 3, 1880,—the former, of course, being the correct one.

[21] Dunmore County was formed in 1772 (H. viii, p. 397), but the name was changed to Shenando[ah] in 1778 (H. ix, p. 424).

[22] Through the generous co-operation of the Hon. H. H. Holt, Clerk of the Circuit Court of Elizabeth City County, we are able to offer the following letter in regard to the destruction of the records of that County:

Hampton, Va.,
March 13th, 1916.

"Mr. Morgan P. Robinson,
Archivist,
Virginia State Library,
Richmond,
Va.,

Dear Sir:—

In reply to your communication of the 10th, I have the honor to say that I am not sure whether the records of this office which have been lost or destroyed were so lost or destroyed during the Revolutionary War, the War of 1812, or the Civil War, or during all of them. The Town of Hampton was burned during each of these wars, but whether or not the records were preserved through any of them I do not know. I do know, however, that our records are very much broken from 1634, the date of the organization of this County, up to 1861, the date of the Civil War. During this period there are only a few scattering books concerning deeds, wills and in some instances Court proceedings and bonds. The beginning of our records which are now complete is 1865, after the end of the Civil War. The others prior to that time, as I said before, are scattering and there are lapses of fifty or sixty years between some of the books.

Regretting that I cannot give you definite information as to the destruction of these records, I am

Very respectfully,

H. H. Holt,
Clerk.

[23] See note 13.

[24] See note 35.

[25] Fincastle County was formed in 1772 (H. viii, p. 600), but became extinct in 1777, when its territory was divided into Kentucky, Montgomery and Washington Counties (H. ix, p. 257).

[26] See note 6; but "'Owing to some delay of the population in these parts, not being able to support a sufficient number of competent men able to officer the new County', the Courts for all this section were held at Orange C. H., until Nov. [11th], 1743, when the first Court was held for Frederick County". (Cartmell's "A History of Frederick County, Virginia", p. 18).

[27] See note 17.

[28] We are indebted to Doctor Lyon G. Tyler, of Williamsburg, Va., for the following data concerning the early history of Gloucester County:

"Lands in Gloucester are shown by the Land Grants previous to 1651 to have been in York. As its first delegates appeared in April, 1652 (H. i, p. 371), it must have been formed in 1651".

[29] The "Act for dividing the County of Henrico" appears in Hening (iv, p. 240) by title only; but reference to Part VI, chapter vi, below, will show the full text of the Act, a copy of which was recently secured by the Library from the Public Record Office in London, for use in this connection. It will be noted that Goochland County,—although authorized by an Act passed in 1727,—came into actual existence in 1728,—the former date being the general and more popular interpretation of the earliest actual existence of this county.

[30] The "Act for dividing New Kent County" appears in Hening (iv, p. 95) by title only, but reference to Part VI, chapter v, below, will show the full text of this Act, a copy of which was recently secured by the Library from the Public Record Office in London, for use in this connection. It will be noted that Hanover County,—although authorized by an Act passed in 1720,—came into actual existence in 1721,—the former date being the general and more popular interpretation of the earliest actual existence of this county.

The following letter throws light upon the destruction of the records of Hanover County:

Richmond, Va.,
December 24th, 1915.

"Mr. Morgan P. Robinson,
  State Library Bldg.,
    CITY.
Dear Sir:—

Your letter of December 23rd, just received.

I note that you ask me to give my recollection or knowledge of the destruction of our Court records during the war between the States.

Responding to your inquiry, I have to say that I was raised in Hanover County, about eight miles east of Hanover C. H., but was rarely at Hanover C. H., until after the close of the war. The lower part of Hanover, reaching within a few miles of Hanover C. H., was occupied by the armies of McClellan and Grant, and was the subject of frequent cavalry raids, which took in Hanover C. H., and the Clerk of the County Court of Hanover County as a precaution against the destruction of the records of that Court removed them to Richmond, and they were deposited in the Court Bldg., which then stood on the Capitol Square just in front of the Franklin Street entrance from the east, just about where the fountain now stands, which building was destroyed, and so far as I know no papers of value were taken or quence all of the records of the County Court of Hanover County were burned. The records of the Circuit Court (which Court then had its own clerk in the same building with the County Court Clerk) were allowed to remain in the Clerk's Office at Hanover C. H. and though that section was several times raided and the Clerk's Office opened, and some few papers probably lost, I do not think any of the record books were destroyed, and, so far as I know, no papers of value were taken or destroyed. Among the records thus preserved two old books bound in raw hide dated about 1730, remained in the office and were not hurt.

I do not know if this answers fully your inquiry, but if you desire any further information and I can obtain it for you will be very glad to answer any inquiry you make make.

Yours very truly,

GEO. P. HAW."

ᵃ Through the generous co-operation of the Hon. S. P. Waddill, Clerk of the Circuit Court of Henrico County, we are able to offer the following letter in regard to the preservation of the records of that county:

Richmond, Va.,
March 3, 1916.

"Mr. Morgan P. Robinson, Archivist,
  Virginia State Library,
    Richmond, Va.
Dear Sir:

Your favor of the 14th ult. received, and in reply—The earliest records of this County begin with the year 1677, and from that date to 1781, we have a good many volumes, but they are not in continuous order, but from 1781 to the present date they are intact.

I have always understood that a great many records of the County were destroyed when Arnold during the Revolution invaded this City, and the fact that there are volumes remaining prior to that date, is due to the fact that the records were carried from the City and stored at a point on James River known as the Powhatan Furnace. Some of the books prior to 1781 have indexes and others have not.

The Board of Supervisors of this County some few years ago took up the matter of indexing them and had an index made of those in the 17th Century, but did not continue it from 1700 to 1781.

It appears that the Governor of the State was authorized to appoint commissioners to set up lost records [Hening x, p. 453], and such a commission was appointed for this County by Governor Benj. Harrison on April 8th, 178—(82), and the Commission held its first session on the 24th day of February, 1783, and some of the records that were destroyed were set up by the commission. It is recited that the Commissioners met pursuant to the Act of the Assembly 'for the relief of persons who have been, or may be, injured by the destruction of the records of the County Courts.' In the proceedings it is stated that such an such a record had been destroyed by the enemy, but the circumstances attending the destruction are not stated.

Some twenty or more years ago under an Act of the General Assembly, passed, I think, at the instance of Hon. Lyon G. Tyler, President of William and Mary College, the records of this office of the 17th Century were copied by the late Chas. M. Wallace, and were deposited in the State Library.

I found these old records when I became connected with this office in a very damp place and hastening to destruction. I changed the location of them and took other means to preserve them and have had a number of them rebound. The paper in many of them is extremely brittle and the least handling damages them. Of late years they have been subjected to a great deal of handling by persons whose prime motive is to secure the information they want, and who have little respect for their preservation, and unless some remedy can be suggested they will finally be destroyed.

All of the records of the Circuit Court of this County were destroyed at the Evacuation of the City on the 3rd day of April, 1865— the Court holding its sessions at the State Courthouse, which was located on the Capitol Square, just opposite the rear of the State Library, at the head of lower Franklin Street. No steps were ever taken to set up these records because the Court had no jurisdiction as to land titles, etc.

Please excuse the delay in replying but I was not conscious of the fact that so much time had elapsed since the receipt of your letter.

Yours truly,

Samuel P. Waddill."

[21,a] The "Journal of the House of Burgesses" (H. B., 1619-59, pp. vii, 3) gives the name as Henricus, but thereafter as Henrico. (See also Brown's "First Republic", pp. 254, 313).

[21,b] See note 29.

[22] Illinois County (1778-1784) was formed by an Act of Assembly passed December 9, 1778, "for the better protection and defence of the county and its inhabitants" (H. ix, p. 554), to "be enforced, from and after the passage of the same, for and during the term of twelve months * * * and no longer." (H. ix, p. 555). By an Act of Assembly passed July 14, 1780, the above Act of 1778 was amended to "continue and be in force for one year after the passing of this act, and from thence to the end of the next session of assembly." (H. x, p. 303). An Act of Congress passed September 6, 1780, "recommended to the several states in the Union, having claims to waste and unappropriated lands in the western country, a liberal cession to the United States, of a portion of their respective claims, for the common benefit of the nation." ("Journals of Congress", 1823, iii, pp. 516-7; H. xi, pp. 571-2). On January 2, 1781, the Virginia Assembly passed certain resolutions, setting forth her offer of "a Cession of the lands on the north west of Ohio to the United States", and the conditions thereto attached (H. x, p. 564). By an Act of Assembly passed December 20, 1783, the Virginia delegates in Congress were authorized "to convey to the United States, in congress assembled, all the right of this commonwealth in the territory north westward of the river Ohio" (H. xi, p. 326). By Deed of Cession of March 1, 1784, this area was conveyed to the United States, in Congress assembled, by the delegates from Virginia for that purpose designated. ("Journals of Congress", 1823, vol. iv, pp. 341-4; H. xi, pp. 571-5).

[23] Illinois County was formed in 1778 (H. ix, p. 554), but ceased to be a county of Virginia in 1784, when it was ceded to the United States (H. xi, pp. 571-5).

[54] We are indebted to Doctor Lyon G. Tyler, of Williamsburg, Va., for the following data concerning the early history of Isle of Wight County:

"The Land Books show that the lands in Isle of Wight lay previously in Warascoyack Co. The name was changed from Warascoyack to Isle of Wight in 1637. For history of Isle of Wight County, see "William and Mary Quarterly", vol. vii, p. 205".

Isle of Wight County appears in Hening (H. i, p. 228) under date of January, 1639-'40,—the bounds having been finally determined under date of 1642/3 (H. i, p. 247),—although the index of this volume (H. i, p. 599), under the caption "Warrosquyoake", says that Warrosquyoake was changed to Isle of Wight in 1637.

We desire to acknowledge with pleasure the generous co-operation of the Hon. A. S. Johnson, Clerk of the Circuit Court of Isle of Wight County, in furnishing data concerning the early history of his county.

[54, a] For full text of this act, see Part V, Chap. ii, below.

[54, b] See note 14, a.

[55] Williams's "Index to Enrolled Bills of the General Assembly of Virginia, 1776-1910" (1911), p. 227, l. 21, says,—under the caption of "Kanawha County",—"Forming Fauquier county from portion of,——1823-4, 16". This "Fauquier" is evidently a typographical error for "Logan", as see A (1823-4), p. 20.

[56] Kentucky District (1779-1792) was formed in 1779, under "An Act for adjusting and settling the titles of claimers to unpatented lands under the present and former government, previous to the establishment of the commonwealth's land office", by the enactment "That the counties on the western waters shall be allotted into districts, to wit: * * *; and the county of Kentucky, shall be another district; * * *" (H. x, p. 43). In 1782, it was enacted "That from and after the first day of August next [1782], the counties of Jefferson, Fayette and Lincoln shall be one district, and called the Kentucky district, for which there shall be a supreme court of judicature of original jurisdiction, * * *" (H. xi, p. 85). In 1786, 1787, 1788 and 1789, the Virginia Assembly passed acts setting forth the "terms on which the district of Kentucky may be erected into an independent state", and several amendments thereto (H. xii, pp. 37, 240, 788; H. xiii, p. 17). By Act of Congress of 1791, consent was given "that a new state be formed within the jurisdiction of Virginia, and admitted to the Union, by the name of the State of Kentucky",—the new state to be admitted on June 1, 1792 (U. S. Stats., 1, p. 189).

[57] Kentucky County was formed in 1777 (H. ix, p. 257), but became extinct in 1780, when its territory was divided into Jefferson, Fayette and Lincoln Counties (H. x, p. 315).

[58] See note 13.

[59] The "Act for dividing Richmond County" appears in Hening (iv, p. 95) by title only, but reference to Part VI, chapter iv, below, will show the full text of this Act, a copy of which was recently secured by the Library from the Public Record Office in London, for use in this connection. It will be noted that King George County,—although authorized by an Act passed in 1720,—came into actual existence in 1721,—the former date being the general and more popular interpretation of the earliest actual existence of this county.

[60] See note 13.

[61] We are indebted to Doctor Lyon G. Tyler, of Williamsburg, Va., for the following data concerning the early history of Lancaster County:

"The books in the Land Office show that the land in Lancaster County was previously in Northumberland and York. The first court was held January 1, 1651/52. It was probably formed at an assembly held in 1651, whose records are not preserved."

Through the generous co-operation of the Hon. Wm. Chilton, Clerk of the Circuit Court of Lancaster, we are able to quote in full an attested copy of the record of the proceedings of that court:

"At a Court holden for Lancaster County at ye house of Mr. More Fantleroy on ye first of Jany 1652.

Present Mr. Toby Smith   Mr. Ja: Williamson
         Mr. James Bagnall   Mr: Geo: Tayloe
         Mr: David Fox   Mr: Geo: Gibson
                    Mr. Wm: Underwood

The Court according to an Act of Assembly in yt case provided hath elected made choyce & appointed John Philips to officiate in ye place & office of Clerke to ye sd Court, he ye sd Philips demeaning himself therein according to ye oath by him taken & ye laws & customs of this Country. And likewise forasmuch as ye sd County beinge in ye infancy & first seating thereof not able to afford a livelyhood & subsistence to him yt shall officiate in ye place and office of Sheriff, the Court hath likewise conferd ye sd place & office on him ye sd Philips, he puting in security acording to Act in yt case provided & whereas the sd Philips having presented Abraham Moone to this Court for his security for ye sd place of Sheriff the Court hath adopted thereof he entering bond to ye Court according to ye Courts bond in like cases.

Whereas Capt More Fantleroy hath made supplication unto the Court yt there is two hundred acres of land due him for transportation of four persons into this country whose names are hearunder inserted the Court doth order yt certificate thereof be made to ye Secretary at James Cittie. [Here follow the four names, but are too much defaced to be deciphered].

The Court hath ordered yt ye next Court for this County be holden at ye house of Mr: Tho: Brise on ye 6th day of August next & yt ye Court hereafter be [hiatus] on yt day unless it be Sunday.
         A Copy-Teste:
                                    Wm. Chilton Clerk.
                                    Feb. 8th. 1916."

⁴⁴ See note 35.

⁴⁵ Through the generous co-operation of Judge Frederick W. Sims, of Louisa, Va., we are able to offer the following letter in regard to the escape of the records of Louisa County:
                                    Louisa, Va.
                                    February 8, 1916.
"Mr. Morgan P. Robinson,
         Archivist of the Virginia
                 State Library, Richmond, Va.

My dear Sir:
    Replying to your letter of the 5th inst., will say that the records of the clerk's office of Louisa County are complete from 1742, when it was cut off from Hanover County, down to the present time, with the exception of one order book of the county court which was in use during the war and was sent to Richmond for preservation, destroyed, it is supposed, at the fall of Richmond.

There was a deed book sent to Richmond at the same time, namely, the deed book from 1860 to 1865. This book had a rather remarkable experience. It was carried away from Richmond by the Federal troops, and a Mr. George E. Bluebaugh, the hotel keeper at Louisa, happened to be in Baltimore soon after the war and saw this deed book on a table in a hotel and he was told by the hotel proprietor that he had bought the book from a negro for $1.00. Bluebaugh on returning home reported this to the Board of Supervisors of Louisa County and the latter bought the book from the Baltimore Hotel man for the sum of $25.00. The following entry appears on the fly leaf of this deed book, in the hand writing of Mr. Jesse J. Porter, who was clerk of this county for a great many years, up until his death, and who is succeeded by his son, Mr. P. B. Porter, the present clerk:

'This book was carried by yankees from Richmond, whence it had been sent to evade them, to Maryland and bought by the county of Louisa for the sum of $25.00.'

The two books above mentioned were the only records from this county that were sent away for safe-keeping during the war of 61 to 65. The other records remained here throughout the war and were not molested.

While it is true that Tarlton on his raid to Charlottesville passed by Louisa Courthouse, none of the records were molested by him.

There are some very interesting orders of court in our old order books in colonial days, one especially in reference to the fining of an Episcopal clergyman for being drunk and swearing 'one profane oath' and also some very interesting records in connection with Patrick Henry when he lived in this county, who, as you will remember, was the Delegate from Louisa County at the time he made his famous utterance of 'Give me liberty or give me death.'

I feel sure that Mr. P. B. Porter, clerk of Louisa, will be glad to give you such further information as you may desire.

With kindest regards and best wishes, I remain

Yours sincerely,

F. W. Sims."

[43, a] For full text of this act, see Part VI, Chap. i, below.

[44] Lower Norfolk County was formed in 1637 (see note 55), but became extinct in 1691, when its territory was divided into Norfolk and Princess Anne Counties (H. iii, p. 95).

[45] The "Journal of the House of Delegates", October, 1792, p. 165, gives this date as December 5, 1792, but H. xiii, p. 558, gives the date as December 4, 1792,—the former, of course, being the correct one.

[46] See note 50.

[47] The title of this act varies in each of the following sources,—"Journal of the House of Delegates", 1834-5, p. 245; *Ibid.*, p. 249; A (1834-5), p. 38.

[48] The "Journal of the House of Delegates", 1803-'04, gives this date as January 3, 1804, while S. iii, p. 77, gives the date as January 2, 1804,—the former, of course, being the correct one.

[49] We are indebted to Doctor Lyon G. Tyler, of Williamsburg, Va., for the following data concerning the early history of Middlesex County:

"The nearest date for its formation is its first court Feb. 2, 1673-'74".

From W. G. Stanard's "Extracts from the Records of the Counties of Old Rappahannock, Essex, Middlesex, King George and Richmond" (manuscript) in the Virginia State Library, we quote the following caption of the first court of Middlesex County:

"Present at a court held Feb. 1673: Richard Perrott Sr; John Branham, Abraham Weeks, Robert Beverley, Henry Thacher, John Foxcroft, Richard Perrott Jr; Walter Whittaker and John Hazlewood, Gentlemen, Justices."

Upon the suggestion of the Hon. M. E. Bristow, of Gloucester, and through the generous co-operation of the Hon. W. W. Woodward, we are able to offer the following letter in regard to the escape of the records of Middlesex County:

Hampton, Va.,
Feb. 10th, 1916.

"Mr. Morgan P. Robinson,
    Virginia State Library,
        Richmond, Va.
Dear Sir:—

Your letter of the 9th inst., is received, relative to the court records in Middlesex County, Va. My father, P. T. Woodward, was the Clerk of Middlesex County for forty years, beginning in 1852. During a portion of this time I was his deputy.

The records of Middlesex County are intact and date back for more than two hundred years. These records were not destroyed during the War between the States.

My father had securely packed and removed the valuable books and papers during the war and concealed them, in an out of the way place upon what is called and known as the Dragon Swamp, which is the head waters of the Piankatank River. The Yankee troops broke in the office, and finding no valuable records pulled down many old worthless papers, cut the strings and scattered them a foot deep on the brick floor. These papers were afterwards burned by order of the Court.

Hon. H. R. Pollard, City Attorney of Richmond, can give you information on the subject.

        Yours very truly,
                W. W. Woodward."

[50] Williams's "Index to the Enrolled Bills of the General Assembly of Virginia, 1776-1910" (1911), p. 294, l. 47, under the caption "Monroe County", carries the entry "Establishing Taylor county from part of,———1843-4, 9",—this entry obviously having been typographically transposed from its proper place amongst the data under "Marion County", as see A (1843-4), p. 34. See also note 17.

[51] The "Journal of the House of Delegates", 1798-9, p. 77, gives this date as January 15, 1799, while S. ii, p. 168, gives the date as January 14, 1799,—the former, of course, being the correct one.

[52] Upper Norfolk was formed in 1637 (see note 55), but the name was changed to Nansemond in 1642. For full-text of the Act of Assembly establishing this new early date for Nansemond, see Part VI, chap. ii, below.

[53] The "Journal of the House of Delegates", 1807-'08, p. 34, gives this date as December 23, 1807, while S. iii, p. 378, gives the date as December 25, 1807 (Christmas Day),—the former, of course, being the correct one. The assembly sat regularly on Christmas Day as late as 1801.

[54] See note 30.

[55] We are indebted to Col. B. O. James, Secretary of the Commonwealth, for the following extract from a letter concerning the records of Norfolk County, written under date of Portsmouth, Va., October 21, 1913, by the Hon. Alvah H. Martin, Clerk of that county:

"You will find that what was known as New Norfolk County was formed in 1636, and embraced the territory [of Elizabeth City County] south of the James River. In 1637 New Norfolk County was divided into Upper and Lower Norfolk County. Upper Norfolk County was then changed to Nansemond County (see First Hening's Statutes, page 321). In 1691 Lower Norfolk County was divided into Princess Anne and Norfolk Counties; but Norfolk County proper retained all the record books to 1636, so that our records here embrace the records of Nansemond and Princess Anne Counties, as well as Norfolk County itself, from 1636. It also embraces the records of Norfolk City up to the time of its incorporation. You can see the proof of the last statement in Third Hening, p. 95." For full text of the Act giving the bounds of Lower Norfolk and Upper Norfolk, see Part VI, chap. i, below.

⁵⁶ New Norfolk County was formed from Elizabeth City County in 1636 (see note 55), but it became extinct in 1637, when its territory was divided into Upper Norfolk and Lower Norfolk Counties (see note 55; H. i, pp. 228, 247).

⁵⁷ "That [1691] is the date of the formation of Princess Anne. But the act declares that the other county mentioned at that time should 'retain' the name of Norfolk County. The act divided 'Lower Norfolk County' into two, but Norfolk County was nothing more than 'Lower Norfolk' reduced by Princess Anne. There had once been an 'Upper Norfolk County', but that had long been known by the name of Nansemond, and it was felt in 1691 that it was useless to retain the adjective 'Lower'. The books in the clerk's office at Portsmouth begin in 1637." "Virginia Magazine of History and Biography", iii, p. 84. (See note 55.)

⁵⁸ The name of Accomack County was changed to Northampton in 1642/3 (H. i, p. 249); see also Green's "Genesis of Counties" in Slaughter's "Brief Sketch of William Green, LL. D.", p. 101.

⁵⁹ We are indebted to Doctor Lyon G. Tyler, of Williamsburg, Va., for the following data concerning the early history of Northumberland County:

"Northumberland was the Indian name given to the Indian district Chickacoan in February, 1645 (H. i, p. 294). It was doubtless then created a county by the governor and council. In October, 1648, this action was formally confirmed by the General Assembly. (H. i, p. 352; see also account of Northumberland in "William and Mary Quarterly", xxiii, p. 182)". See also "Virginia Magazine of History and Biography", xxiii, pp. 249, 250.

⁶⁰ Northumberland and Westmoreland were united for "civill and millitary" purposes, by an Act of March 1661/2 (H. ii, p. 151).

⁶¹ The "Journal of the House of Delegates", October, 1788, 117, gives this date as December 23, 1788, while Hening (xii, p. 723) gives the date as December 22, 1788,—the former, of course, being the correct one.

⁶² The "Act for Dividing Charles City County" appears in Hening (iii, p. 223) by title only; but reference to Part VI, chapter iii, below, will show the full text of this Act, a copy of which was recently secured by the Library from the Public Record Office in London, for use in this connection. It will be noted that Prince George County,—although authorized by an Act passed in 1702,—came into actual existence in 1703,—the former date being the general and more popular interpretation of the earliest actual existence of this county. "* * *, but is is certain that in addition to the present County of Prince George, the Counties of Dinwiddie, Amelia, Nottoway and Prince Edward were included." ("Virginia Magazine of History and Biography", iv, p. 272). See also Part IV, chart 2, below.

⁶³ See note 55.

⁶⁴ The enrolled bills (1839, '58), and the Acts (1839, p. 30) give this order as "Montgomery and Wythe", while a typographical error makes Williams's "Index to Enrolled Bills" (p. 367, l. 31), under the caption "Pulaski County", give the order as "Wythe and Montgomery".

⁶⁵ We are indebted to Doctor Lyon G .Tyler, of Williamsburg, Va., for the following data concerning the early history of old Rappahannock County:

"Rappahannock County was formed, as shown by the county records, by Act of Assembly, December 11, 1656".
See also "Virginia Magazine of History and Biography", ii, pp. 72 and 235, where this date is given as December 13, 1656.

⁶⁶ Rappahannock County was formed in 1656 (see note 65), but became extinct in 1692, when it was divided into Essex and Richmond Counties (H. iii, p. 104).

[67] The "Journal of the House of Delegates", 1832-3, p. 190, gives this date as February 18, 1833, but A (1832-3), p. 44, gives the date as February 8, 1833,—the former, of course, being the correct one.

[68] See note 39.

[69] See note 17.

[70] The Acts of Assembly, 1814-5, p. 85, give this date as November 24, 1815, and the Acts of the same session, p. 87,—in referring to this act,—says "passed the twenty fourth day of November eighteen hundred and fourteen" (the date written out in full), which latter date is confirmed by the "Journal of the House of Delegates" of that session, p. 88.

[71] The "Act for dividing the County of Isle of Wight into two distinct Counties and for other purposes therein mentioned" does not appear in Hening (1748,—vols 5 and 6) either by title or in full text; but reference to Part VI, chapter x, below, will show the full text of this Act, a copy of which was recently secured by the Library from the Public Record Office in London, for use in this connection. It will be noted that Southampton County,—although authorized by an Act passed in 1748,—came into actual existence in 1749,—the former date being the general and more popular interpretation of the earliest actual existence of this county.

[72] Upon a suggestion of Mr. William G. Stanard, Secretary of the Virginia Historical Society, and through the generous co-operation of the Hon. George W. Herring, Clerk of the Circuit Court of Stafford County, we are enabled to quote in full the record of the proceedings of the first court of that county, which are to be found in "Stafford Co. Va. Court Book", p. 1, under date of 1664, and thus prove that Stafford was in actual existence at least two years prior to the generally accepted date of 1666:

"At a Court held for the County of Stafford, the 27, May, 1664,
Present: Lt. Colo. Robert Williams, Capt. John Alexander, Mr. Richard Heabeard, Mr. Richard Perfitt, Mr. Richard Fassaker, Justices;
Colo. John Dodman was sworne Sheriff, for this County, for this year as Mr. Secretary Ludwell, signified by his letter to the Court, that it was the Governors pleasure, the said Colonel Dodman having entered into Bond to perform the said Office.
Attorney Bridges was this day sworne Clerk of this County Court by grant of the Honorable Secretary of Virginia.
John Samwaies was this day sworne under Sheriff of this County.
The Court doth order that Capt. John Alexander shall forthwith cresse six men and horse & goe to the Manfattero Indians to see if he can Discover what Indians they were that had Lately committed that Murther above Potomeck.
Let noe will be proved (if any made) nor administcon granted of the Estate of Jacob Porter Deceased unless John Whitston Principal Creditor of the said Deceased be first called—
14th, June 1664 this Coveat was entered:"

[73] We are indebted to Doctor Lyon G. Tyler, of Williamsburg, Va., for the following data concerning the early history of Surry County:

"Lands in Surry are shown by the Land Grants to have been in James City County previous to December 6, 1651. Its first justices were appointed in April, as shown by the county records. (See "William and Mary Quarterly", viii, 165). So it was certainly formed at the assembly which met at this time, April, 1652."

[74] See note 50.

[75] The "Journal of the House of Delegates", 1799-1800, p. 32, gives this date as December 20, 1799, while S. ii, p. 217, gives the date as December 19, 1799,—the former, of course, being the correct one.

⁷⁵ The "Journal of the House of Delegates", 1814-5, p. 105, gives this date as December 3, 1814, while A (1814-5), p. 87, gives this date as December 6, 1814,— the former, of course, being the correct one.

⁷⁶, ᵃ For full text of this act, see Part VI, chap. i, below.

⁷⁷ Upper Norfolk County was formed in 1637 (see note 55), but the name was changed to Nansemond in 1642 (see note 52).

⁷⁸ The "Journal of the House of Delegates", 1850-1, p. 449, gives this date as March 27, 1851, while A (1850-1), p. 23, gives the date as March 26, 1651,— the former, of course, being the correct one.

⁷⁹ Warrosquyoake County was formed in 1634 (H. i, p. 224), but the name was changed to Isle of Wight in 1637 (see note 34; H. i, p. 228).

⁸⁰ The name of Warwick River was changed to Warwick in 1642/3 (H. i, p. 249).

⁸¹ Warwick River County was formed in 1634 (H. i, p. 224), but the name was changed to Warwick in 1642/3 (H. i, p. 249).

⁸² We are indebted to Doctor Lyon G. Tyler, of Williamsburg, Va., for the following data concerning the early history of Westmoreland County:

"Westmoreland County was formed from Northumberland in July, 1653 (H. i, p. 381)".

⁸³ See note 60.

⁸⁴ The "Journal of the House of Delegates", 1845-6, pp. 52, 82, as well as the title and the entire text of the enrolled bill itself carry the spelling "Whetsell"; the index to the House Journal for this session carries the spelling "Whetzel", while the A (1845-6), p. 51, and Williams's "Enrolled Bills of the General Assembly of Virginia, 1776-1910" (1911), p. 488, carry the spelling "Wetzel".

⁸⁵ The "Journal of the House of Delegates", 1798-9, p. 35, gives this date as December 22, 1798, while S. ii, p. 170, gives the date as December 21, 1798,—the former, of course, being the correct one.

⁸⁶ Yohogania County was formed in 1776 (H. ix, p. 262), but was abolished in 1786 (J. Jan. 6, 1786), by legislation resulting from the fact that "by the extension of the western boundary between the State of Pennsylvania and this commonwealth, the greater part of the County of Yohogania has fallen within the limits of the former, whereby the remainder of the said county is rendered too small and inconsiderable for a separate county", and this small remaining portion was "hereby added to the County of Ohio" (H. xii, p. 114).

⁸⁷ Yohogania County was formed in 1776 (H. ix, p. 262), but became extinct in 1786 (H. xii, 114).

⁸⁸ The name of Charles River County was changed to York in 1642/3 (H. i, p. 249).

PART II.

CHRONOLOGICAL ARRANGEMENT

The Notes are assembled in series at the end of Part I, Alphabetical Arrangement.

In the Chronological Arrangement, the date of the operation of the Act of Assembly has, of course, been the guide, but when several Acts became operative in the same year, the dates of the final passage of these Acts decide the chronology; while resort has been had to alphabetizing the names when two or more counties came into actual existence in the same year as the result of Acts finally passed on the same date. Striking illustrations of this appear under the years 1777, 1778 and 1786. Kentucky, Montgomery and Washington came into actual existence in 1777 as the result of an Act passed Dec. 7, 1776. Hence these counties appear under this date in the order named. Fluvanna and Powhatan came into actual existence in 1777 as the result of *two Acts* finally passed on June 3, 1777, and therefore appear in alphabetical order under the latter date. Henry, however, is the first of those listed under 1777, because it came into actual existence that year, and the Act forming it was passed earlier than any of the other three.

The following abbreviations are used in this Part:

- A.: Acts of the General Assembly of Virginia, for the session indicated.
- E. (superior): resulted from Virginia legislation, but now extinct, as shown by accompanying limiting dates.
- H.: Hening's "Statutes at Large".
- H. B.: "Journals of the House of Burgesses", 1619-1776 (Virginia State Library: 1905-1915).
- J.: "Journal of the House" (Burgesses or Delegates, as the case may be), as interpreted in the note on the subject under the "General" section of the Preface.
- K. (superior): resulted from Virginia legislation, but now in Kentucky.
- S.: Shepherd's "Statutes at Large" (continuation of Hening).
- U. S. Stats.: United States Statutes.
- W. (superior): resulted from Virginia legislation, but now in West Virginia.

Formed	County	Land formed from	References
1634 (See note 1.);	[a]Accawmack; (1634-1642/3)[89]	Original Shire;	H. i, 224; H. i, 249.
1634 (See note 1.);	Charles City;	Original Shire; and enlarged, but no metes or bounds given;	H. i, 224; H. iii, 223.[90] H. iv, 94.[90,a]
1634 (See note 1.);	[a]Charles River; (1634-1642/3)[91]	Original Shire;	H. i, 224; H. i, 249.
1634 (See note 1.);	Elizabeth City;[92]	Original Shire;	H. i, 224; A (1881-2), 43.
1634 (See note 1.);	Henrico;[93]	Original Shire;	H. i, 224; (See note 16.); H. iv, 240;[94] H. xii, 620.
1634 (See note 1.);	James City;	Original Shire; and part of New Kent; and part of York;	H. i, 224; H. iv, 94;[94,a] H. viii, 208; H. viii, 405; H. viii, 419; A (1852), 31.

[89,a] See note 14, a.
[89] See note 15.
[90] See note 2.
[90] See note 62.

[94] See note 22.
[94] See note 31.
[94,a] See note 29.
[94,a] See note 14, a.

Virginia Counties

1634 (See note 1.);	•Warrosquyoake; (1634-1637)[95]	Original Shire;	H. 1, 224; (See note 34.)
1634 (See note 1.);	•Warwick River; (1634-1642/3)[96]	Original Shire;	H. 1, 224; H. 1, 249.
1636 (See note 55.);	•New Norfolk; (1636-1637)[97]	Elizabeth City;	(See note 55.).
1637 (See note 34.);	Isle of Wight;	Formerly Warrosquyoake; and part of Upper Norfolk;	H. 1, 228:97,a; H. 1, 247; H. 1, 423; H. iv, 355; (See note 71.); H. viii, 405; H. viii, 602.
1637 (See note 55.);	•Lower Norfolk; (1637-1691)[98]	and part of Nansemond; New Norfolk;	H. 1, 228:97,a; H. 1, 247; (See note 55.).
1637 (See note 55.);	•Upper Norfolk; (1637-1642)[99]	and part of Nansemond; New Norfolk;	H. 1, 228:97,a; H. 1, 247; H. 1, 423; (See note 55.).
1642 (See note 52);	Nansemond;	Formerly Upper Norfolk;	H. 1, 321; Va. Mag. of Hist. and Biog., xxiii, 254; H. viii, 405; H. viii, 602; H. xii, 69.

[95] See note 79.
[96] See note 81.
[97],* For full text of this act, see Part vi, chap l, below.
[98] See note 44.
[99] See note 77.

Formed	County	Land formed from	References
1642/3 (See note 58);	Northampton;	Formerly Accomack;	H. 1, 249.
1642/3 (See note 80);	Warwick;	Formerly Warwick River;	H. 1, 249; A. (1881-2), 43.
1642/3 (See note 88);	York;	Formerly Charles River;	H. 1, 249; H. viii, 405; H. viii, 419; A. (1852), 31.
1648 (See note 59);	Northumberland;[100]	Chickacoan;	H. 1, 294, n; H. 1, 299; H. 1, 337-8; H. 1, 340; H. 1, 352; H. 1, 353; H. 1, 362.
1651 (See note 28);	Gloucester;	York;	H. 1, 374; H. xiii, 162.
1651 (See note 41);	Lancaster;	Northumberland and York;	H. 1, 374; (See note 41).
1652 (See note 73);	Surry;	James City;	H. 1, 373; H. iv, 355; H. vi, 384;

[100] See note 60.

1653 (See note 82);	Westmoreland;[101]	Northumberland; and part of King George;	H. i, 381. H. ix, 432.
1654 (————);	New Kent;	York; and part of James City;	H. i, 387-8; H. iv, 95;[102] H. viii, 208.
1656 (See note 65);	•Rappahannock; (1656-1692)[103]	Lancaster;	H. i, 427; H. iii, 104.
1663 (See note 3);	Accomack;	Northampton;	H. ii, 122; H. ii, 186.
1664 (See note 72);	Stafford;	Westmoreland;	H. ii, 239; H. ii, 250; H. iv, 303; H. ix, 244.
1673 (See note 49);	Middlesex;	Lancaster;	H. ii, 327.
1691 (J. May 12, 1691);	King and Queen;	New Kent;	H. iii, 94; H. iii, 211; H. iv, 77; H. iv, 240;[104] H. v, 185; H. vii, 620.
1691 (J. May 16, 1691);	Norfolk;[105]	Lower Norfolk;	H. iii, 95.

[101] See note 60.
[103] See note 30.
[102] See note 86.
[104] See note 13.
[105] See notes 55 and 57.

Formed	County	Land formed from	References
1691 (J. May 16, 1691);	Princess Anne;[106]	Lower Norfolk;	H. iii, 95.
1692 (J. Apl. 26, 1692);	Essex;	Rappahannock;	H. iii, 104; H. iv, 77; H. iv, 240.[107]
1692 (J. Apl. 26, 1692);	Richmond;	Rappahannock;	H. iii, 104; H. iv, 95.[108]
1702 (J. Sep. 12, 1701);	King William;	King and Queen;	H. B. (1695-1702), 398; H. iii, 211; H. iv, 77; H. iv, 240.[109]
1703 (J. Aug. 25, 1702);	Prince George;[110]	Charles City;	H. iii, 223; H. iv, 467; H. vi, 254.
1721 (J. Nov. 24, 1720);	King George;[111]	Richmond; and part of Westmoreland;	H. B. (1712-26), 279; H. iv, 95; H. iv, 303; H. ix, 244; H. ix, 432.

[105] See notes 55 and 57.
[107] See note 13.
[108] See note 39.
[109] See note 13.
[110] See note 62.
[111] See note 39.

Virginia Counties

Date	County	Formed from	References
1721 (J. Nov. 20 [26], 1720);	Hanover;[112]	New Kent;	H. B. (1712-26), 281; H. Iv, 95; H. v, 208; H. xii, 620.
1721 (J. Dec. 17, 1720);	Spotsylvania;	Essex, King and Queen and King William;	H. Iv, 77; H. Iv, 450.
1728 (J. Mar. 6, 1727);	Goochland;[113]	Henrico;	H. B. (1727-40), 33; H. Iv, 240; H. v, 266; (See note 19); H. xii, 71.
1728 (J. Mar. 15, 1727);	Caroline;[114]	Essex, King and Queen and King William; and part of King and Queen; and part of King and Queen;	H. B. (1727-40), 39; H. Iv, 240; H. v, 185; H. vii, 620;
1731 (J. June 19, 1730);	Prince William;	Stafford and King George;	H. Iv, 303; H. v, 207; H. vii, 311;
1732 (J. Dec. 17, 1720);	Brunswick;[115]	Area not named [Prince George][115,a] and parts of Surry and Isle of Wight;	H. Iv, 77; H. Iv, 355; H. Iv, 467; H. v, 383; H. x, 363; H. xii, 596.

[112] See note 13.
[113] See note 11.
[114] See note 30.
[115] See note 29.
[115,a] See note 11, a.

Formed	County	Land formed from	References
1734 (J. Sep. 20, 1734);	Orange;	Spotsylvania;	H. iv, 450; H. v, 78; (See note 18); A (1838), 52.
1735 (J. Sep. 30, 1734);	Amelia;	Prince George and Brunswick;	H. iv, 467; H. vi, 379; H. xii, 723; H. xiii, 561.
1742 (J. May 27, 1742);	Fairfax;	Prince William; and part of Loudoun;	H. v, 207; H. vii, 148; S. ii, 107; U. S. Stats. i, 130, 214; U. S. Stats. ii, 103, 115; A (1845-6), 50; A (1846-7), 41; A (1846-7), 48.
1742 (J. June 2, 1742);	Louisa;[118]	Hanover;	H. v, 208; H. vii, 419; A (1836-7), 33; A (1838), 57; A (1876-7), 20; A (1876-7), 21; A (1876-7), 228.

[118] See note 43.

1743 (J. Dec. 15, 1738);	Frederick;[117]	Orange; and part of Augusta;	H. v, 78; H. vi, 376; H. viii, 597; A (1827-8), 51; A (1835-6), 20; A (1835-6), 22; A (1847-8), 43; A (1862, Wheeling), 3; A (1865-6), 194; A (1865-6), 195.
1744 (J. Oct. 16, 1744);	Albemarle;[118]	Goochland; and part of Louisa; "and certain islands in the Fluvanna River";	H. v, 266; H. vi, 441; H. vii, 419; H. viii, 395; H. ix, 325; A (1836-7), 83; A (1838), 57; A (1855-6), 99; A (1861), 151; A (1871-2), 342; A (1876-7), 21; A (1876-7), 228.

[117] See note 25.   [118] See note 4.

Formed	County	Land formed from	References
1745 (J. Dec. 15, 1738);	Augusta;[119]	Orange;	H. v, 78; H. vi, 376; H. viii, 395; H. ix, 262; H. ix, 420; H. x, 114; H. x, 351; H. xii, 637; H. xiii, 165.
1746 (J. Apl. 1, 1746);	Lunenburg;	Brunswick; and part of Charlotte;	H. v, 383; H. vi, 252; H. vi, 381; H. vi, 441; H. viii, 41; H. ix, 327.
1749 (J. Mar. 23, 1748);	Culpeper;[120]	Orange;	H. B. (1742-9), 346; H. xiii, 558; A (1832-3), 44.
1749 (J. Mar. 23, 1748);	Cumberland;[121]	Goochland; and part of Buckingham;	H. B. (1742-9), 346; H. ix, 322; H. ix, 559.

[119] See note 6.   [120] See note 18.   [121] See note 19.

Virginia Counties

1749 (J. Apl. 20, 1749);	Southampton;[122]	Isle of Wight; and part of Nansemond;	H. B. (1742-9), 371; H. xll, 69.
1749 (J. May 1, 1749);	Chesterfield;[123]	Henrico;	H. B. (1742-9), 384; A (1849-0), 26.
1752 (J. Mar. 9, 1752);	Dinwiddie;	Prince George;	H. vi, 254.
1752 (J. Apl. 17, 1752);	Halifax;	Lunenburg;	H. vi, 252; H. viii, 205.
1754 (J. Nov. 17, 1753);	Prince Edward;	Amelia;	H. vi, 379; A (1844-5), 38.
1754 (J. Nov. 28, 1753);	Sussex;	Surry;	H. vi, 384; S. ii, 347.
1754 (J. Dec. 13, 1753);	Bedford;[124]	Lunenburg; and parts of Albemarle and Lunenburg;	H. vi, 381.
1754 (J. Dec. 13, 1753);	w Hampshire;	Augusta and Frederick; and part of Augusta; and part of Hardy;	H. vi, 441; H. x, 447; H. xii, 70. H. vi, 376; H. ix, 420; H. xii, 86; H. xii, 597; A (1819-0), 27; A (1820-1), 120; A (1823-4), 83.

[122] See note 71.

[123] See note 16.

[124] See note 7.

Formed	County	Land formed from	References
1757 (J. May 17, 1757);	Loudoun;	Fairfax;	H. vii, 148; S. ii, 107; A (1823-4), 82.
1759 (J. Apl. 5, 1759);	Fauquier;[128]	Prince William;	H. vii, 311; A (1823-4), 82.
1761 (J. Apl. 7, 1761);	Amherst;	Albemarle; "and certain islands in the Fluvanna River;"	H. vii, 419
1761 (J. Apl. 7, 1761);	Buckingham;	Albemarle; and part of Appomattox;	H. viii, 395; S. iii, 378.
1765 (J. Nov. 27, 1764);	Charlotte;	Lunenburg;	H. vii, 419; H. xi, 559; A (1844-5), 38; A (1859-0), 171.
1765 (J. Nov. 27, 1764);	Mecklenburg;	Lunenburg;	H. viii, 41; H. ix, 327; A (1844-5), 38.
1767 (J. Dec. 15, 1766);	Pittsylvania;	Halifax;	H. viii, 41.
			H. viii, 205; H. ix, 241.

[128] See note 25.

Virginia Counties 101

1770 (J. Nov. 28, 1769):	Botetourt;[126]	H. viii, 395;
		H. viii, 600;
		H. ix, 420;
		H. xii, 74;
		H. xiii, 76;
		H. xiii, 165;
	Augusta;	S. i, 406;
		S. ii, 64;
	and part of Bockbridge;	S. ii, 345;
		A (1821-2), 28;
		A (1838), 54;
		A (1850-1), 21;
		A (1887-8), 556.
1772 (J. Mar. 24, 1772):	w Berkeley;	H. viii, 597;
		S. ii, 271;
	Frederick;	A (1819-0), 27;
		A (1862, Wheeling), 3;
		A (1865-6), 194;
		A (1865-6), 195.
1772 (J. Mar. 24, 1772):	e Dunmore;	H. viii, 597;
	(1772-1778)[127] Frederick;	H. ix, 424.
1772 (J. Apl. 8, 1772):	e Fincastle;	H. viii, 600;
	(1772-1777)[128] Botetourt;	H. ix, 257.

[126] See note 17.   [127] See note 21.   [128] See note 25.

Formed	County	Land formed from	References
1776 (J. Nov. 6, 1776);	w Monongalia;	Augusta; and part of Augusta; and part of Augusta;	H. ix, 262; H. x, 114; H. x, 351; H. xi, 366; S. ii, 203; A (1817-8), 32; A (1818-9), 141; A (1840-1), 61; A (1841-2), 34; A (1846-7), 57.
1776 (J. Nov. 6, 1776);	w Ohio;	and part of Preston; Augusta; and part of Yohogania;	H. ix, 262; H. xii, 114; S. ii, 54; S. iii, 174; A (1814-5), 87; A (1832-3), 48; A (1834-5), 38.
1776 (J. Nov. 6, 1776);	e Yohogania;[119] (1776-1786)[120]	Augusta;	H. ix, 262; H. xii, 114.
1777 (J. Oct. 23, 1776);	Henry;	Pittsylvania; and part of Patrick;	H. ix, 241; H. xii, 70; H. xiii, 160; H. xiii, 290; A (1857-8), 113.

[119] See note 86.   [120] See note 87.

1777 (J. Dec. 7, 1776);	•Kentucky;[131] (1777-1780)[132]	Fincastle;	H. ix, 257; H. x, 315.
1777 (J. Dec. 7, 1776);	Montgomery;	Fincastle; and part of Botetourt; and part of Pulaski;	H. ix, 257; H. ix, 330; H. ix, 420; H. xii, 670; H. xiii, 76; S. i, 315; S. i, 406; S. ii, 64; S. iii, 244; A (1830-1), 137; A (1839), 30; A (1839-0), 35; A (1841-2), 39; A (1848-9), 28; A (1852-3), 130.
1777 (J. Dec. 7, 1776);	Washington;	Fincastle; and part of Montgomery;	H. ix, 257; H. ix, 330; H. xii, 110; S. i, 315; A (1814-5), 85; A (1814-5), 87; A (1823-4), 83; A (1824-5), 76; A (1825-6), 40; A (1831-2), 47.

[131] See note 36. [132] See note 37.

Formed	County	Land formed from	References
1777 (J. June 3, 1777);	Fluvanna;	Albemarle;	H. ix, 325; H. xii, 71; A (1836-7), 33; A (1838), 57; A (1855-6), 99; A (1861), 151; A (1871-2), 342; A (1876-7), 20; A (1876-7), 228.
1777 (J. June 3, 1777);	Powhatan;	Cumberland; and part of Chesterfield;	H. ix, 322; A (1849-0), 26.
1778 (J. Jan. 12, 1778);	w Greenbrier;	Botetourt and Montgomery; and part of Monroe; and part of Fayette; and part of Fayette;	H. ix, 420; H. xii, 670; H. xiii, 165; S. i, 388; S. ii, 168; A (1817-8), 54; A (1824-5), 73; A (1826-7), 41; A (1830-1), 134; A (1830-1), 136; A (1832-3), 47.
1778 (J. Jan. 12, 1778);	Rockbridge;	Augusta and Botetourt; and part of Botetourt;	H. ix, 420; H. xii, 74; A (1887-8), 556.

Virginia Counties 105

1778 (J. Jan. 12, 1778);	Rockingham;	Augusta;	H. ix, 420; H. xii, 637; A. (1830-1), 140.
1778 (J. Jan. 12, 1778);	Shenando[ah];	Formerly Dunmore;	H. ix, 424; A. (1830-1), 140; A. (1835-6), 22; A. (1847-8), 43.
1778 (J. Dec. 9, 1778);	ͤIllinois;[123] (1778-1784)[124]	"on the western side of the Ohio River" [Augusta];	H. ix, 552; H. x, 303; "Journals of Congress", 1823, iii, 516-7; H. x, 564; H. xi, 571-5; "Journals of Congress", 1823, iv, 341-4.
1780 (J. June 30, 1780);	ᵏFayette;	Kentucky;	H. x, 315; H. xii, 89; H. xii, 663.
1780 (J. June 30, 1780);	ᵏJefferson;	Kentucky;	H. x, 315; H. xi, 469.
1780 (J. June 30, 1780);	ᵏLincoln;	Kentucky;	H. x, 315; H. xii, 118.

[123] See note 32.
[124] See note 33.

Formed	County	Land formed from	References
1781 (J. Nov. 28, 1780);	Greensville;	Brunswick; and part of Brunswick; and part of Sussex;	H. x, 363; H. xii, 596; S. ii, 347.
1782 (J. Dec. 15, 1781);	Campbell;	Bedford;	H. x, 447; A. (1844-5), 58; A. (1847-8), 41.
1784 (J. June 4, 1784);	w Harrison;	Monongalia; and part of Monongalia; and part of Randolph; and part of Ohio;	H. xi, 366; H. xii, 393; S. ii, 170; S. ii, 203; S. ii, 345; S. iii, 174; A. (1816-7), 152; A. (1816-7), 154; A. (1818-9), 142; A. (1841-2), 54; A. (1842-3), 35; A. (1842-3), 37; A. (1843-4), 34; A. (1844-5), 42; A. (1849-0), 53.
1785 (J. Nov. 29, 1784);	k Nelson;	Jefferson;	H xi, 469.

1786 (J. Nov. 29, 1785);	Franklin;	Bedford and Henry; and part of Patrick;	H. xti, 70; A (1847-8), 42; A (1872-3), 85.
1786 (J. Dec. 10, 1785);	w Hardy;	Hampshire;	H. xti, 86; H. xti, 597; H. xti, 637; A (1823-4), 83.
1786 (J. Dec. 15, 1785);	k Madison;	Lincoln;	H. xti, 118.
1786 (J. Dec. 15, 1785);	k Mercer;	Lincoln;	H. xti, 118.
1786 (J. Dec. 29, 1785);	k Bourbon;	Fayette;	H. xti, 89; H. xti, 658.
1786 (J. Jan. 6, 1786);	Russell;	Washington;	H. xti, 110; H. xti, 556; S. H, 217; S. III, 310; A (1812-3), 110; A (1814-5), 85; A (1814-5), 87; A (1823-4), 83; A (1824-5), 76; A (1834-5), 40; A (1855-6), 87; A (1857-8), 108; A (1879-0), 125.

Formed	County	Land formed from	References
1787 (J. Nov. 29, 1786);	w Randolph;	Harrison;	H. xii, 393; S. ii, 345; A (1817-8), 34; A (1817-8), 184; A (1821-2), 27; A (1827-8), 53; A (1838), 57; A (1842-3), 37; A (1848-9), 30; A (1850-1), 23; A (1855-6), 95; A (1859-0), 151.
1788 (J. Dec. 4, 1787);	w Pendleton;	Augusta, Hardy and Rockingham; and part of Bath;	H. xii, 637; S. ii, 53; A (1821-2), 27; A (1846-7), 52.
1789 (J. Nov. 5, 1788);	k Mason;	Bourbon;	H. xii, 658.
1789 (J. Nov. 12, 1788);	k Woodford;	Fayette;	H. xii, 663.

1789 (J. Nov. 14, 1788);	w Kanawha;[155] Greenbrier and Montgomery; and part of Fayette;	H. xii, 670; S. i, 388; S. ii, 263; S. iii, 77; A (1808-9), 44; A (1816-7), 157; A (1817-8), 24; A (1817-8), 185; A (1823-4), 20; A (1823-4), 80; A (1823-4), 81; A (1829-0), 117; A (1830-1), 134; A (1830-1), 138; A (1835-6), 18; A (1839), 33; A (1843-4), 37; A (1844-5), 45; A (1846-7), 49; A (1847-8), 34; A (1849-0), 24; A (1849-0), 25; A (1855-6), 91.
1789 (J. Dec. 23, 1788);[156]	Nottoway;	Amelia;	H. xii, 723; H. xiii, 561.

[155] See note 35.

[156] See note 61.

Formed	County	Land formed from	References
1790 (J. Dec. 1, 1789);	Wythe;	Montgomery; and part of Grayson;	H. xiii, 76; H. xiii, 559; S. ii, 217; S. iii, 389; A. (1824-5), 75; A. (1825-6), 40; A. (1831-2), 47; A. (1839), 30; A. (1839-0), 35; A. (1840-1), 62; A. (1861), 45; A. (1861-2), 106; A. (1874-5), 26.
1791 (J. Nov. 26, 1790);	Patrick;	Henry; and part of Henry;	H. xiii, 160; H. xiii, 290; S. i, 315; A. (1809-10), 58; A. (1817-8), 185; A. (1847-8), 42; A. (1855-6), 98; A. (1857-8), 113.
1791 (J. Dec. 14, 1790);	Bath;	Augusta, Botetourt and Greenbrier;	H. xiii, 165; S. ii, 53; A. (1821-2), 27; A. (1821-2), 28; A. (1822-3), 88; A. (1846-7), 52; A. (1846-7), 57.

1791 (J. Dec. 16, 1790);	Mathews;	Gloucester;	H. xiii, 162.
1793 (J. Oct. 25, 1792);	Lee;	Russell;	H. xiii, 556;
			A (1812-3), 110;
			A (1814-5), 85;
			A (1814-5), 87;
		and part of Scott;	A (1822-3), 90;
			A (1836-7), 34;
			A (1855-6), 87.
1793 (J. Nov. 7, 1792);	Grayson;	Wythe;	H. xiii, 559;
			S. i, 315;
			A (1809-0), 58;
		and part of Patrick;	A (1817-8), 185;
			A (1824-5), 75;
			A (1840-1), 62;
			A (1841-2), 32;
			A (1874-5), 26;
			A (1874-5), 330.
1793 (J. Dec. 5, 1792);[137]	Madison;	Culpeper;	H. xiii, 558.
1797 (J. Nov. 30, 1796);[138]	w Brooke;	Ohio;	S. ii, 54;
			A (1847-8), 30.
1798 (J. Dec. 22, 1798);[139]	w Wood;	Harrison;	S. ii, 170;
		and part of Kenawha;	S. ii, 263;
			A (1830-1), 138;
			A (1842-3), 35;
			A (1843-4), 34;
			A (1847-8), 38;
			A (1850-1), 25.

[137] See note 45. [138] See note 10. [139] See note 85.

Formed	County	Land formed from	References
1799 (J. Jan. 15, 1799);[140]	ᵛMonroe (Munroe);[141]	Greenbrier; and part of Botetourt;	S. ii, 168; S. ii, 345; S. iii, 244; A (1821-2), 28; A (1826-7), 41; A (1826-7), 42; A (1828-9), 119; A (1842-3), 40; A (1850-1), 21; A (1852-3), 130; A (1855-6), 97; A (1855-6), 383.
1800 (J. Dec. 20, 1799);[143]	Tazewell;	Wythe and Russell; and part of Russell; and parts of Washington and Wythe; and part of Logan; and part of Russell;	S. ii, 217; S. iii, 310; S. iii, 244; A (1823-4), 20; A (1825-6), 39; A (1825-6), 40; A (1827-8), 52; A (1833-4), 73; A (1834-5), 40; A (1835-6), 24; A (1836-7), 31; A (1857-8), 106; A (1857-8), 108; A (1859-0), 169; A (1861), 45.

[140] See note 51.   [141] See note 50.   [143] See note 75.

Virginia Counties 113

1801 (J. Jan. 8, 1801);	w Jefferson;	Berkeley;	S. ii, 271; A (1862, Wheeling), 3; A (1865-6), 194; A (1865-6), 195.
1804 (J. Jan. 3, 1804);[145]	w Mason;	Kanawha;	S. iii, 77; A (1816-7), 157; A (1823-4), 81; A (1830-1), 138; A (1847-8), 34.
1806 (J. Jan. 16, 1806);	Giles;[146]	Montgomery, Monroe and Tazewell; and part of Wythe; and part of Tazewell; and part of Monroe; and part of Tazewell; and part of Mercer; and part of Craig;	S. iii, 244; S. iii, 389; A (1823-4), 20; A (1825-6), 39; A (1826-7), 42; A (1827-8), 52; A (1828-9), 119; A (1835-6), 24; A (1836-7), 31; A (1840-1), 61; A (1850-1), 21; A (1857-8), 114; A (1861), 45; A (1879-0), 183; A (1899-00), 665.

---

[145] See note 48.   [146] See note 17.

Formed	County	Land formed from	References
1808 (J. Dec. 23, 1807);[145]	Nelson;	Amherst;	S. iii, 378.
1809 (J. Jan. 2, 1809);	w Cabell;	Kanawha;	A (1803-9), 44; A (1817-8), 185; A (1823-4), 20; A (1829-0), 117; A (1841-2), 36; A (1846-7), 49; A (1847-8), 34; A (1849-0), 24.
1814 (J. Nov. 24, 1814);[146]	Scott;	Lee, Russell and Washington;	A (1814-5), 85; A (1814-5), 87; A (1822-3), 90; A (1836-7), 34; A (1855-6), 87.
1814. (J. Dec. 3, 1814);[147]	w Tyler;	Ohio;	A (1814-5), 87; A (1815-6), 154; A (1832-3), 48; A (1844-5), 42; A (1845-6), 51; A (1849-0), 38; A (1850-1), 25.

[145] See note 53. [146] See note 70. [147] See note 76.

Virginia Counties

1816 (J. Dec. 18, 1816); w Lewis; Harrison; and part of Randolph;
A (1816-7), 152;
A (1817-8), 184;
A (1818-9), 142;
A (1835-6), 18;
A (1842-3), 35;
A (1843-4), 37;
A (1844-5), 42;
A (1844-5), 45;
A (1846-7), 58;
A (1849-0), 33;
A (1850-1), 23.

1818 (J. Jan. 19, 1818); w Preston; Monongalia;
and part of Randolph;
and part of Randolph;
and part of Monongalia;
A (1817-8), 32;
A (1818-9), 141;
A (1827-8), 53;
A (1838), 57;
A (1840-1), 61.

1818 (J. Jan. 30, 1818); w Nicholas; Greenbrier, Kanawha and Randolph;
and part of Kanawha;
A (1817-8), 34;
A (1819-0), 72;
A (1819-0), 91;
A (1823-4), 80;
A (1830-1), 134;
A (1835-6), 18;
A (1843-4), 37;
A (1857-8), 111;
A (1859-0), 151.

1820 (J. Feb. 9, 1820); w Morgan; Berkeley and Hampshire;
A (1819-0), 27;
A (1820-1), 120;
A (1827-8), 51.

Formed	County	Land formed from	References
1821 (J. Dec. 21, 1821);	w Pocahontas;	Bath, Pendleton and Randolph; and part of Greenbrier;	A (1821-2), 27; A (1824-5), 73.
1822 (J. Jan. 5, 1822);	Alleghany;	Bath, Botetourt and Monroe; and part of Monroe; and part of Bath;	A (1821-2), 28; A (1822-3), 88; A (1842-3), 40; A (1846-7), 57; A (1855-6), 97; A (1885-6), 383.
1824 (J. Jan. 12, 1824);	w Logan;[148]	Giles, Cabell, Tazewell and Kanawha; and parts of Kanawha and Cabell;	A (1823-4), 20; A (1829-0), 117; A (1830-1), 134; A (1833-4), 33; A (1846-7), 49; A (1849-0), 21.
1831 (J. Jan. 15, 1831);	Floyd;	Montgomery; and part of Franklin;	A (1830-1), 137; A (1872-3), 85.
1831 (J. Feb. 28, 1831);	w Fayette;	Logan, Greenbrier, Nicholas and Kanawha; and part of Kanawha;	A (1830-1), 134; A (1830-1), 136; A (1832-3), 47; A (1839), 33; A (1849-0), 19; A (1849-0), 25; A (1850-1), 26.

[148] See note 35.

1831 (J. Mar. 1, 1831);	w Jackson;	Mason, Kanawha and Wood; and part of Wirt;	A (1830-1), 138; A (1847-8), 38; A (1852-3), 130; A (1855-6), 91.
1831 (J. Mar. 30, 1831);	Page;	Rockingham and Shenandoah;	A (1830-1), 140.
1832 (J. Feb. 23, 1832);	Smyth;	Washington and Wythe;	A (1831-2), 47; A (1874-5), 330.
1833 (J. Feb. 18, 1833);[149]	Rappahannock;	Culpeper;	A (1832-3), 44.
1835 (J. Mar. 12, 1835);	w Marshall;[150]	Ohio;	A (1834-5), 38.
1836 (J. Jan. 15, 1836);	w Braxton;	Lewis, Kanawha and Nicholas; and part of Randolph;	A (1835-6), 18; A (1843-4), 37; A (1848-9), 30; A (1857-8), 111; A (1859-0), 151.
1836 (J. Mar. 8, 1836);	Clarke;	Frederick; and part of Warren;	A (1835-6), 20; A (1859-0), 496.
1836 (J. Mar. 9, 1836);	Warren;	Shenandoah and Frederick;	A (1835-6), 22; A (1859-0), 496.
1837 (J. Mar. 17, 1837);	w Mercer;	Giles and Tazewell;	A (1836-7), 31; A (1840-1), 61; A (1846-7), 57.

[149] See note 67.

[150] See note 47.

Formed	County	Land formed from	References
1838 (J. Jan. 24, 1838);	Greene;	Orange;	A (1838), 52.
1838 (J. Mar. 30, 1838);	Roanoke;[151]	Botetourt; and part of Montgomery;	A (1838), 54; A (1848-9), 28; A (1850-1), 21.
1839 (J. Mar. 30, 1839);	Pulaski;	Montgomery and Wythe;[152]	A (1839), 30; A (1839-0), 35; A (1841-2), 39; A (1861-2), 106.
1842 (J. Jan. 14, 1842);	w Marion;[153]	Monongalia and Harrison; and part of Monongalia;	A (1841-2), 34; A (1842-3), 40; A (1843-4), 34; A (1846-7), 57; A (1855-6), 98.
1842 (J. Jan. 17, 1842);	Carroll;	Grayson; and part of Patrick;	A (1841-2), 32; A (1855-6), 98.
1842 (J. Jan. 18, 1842);	w Wayne;	Cabell;	A (1841-2), 36.
1843 (J. Feb. 18, 1843);	w Ritchie;	Harrison, Lewis and Wood;	A (1842-3), 35; A (1843-4), 34; A (1844-5), 42; A (1849-0), 33; A (1850-1), 25.

[151] See note 17.

[152] See note 64.

[153] See note 50.

Virginia Counties 119

1843 (J. Mar. 3, 1843);	w Barbour;	Harrison, Lewis and Randolph;	A (1842-3), 37; A (1843-4), 34; A (1850-1), 23.
1844 (J. Jan. 19, 1844);	w Taylor;[154]	Harrison, Barbour and Marion; and part of Marion;	A (1843-4), 34; A (1855-6), 98.
1845 (J. Feb. 3, 1845);	w Gilmer;	Lewis and Kanawha;	A (1844-5), 45; A (1846-7), 56; A (1855-6), 90; A (1855-6), 91.
1845 (J. Feb. 4, 1845);	w Doddridge;	Harrison, Tyler, Ritchie and Lewis;	A (1844-5), 42; A (1849-0), 33.
1845 (J. Feb. 8, 1845);	Appomattox;	Buckingham, Prince Edward, Charlotte and Campbell; and part of Campbell;	A (1844-5), 38; A (1847-8), 41; A (1859-0), 171.
1846 (J. Jan. 10, 1846);	w Wetzel;[155]	Tyler;	A (1845-6), 51.
1847 (J. Mar. 11, 1847);	w Boone;	Kanawha, Cabell and Logan;	A (1846-7), 49.
1847 (J. Mar. 13, 1847);	Alexandria;[156]	District of Columbia; (that portion of it which was formerly a part of Fairfax County);	U. S. Stats. l, 130, 214; U. S. Stats. ll, 103, 115; A (1845-6), 50; A (1846-7), 41; A (1846-7), 48.

[154] See note 50.   [155] See note 84.   [156] See note 5.

Formed	County	Land formed from	References
1847 (J. Mar. 19, 1847);	Highland;	Pendleton and Bath;	A (1846-7), 52.
1848 (J. Jan. 15, 1848);	w Hancock;	Brooke;	A (1847-8), 30.
1848 (J. Jan. 19, 1848);	w Wirt;	Wood and Jackson;	A (1847-8), 38; A (1852-3), 130.
1848 (J. Mar. 11, 1848);	w Putnam;	Kanawha, Cabell and Mason; and parts of Cabell and Kanawha;	A (1847-8), 34; A (1849-0), 24.
1850 (J. Jan. 23, 1850);	w Raleigh;	Fayette;	A (1849-0), 19; A (1850-1), 26.
1850 (J. Jan. 26, 1850);	w Wyoming;	Logan;	A (1849-0), 21.
1851 (J. Mar. 21, 1851);	Craig;	Botetourt, Roanoke, Giles and Monroe;[157] and part of Monroe; and part of Montgomery; and part of Alleghany; and part of Monroe; and part of Giles;	A (1850-1), 21; A (1852-3), 130; A (1852-3), 130; A (1855-6), 97; A (1855-6), 97; A (1857-8), 114; A (1879-0), 183.
1851 (J. Mar. 27, 1851);[158]	w Upshur;	Randolph, Barbour and Lewis;	A (1850-1), 23.

[157] See note 17.
[158] See note 78.

1851 (J. Mar. 29, 1851);	w Pleasants;	Wood, Tyler and Ritchie;	A (1850-1), 25;
1856 (J. Feb. 16, 1856);	Wise;	Lee, Scott and Russell;	A (1855-6), 87; A (1879-0), 125.
1856 (J. Mar. 5, 1856);	w Calhoun;	Gilmer;	A (1855-6), 90.
1856 (J. Mar. 7, 1856);	w Roane;	Kanawha, Jackson and Gilmer;	A (1855-6), 91.
1856 (J. Mar. 11, 1856);	w Tucker;	Randolph;	A (1855-6), 95.
1858 (J. Feb. 16, 1858);[158]	Buchanan;	Tazewell and Russell;	A (1857-8), 108; A (1879-0), 125.
1858 (J. Feb. 20, 1858);	w McDowell;	Tazewell;	A (1857-8), 106; A (1859-0), 169.
1858 (J. Mar. 29, 1858);	w Clay;	Braxton and Nicholas;	A (1857-8), 111.
1860 (J. Jan. 10, 1860);	w Webster;	Nicholas, Braxton and Randolph;	A (1859-0), 151; A (1861), 50.
1861 (J. Mar. 30, 1861);[160]	Bland;	Giles, Wythe and Tazewell; and part of Giles;	A (1861), 45; A (1899-00), 665.
1880 (J. Feb. 27, 1880);[161]	Dickenson;	Russell, Wise and Buchanan;	A (1879-0), 125.

[158] See note 8.

[160] See note 20.

[159] See note 12.

PART III.

GEOGRAPHICAL ARRANGEMENT

The Notes are assembled in series under Part I, Alphabetical Arrangement.

As the rivers, streams, mountain barriers and natural defences influenced the routes of migration into the wilderness more than anything else, it seems appropriate to base the geographical treatment of the counties upon the grand geological divisions of the State,—the counties in each of these geological divisions being arranged chronologically in accordance with the plan used in Part II,—as the best manner in which to show the gradual development of population in each of these sections, and how the ever-restless settler pushed on into the wilderness, as each section was once securely peopled.

Disregarding the popular interpretation of "Southside" and "Southwest", and following the geological divisions of the State in a general, 'though not in a technical, sense, the counties fall into the following groups:

(For map illustrating these geological divisions, see frontispiece.)

Tidewater (Coastal Plain), extending from the ocean to the fall-line, containing counties to the number of,................... 39.
Piedmont, extending from the fall-line to the crest of the Blue Ridge Mountains, containing counties to the number of,........ 41.
Valley, extending from the crest of the Blue Ridge to the crest of the Alleghanies, containing counties to the number of,........ 17.
Trans-Alleghany, extending from the crest of the Alleghanies westward to the limits of Virginia jurisdiction, and containing counties to the number of,.. 75.

Counties here listed,....................................172.

The popular interpretations having been disregarded, it will doubtless not seem so odd to have Hanover and Henrico classified as Tidewater Counties, and to find that Chesterfield, Grayson, Floyd and Carroll have been assigned to the Piedmont section. We believe that an examination of the geology of the State will justify this rather unusual classification. One should not omit to note that the "Southside" has fallen mostly in the geological Piedmont Plateau, while the "Southwest" is given its natural geological position as a portion of the Valley and Trans-Alleghany areas.

The maps (# 1 to 9) show the settlement of the Coastal Plain up to 1702, and # 10 shows the drift of population on through the Piedmont Plateau to the Blue Ridge Mountains up to 1729, except that Brunswick and Caroline are not indicated; while # 11 shows the complete occupation of the present limits of Virginia by county formations up to 1775, except that the following are not indicated: Amherst, Bedford, Botetourt, Buckingham, Charlotte, Dinwiddie, Dunmore, Fauquier, Fincastle, Halifax, Loudoun, Mecklenburg, Pittsylvania, Prince Edward, Prince William and Sussex.

The variations of names and dates on these maps from those used in the text are those noted in the "Geographical" section of the Preface.

The following abbreviations are used in this Part:

- A.: Acts of the General Assembly of Virginia, for the session indicated.
- E. (superior): resulted from Virginia legislation, but now extinct, as shown by accompanying limiting dates.
- H.: Hening's "Statutes at Large".
- H. B.: "Journals of the House of Burgesses", 1619-1776 (Virginia State Library: 1905-1915).
- J.: "Journal of the House" (Burgesses or Delegates, as the case may be), as interpreted in the note on the subject under the "General" section of the Preface, p. 12.
- K. (superior): resulted from Virginia legislation, but now in Kentucky.
- S.: Shepherd's "Statutes at Large" (continuation of Hening).
- U. S. Stats.: "United States Statutes at Large".
- W. (superior): resulted from Virginia legislation, but now in West Virginia.

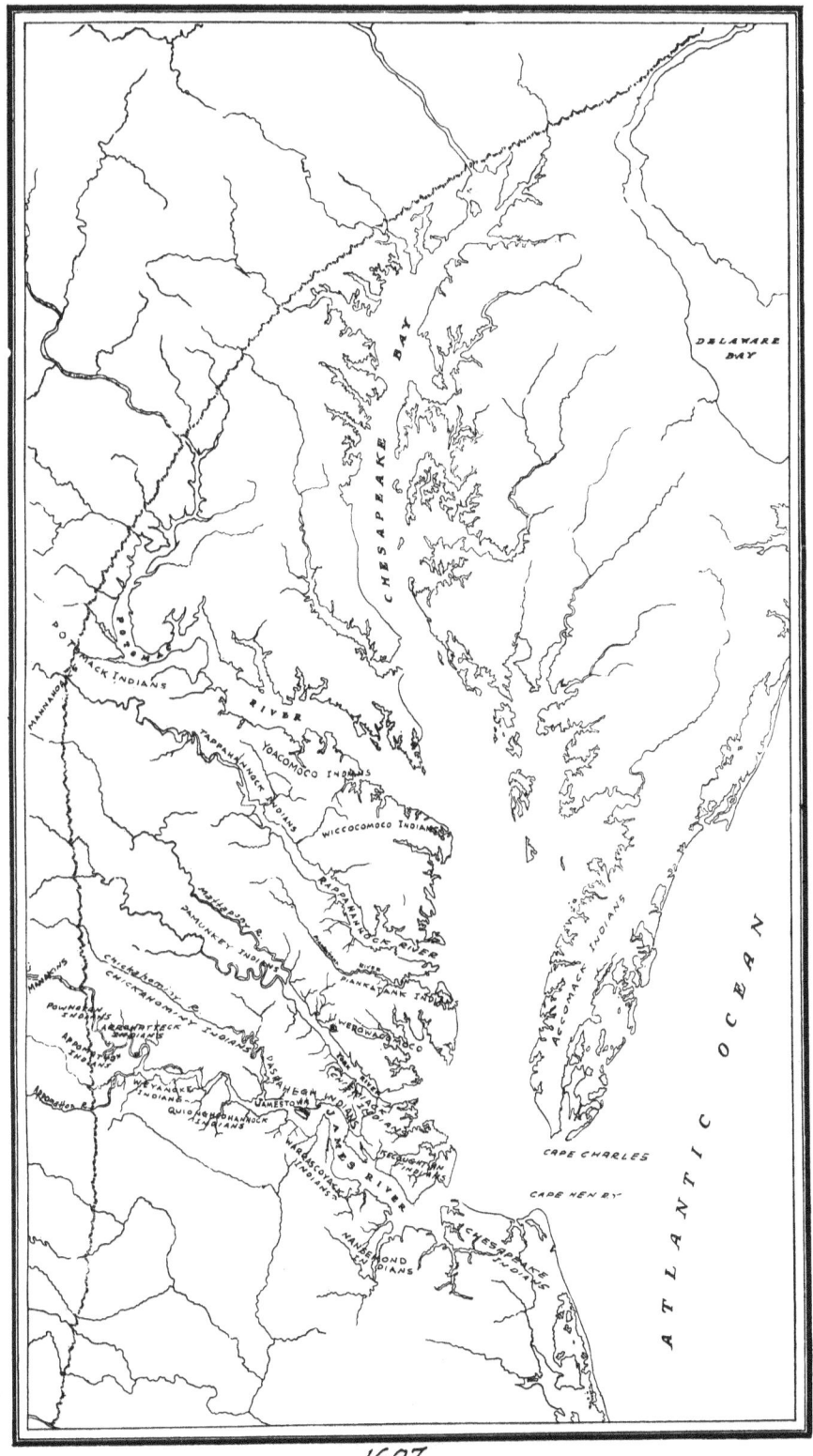

1607
JAMESTOWN
First permanent English Settlement in America.

No. 2.

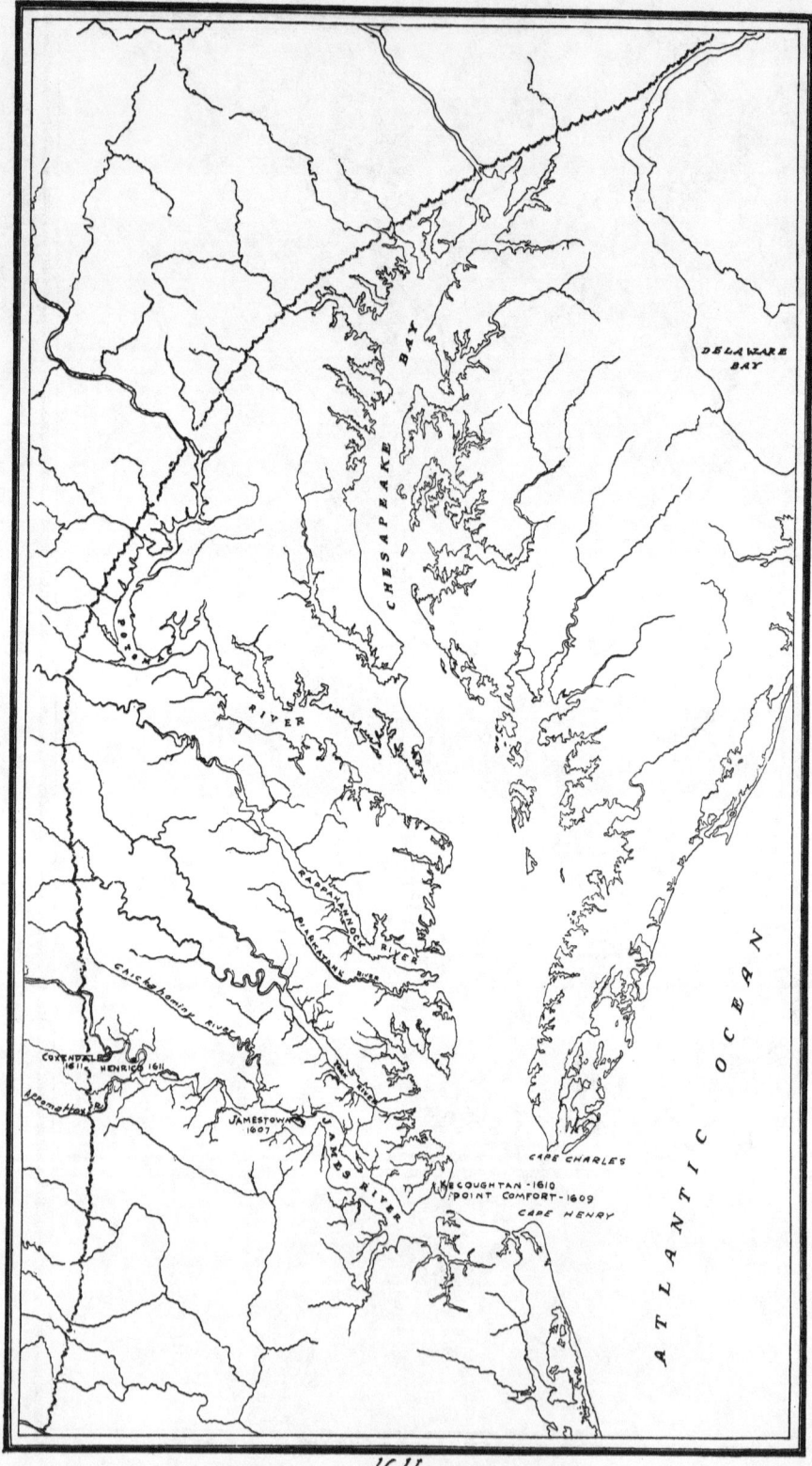

1611
From Point Comfort to Henrico
Plantations on the James River.

No. 3.

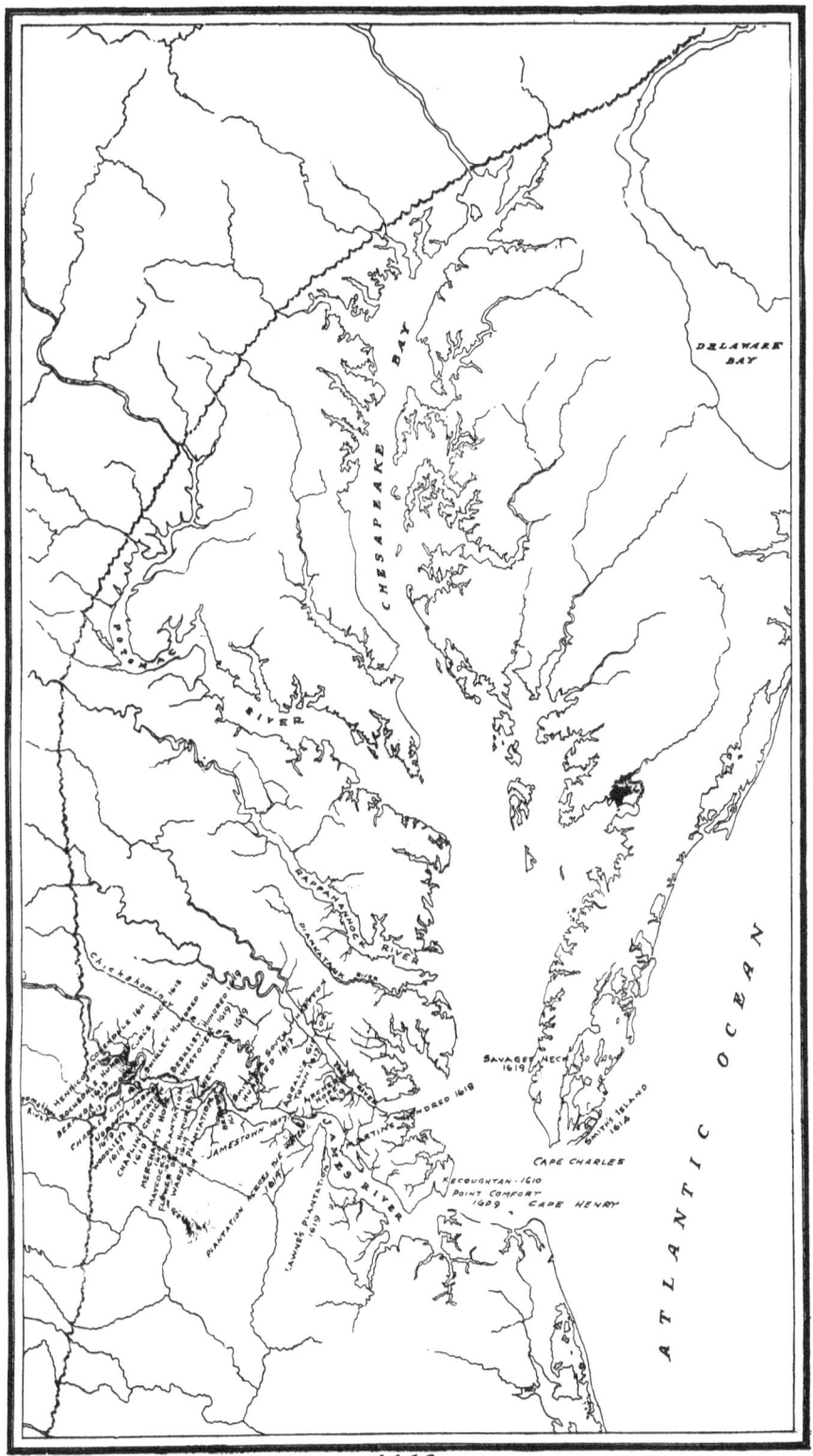

1619
Rapid Growth of Settlement along the James River
Marked by introduction of Representative Government.

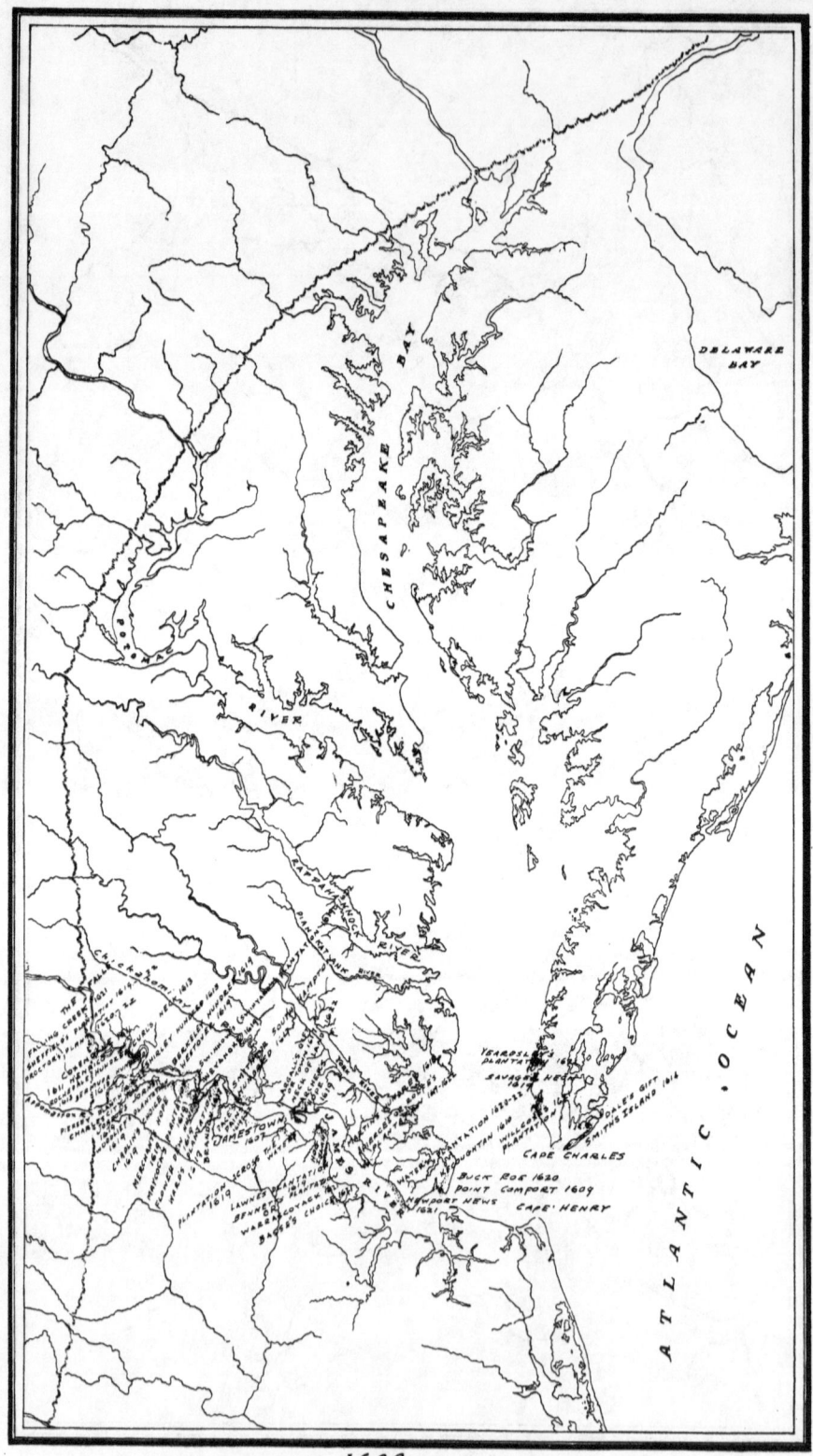

1622
Extension of Settlement prior to
The Indian Massacre

No. 5.

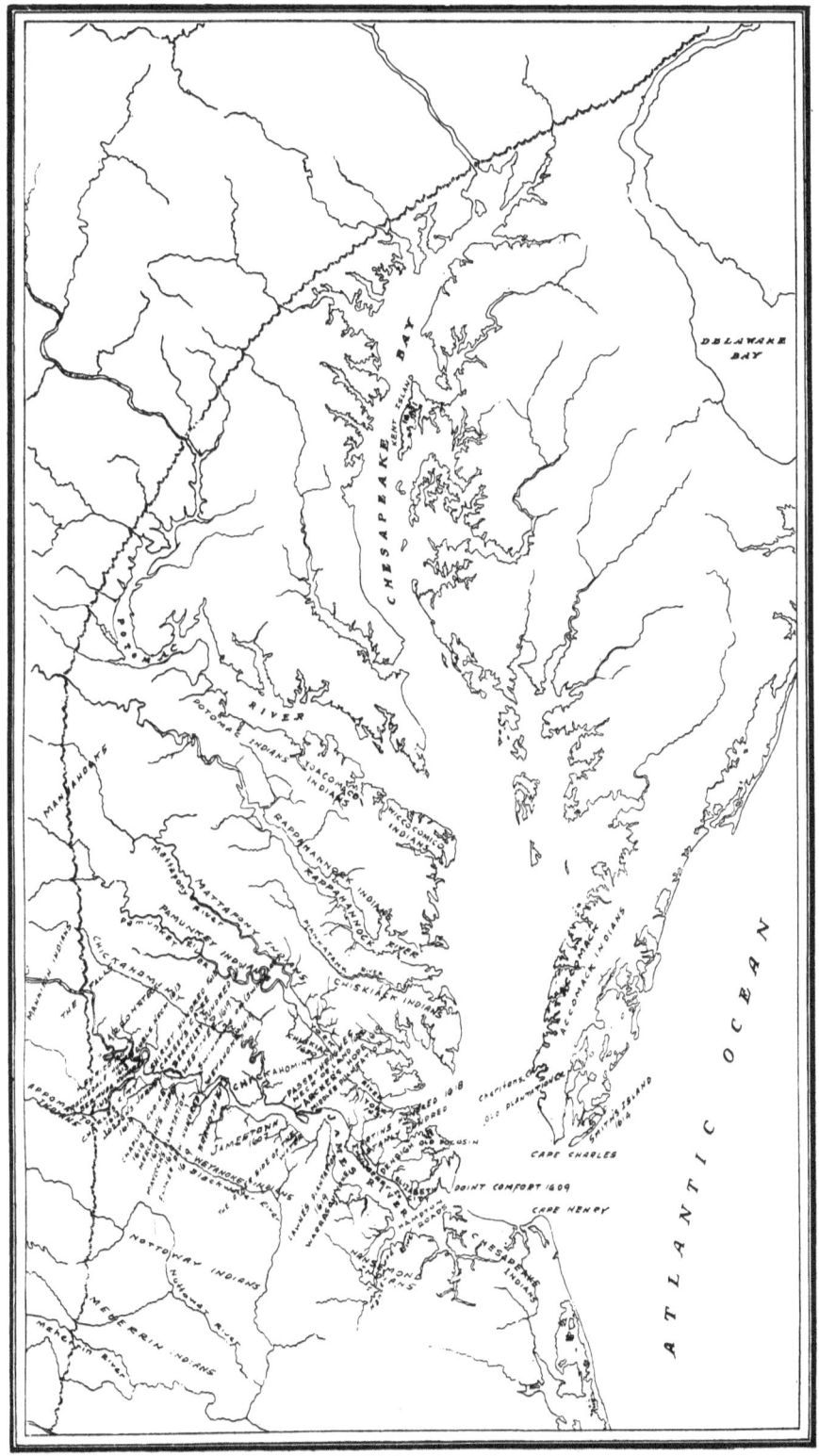

1632
James River and Eastern Shore Plantations Multiplied
Plantations on York River

No. 6.

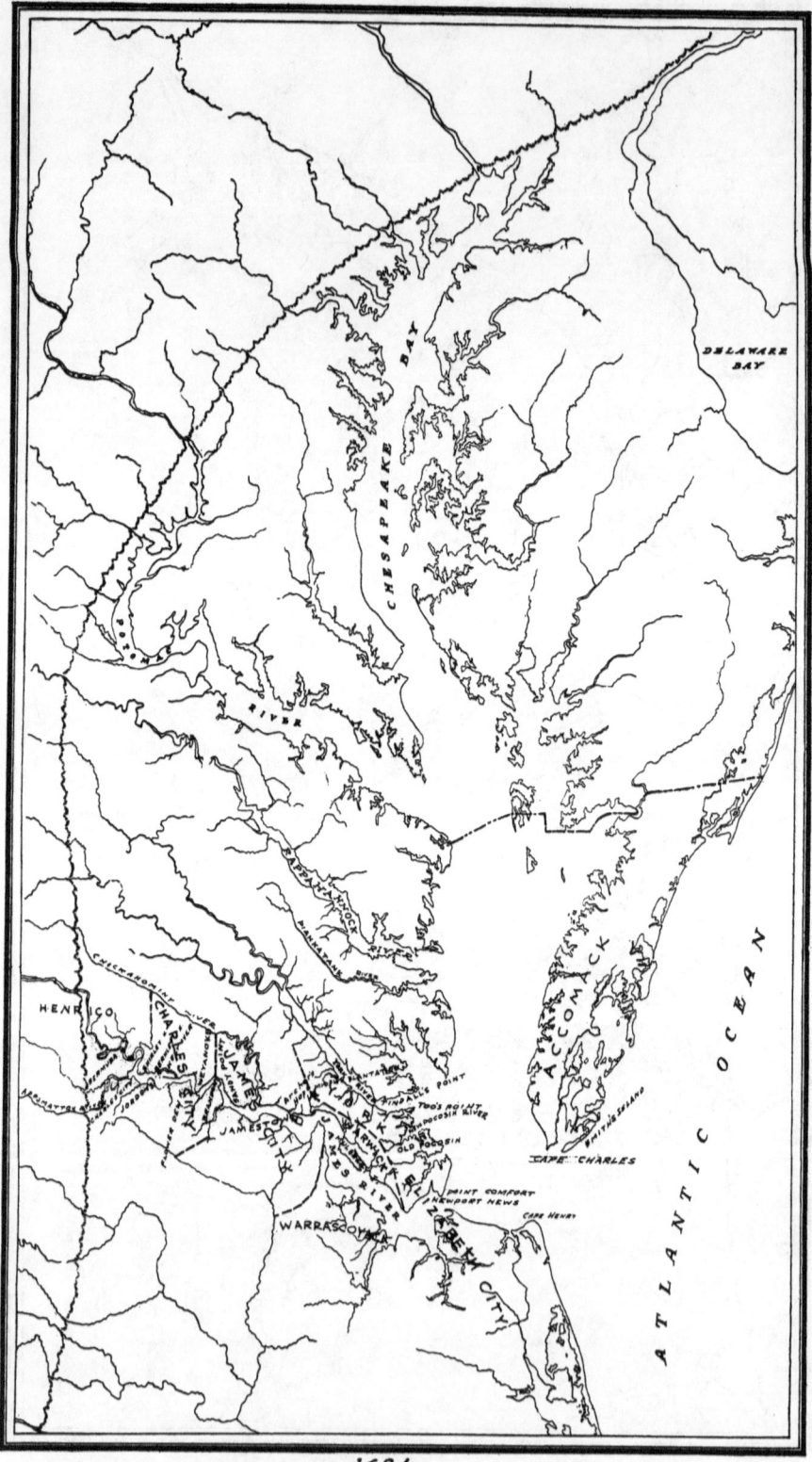

1634
The Peninsula filled in
Counties Established.

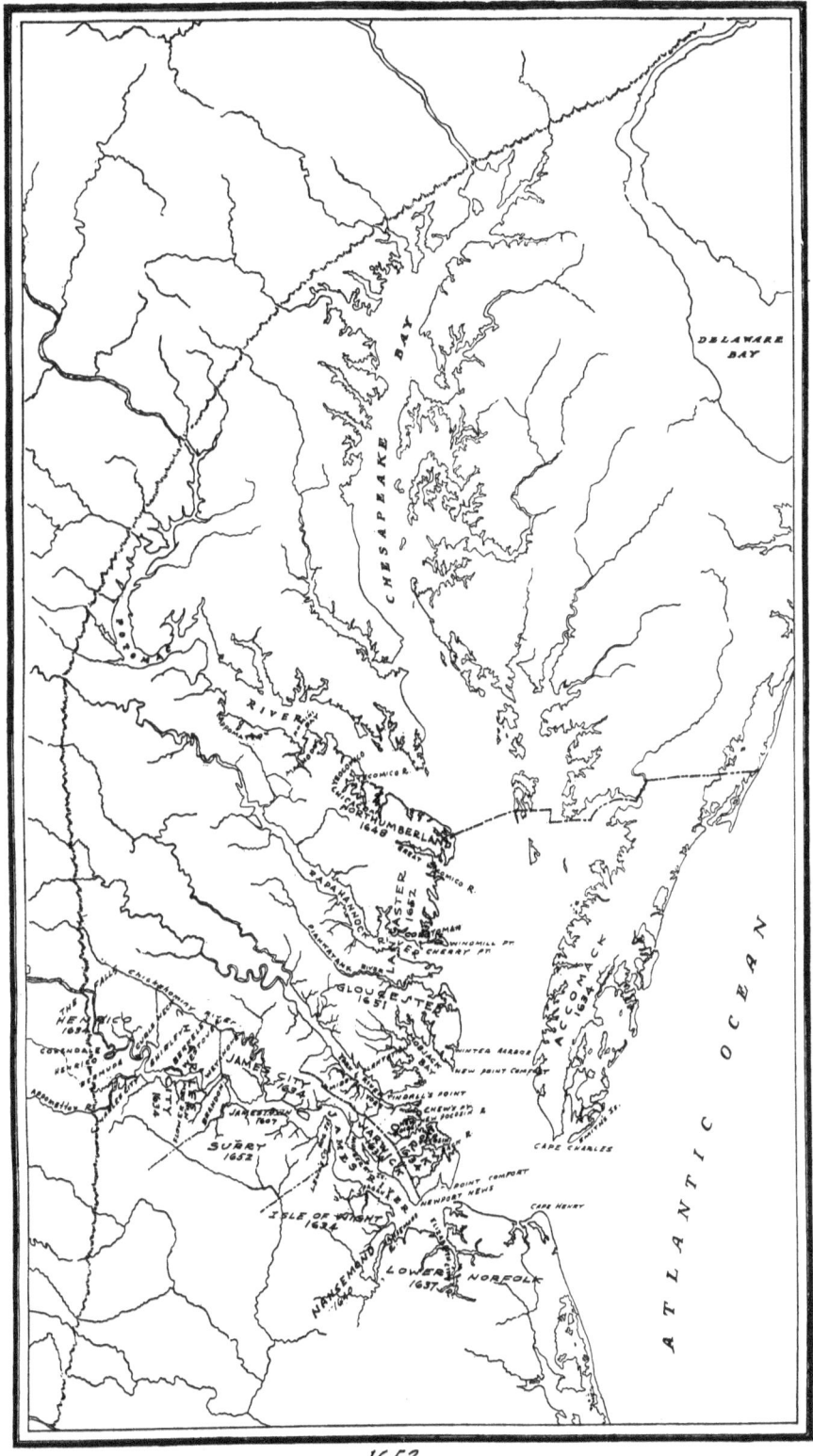

1652
THE ENGLISH COMMONWEALTH PERIOD
Marked by numerous settlements along the Chesapeake and its tributaries

No. 8.

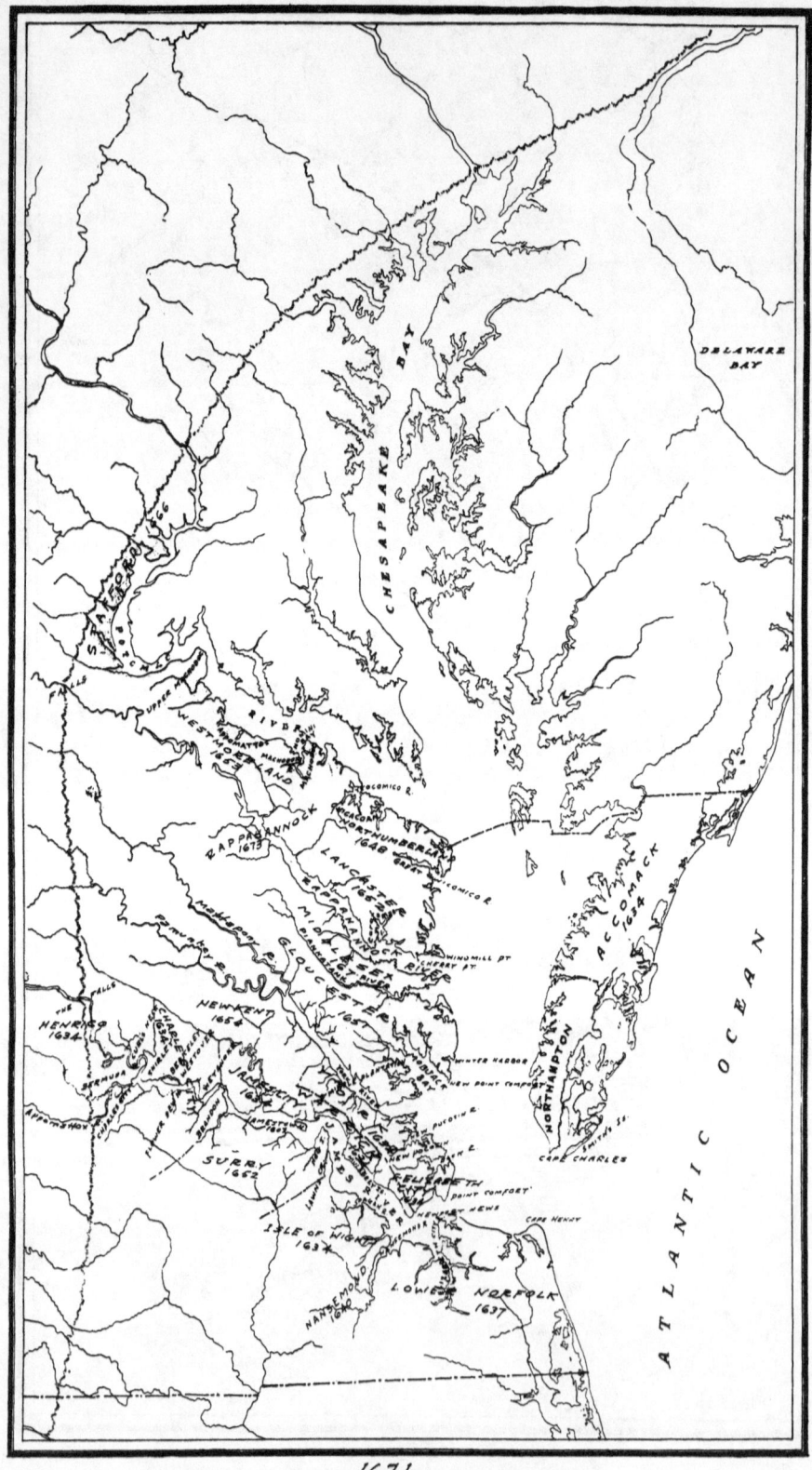

1671
Practically all of Tidewater Virginia Settled.

TIDEWATER

Formed	County	Land formed from	References
1634 (See note 1.);	•Accawmack; (1634-1642/3)[163]	Original Shire;	H. i, 224; H. i, 249.
1634 (See note 1.);	Charles City;	Original Shire; and enlarged, but no metes or bounds given;[163, a]	H. i, 224; H.iii, 223;[163] H. iv, 94. 163, a
1634 (See note 1.);	•Charles River; (1634-1642/3)[164]	Original Shire;	H. i, 224; H. i, 249.
1634 (See note 1.);	Elizabeth City;[165]	Original Shire;	H. i, 224; A (1881-2), 43.
1634 (See note 1.);	Henrico;[166]	Original Shire;	H. i, 224; (See note 16); H. iv, 240;[167] H. xii, 620.
1634 (See note 1.);	James City;	Original Shire; and part of New Kent; and part of York;	H. i, 224; H. iv, 94;[167, a] H. viii, 208; H. viii, 405; H. viii, 419; A (1852), 31.

[163] See note 2.   [163, a] See note 14, a.   [165] See note 22.   [167] See note 29.
[162] See note 62.   [164] See note 15.   [166] See note 21.   [167, a] See note 14, a.

Formed	County	Land formed from	References
1634 (See note 1.);	•Warrosquyoake; (1634-1637)[168]	Original Shire;	H. 1, 224; (See note 34).
1634 (See note 1.);	•Warwick River; (1634-1642/3)[169]	Original Shire;	H. 1, 224; H. 1, 249.
1636 (See note 55.);	•New Norfolk; (1636-1637)[170]	Elizabeth City;	(See note 55).
1637 (See note 34);	Isle of Wight;	Formerly Warrosquyoake; and part of Upper Norfolk; and part of Nansemond; and part of Nansemond;	H. 1, 228;[170, a] H. 1, 247; H. 1, 423; (See note 71); H. 1v, 355; H. vlii, 405; H. vlii, 602.
1637 (See note 55);	•Lower Norfolk; (1637-1691)[171]	New Norfolk;	H. 1, 228;[170, a] H. 1, 247; (See note 55).
1637 (See note 55);	•Upper Norfolk; (1637-1642)[172]	New Norfolk;	H. 1, 228;[170, a] H. 1, 247; H. 1, 423; (See note 55).

[168] See note 79.
[169] See note 81.
[170] See note 56.
[170, a] For full text of this act, see Part V, chap. 1, below.
[171] See note 44.
[172] See note 77.

Virginia Counties 127

1642 (See note 52);	Nansemond;	Formerly Upper Norfolk;	Va. Mag. of Hist. and Biog., xiii, 254; H. i, 321; H. viii, 405; H. viii, 602; H. xii, 69.
1642/3 (See note 58);	Northampton;	Formerly Accomack;	H. i, 249.
1642/3 (See note 80);	Warwick;	Formerly Warwick River;	H. i, 249. A (1881-2), 43.
1642/3 (See note 88);	York;	Formerly Charles River;	H. i, 249; H. viii, 405; H. viii, 419; A (1852), 31.
1648 (See note 59);	Northumberland;[173]	Chickacoan;	H. i, 294, n; H. i, 299; H. i, 337-8; H. i, 340; H. i, 352; H. i, 353; H. i, 362.
1651 (See note 28);	Gloucester;	York;	H. i, 374; H. xiii, 162.
1651 (See note 41);	Lancaster;	Northumberland and York;	H. i, 374; (See note 41).

---
[173] See note 60.

Formed	County	Land formed from	References
1652 (See note 73);	Surry;	James City;	H. i, 373; H. iv, 355; H. vi, 384.
1653 (See note 82);	Westmoreland;[174]	Northumberland; and part of King George;	H. i, 381; H. ix, 432.
1654 (———);	New Kent;	York; and part of James City;	H. i, 387-8; H. iv, 95;[175] H. viii, 208.
1656 (See note 65);	*Rappahannock; (1656-1692)[176]	Lancaster;	H. i, 427; H. iii, 104.
1663 (See note 3);	Accomack;	Northampton;	H. ii, 122; H. ii, 186.
1673 (See note 49);	Middlesex;	Lancaster;	H. ii, 327.
1691 (J. May 12, 1691);	King and Queen;	New Kent;	H. iii, 94; H. iii, 211; H. iv, 77; H. iv, 240;[177] H. v, 185; H. vii, 620.

[174] See note 60.   [175] See note 30.   [176] See note 66.   [177] See note 13.

Virginia Counties

1691 (J. May 16, 1691);	Norfolk;[178]	Lower Norfolk; H. iii, 95.
1691 (J. May 16, 1691);	Princess Anne;[179]	Lower Norfolk; H. iii, 95.
1692 (J. Apl. 26, 1692);	Essex;	Rappahannock; H. iii, 104; H. iv, 77; H. iv, 240.[180]
1692 (J. Apl. 26, 1692);	Richmond;	Rappahannock; H. iii, 104; H. iv, 95.[181]
1702 (J. Sep. 12, 1701);	King William;	King and Queen; H. iii, 211; H. iv, 77; H. iv, 240.[182]
1703 (J. Aug. 25, 1702);	Prince George;[183]	Charles City; H. B. (1695-1702), 393; H. iii, 223; H. iv, 467; H. vi, 254.
1721 (J. Nov. 20 [26], 1720);	Hanover;[184]	New Kent; H. B. (1712-26), 281; H. iv, 95; H. v, 208; H. xii, 620.
1721 (J. Nov. 24, 1720);	King George;[185]	Richmond; and part of Westmoreland; H. B. (1712-26), 279; H. iv, 95; H. iv, 303; H. ix, 244; H. ix, 432.

[178] See note 13.
[179] See notes 55 and 57.
[180] See note 13.
[181] See notes 55 and 57.
[182] See note 39.
[183] See note 62.
[184] See note 30.
[185] See note 39.

Formed	County	Land formed from	References
1728 (J. Mar. 15, 1727);	Caroline;[186]	Essex, King and Queen and King William; and part of King and Queen; and part of King and Queen;	H. B. (1727-40), 39; H. iv, 240; H. v, 185; H. vii, 620.
1749 (J. Apl. 20, 1749);	Southampton;[187]	Isle of Wight; and part of Nansemond;	H. B. (1742-9), 371; H. xii, 69.
1754 (J. Nov. 28, 1753);	Sussex;	Surry;	H. vi, 384; S. ii, 347.
1781 (J. Nov. 28, 1780);	Greensville;	Brunswick; and part of Brunswick; and part of Sussex;	H. x, 363; H. xii, 596; S. ii, 347.
1791 (J. Dec. 16, 1790);	Mathews;	Gloucester;	H. xiii, 162.

[186] See note 13.

[187] See note 71.

PIEDMONT

Formed	County	Land formed from	References
1664 (See note 72);	Stafford;	Westmoreland;	H. ii, 239; H. ii, 250; H. iv, 303; H. ix, 244.
1721 (J. Dec. 17, 1720);	Spotsylvania;	Essex, King and Queen and King William;	H. iv, 77; H. iv, 450.
1728 (J. Mar. 6, 1727);	Goochland;[188]	Henrico;	H. B. (1727-40), 33; H. iv, 240; H. v, 266; (See note 19); H. xii, 71.
1731 (J. June 19, 1730);	Prince William;	Stafford and King George;	H. iv, 303; H. v, 207; H. vii, 311.
1732 (J. Dec. 17, 1720);	Brunswick;[189]	Area not named [Prince George];[189,a] and parts of Surry and Isle of Wight;	H. iv, 77; H. iv, 355; H. iv, 467; H. v, 383; H. x, 363; H. xii, 596.

[188] See note 29.   [189] See note 11.   [189,a] See note 11, a.

Formed	County	Land formed from	References
1734 (J. Sep. 20, 1734);	Orange;	Spotsylvania;	H. iv, 450; H. v, 78; (See note 18); A. (1838), 52.
1735 (J. Sep. 30, 1734);	Amelia;	Prince George and Brunswick;	H. iv, 467; H. vi, 379; H. xii, 723; H. xiii, 561.
1742 (J. May. 27, 1742);	Fairfax;	Prince William; and part of Loudoun;	H. v, 207; H. vii, 148; S. ii, 107; U. S. Stats. i, 130, 214; U. S. Stats. ii, 103, 115; A. (1845-6), 50; A. (1846-7), 41; A. (1846-7), 48.
1742 (J. June 2, 1742);	Louisa;[130]	Hanover;	H. v, 208; H. vii, 419; A. (1836-7), 33; A. (1838), 57; A. (1876-7), 20; A. (1876-7), 21; A. (1876-7), 228.

[130] See note 43.

Virginia Counties

1744 (J. Oct. 16, 1744);	Albemarle;[191]	Goochland;	H. v, 266; H. vi, 441; H. vii, 419;
		and part of Louisa; "and certain islands in the Fluvanna River";	H. viii, 395; H. ix, 325; A (1836-7), 33; A (1838), 57; A (1855-6), 99; A (1861), 151; A (1871-2), 342; A (1876-7), 21; A (1876-7), 228.
1746 (J. Apl. 1, 1746);	Lunenburg;	Brunswick;	H. v, 383; H. vi, 252; H. vi, 381; H. vi, 441; H. viii, 41; H. ix, 327.
1749 (J. Mar. 23, 1748);	Culpeper;[192]	Orange;	H. B. (1742-9), 346; H. xiii, 558; A (1832-3), 44;
1749 (J. Mar. 23, 1748);	Cumberland;[193]	Goochland; and part of Buckingham;	H. B. (1742-9), 346; H. ix, 322; H. ix, 559.

[191] See note 4.   [192] See note 18.   [193] See note 19.

Formed	County	Land formed from	References
1749 (J. May 1, 1749);	Chesterfield;[194]	Henrico;	H. B. (1742-9), 384; A (1849-0), 26.
1752 (J. Mar. 9, 1752);	Dinwiddie;	Prince George;	H. vi, 254.
1752 (J. Apl. 17, 1752);	Halifax;	Lunenburg;	H. vi, 252; H. viii, 205.
1754 (J. Nov. 17, 1753);	Prince Edward;	Amelia;	H. vi, 379; A (1844-5), 38.
1754 (J. Dec. 13, 1753);	Bedford;[195]	Lunenburg; and parts of Albemarle and Lunenburg;	H. vi, 381;
1757 (J. May 17, 1757);	Loudoun;	Fairfax;	H. vi, 441; H. x, 447; H. xii, 70.
1759 (J. Apl. 5, 1759);	Fauquier;[196]	Prince William;	H. vii, 148; S. H, 107; A (1823-4), 52.
			H. vii, 311; A (1823-4), 82.

[194] See note 16.   [195] See note 7.   [196] See note 35.

1761 (J. Apl. 7, 1761);	Amherst;	Albemarle; "and certain islands in the Fluvanna River".	H. vii, 419; H. viii, 395; S. iii, 378.
1761 (J. Apl. 7, 1761);	Buckingham;	Albemarle; and part of Appomattox;	H. vii, 419; H. ix, 559; A (1844-5), 38; A (1859-0), 171.
1765 (J. Nov. 27, 1764);	Charlotte;	Lunenburg;	H. viii, 41; H. ix, 327; A (1844-5), 36.
1765 (J. Nov. 27, 1764);	Mecklenburg;	Lunenburg;	H. viii, 41.
1767 (J. Dec. 15, 1766);	Pittsylvania;	Halifax;	H. viii, 205; H. ix, 241.
1777 (J. Oct. 23, 1776);	Henry;	Pittsylvania; and part of Patrick;	H. ix, 241; H. xii, 70; H. xiii, 160; H. xiii, 290; A (1857-8), 113.

Formed	County	Land formed from	References
1777 (J. June 8, 1777);	Fluvanna;	Albemarle;	H. ix, 325; H. xii, 71; A (1836-7), 33; A (1838), 57; A (1855-6), 99; A (1861), 151; A (1871-2), 342; A (1876-7), 20; A (1876-7), 228.
1777 (J. June 3, 1777);	Powhatan;	Cumberland; and part of Chesterfield;	H. ix, 322; A (1849-0), 26.
1782 (J. Dec. 15, 1781);	Campbell;	Bedford;	H. x, 447; A (1844-5), 38; A (1847-8), 41.
1786 (J. Nov. 29, 1785);	Franklin;	Bedford and Henry; and part of Patrick;	H. xii, 70; A (1847-8), 42; A (1872-3), 85.
1789 (J. Dec. 23, 1788);[197]	Nottoway;	Amelia;	H. xii, 723; H. xiii, 561.

[197] See note 61.

1791 (J. Nov. 26, 1790);	Patrick;	H. xiii, 160; H. xiii, 290; S. i, 315; A (1809-10), 58; A (1817-8), 185; A (1847-8), 42; A (1855-6), 98; A (1857-8), 113.
	Henry; and part of Henry;	
1793 (J. Nov. 7, 1792);	Grayson;	H. xiii, 559; S. i, 315; A (1809-10), 58; A (1817-8), 185; A (1824-5), 75; A (1840-1), 62; A (1841-2), 32; A (1874-5), 26; A (1874-5), 330.
	Wythe; and part of Patrick;	
1793 (J. Dec. 5, 1792);[198]	Madison;	H. xiii, 558.
1808 (J. Dec. 23, 1807);[199]	Nelson;	
1831 (J. Jan. 15, 1831);	Floyd;	S. iii, 378.
	Culpeper; Amherst; Montgomery; and part of Franklin;	A (1830-1), 137; A (1872-3), 85.
1833 (J. Feb. 18, 1833);[200]	Rappahannock;	A (1832-3), 44.
	Culpeper;	
1838 (J. Jan. 24, 1838);	Greene;	A (1838), 52.
	Orange;	

[198] See note 45.   [199] See note 58.   [200] See note 67.

Formed	County	Land formed from	References
1842 (J. Jan. 17, 1842);	Carroll;	Grayson; and part of Patrick;	A (1841-2), 32; A (1855-6), 98.
1845 (J. Feb. 8, 1845);	Appomattox;	Buckingham, Prince Edward, Charlotte and Campbell; and part of Campbell;	A (1844-5), 38; A (1847-8), 41; A (1859-0), 171.
1847 (J. Mar. 13, 1847);	Alexandria;[201]	District of Columbia; (that portion of it which was formerly a part of Fairfax County);	U. S. Stats. I, 130, 214; U. S. Stats. II, 103, 115; A (1845-6), 50; A (1846-7), 41; A (1846-7), 48.

[201] See note 5.

VALLEY

Formed	County	Land formed from	References
1743 (J. Dec. 15, 1738);	Frederick;[203]	Orange; and part of Augusta;	H. v, 78; H. vi, 376; H. viii, 597; A (1827-8), t1; A (1835-6), 20; A (1835-6), 22; A (1847-8), 43; A (1862, Wheeling), 3; A (1865-6), 194; A (1865-6), 195.
1745 (J. Dec. 15, 1738);	Augusta;[203]	Orange;	H. v, 78; H. vi, 376; H. viii, 395; H. ix, 262; H. ix, 420; H. x, 114; H. x, 351; H. xii, 637; H. xiii, 165.

[202] See note 26. [203] See note 6.

Formed	County	Land formed from	References
1770 (J. Nov. 28, 1769);	Botetourt;[204]	Augusta; and part of Rockbridge;	H. viii, 395; H. viii, 600; H. ix, 420; H. xii, 74; H. xiii, 76; H. xiii, 165; S. i, 406; S. ii, 64; S. ii, 345; A. (1821-2), 28; A. (1838), 54; A. (1850-1), 21; A. (1887-8), 556.
1772 (J. Mar. 24, 1772);	• Dunmore; (1772-1778)[205]	Frederick;	H. viii, 597.
1772 (J. Apl. 8, 1772);	e Fincastle; (1772-1777)[206]	Botetourt;	H. viii, 600; H. ix, 257.

[204] See note 17.　[205] See note 21.　[206] See note 25.

1777 (J. Dec. 7, 1776);	Montgomery;	Fincastle;
		and part of Botetourt;
		H. ix, 257; H. ix, 330; H. ix, 420; H. xii, 670; H. xiii, 76; S. i, 315; S. i, 406; S. ii, 64; S. iii, 244; A. (1830-1), 137; A. (1839), 30; A. (1839-0), 35; A. (1841-2), 39; A. (1848-9), 28; A. (1852-3), 130.
1777 (J. Dec. 7, 1776);	Washington;	Fincastle; and part of Montgomery;
		H. ix, 257; H. ix, 330; H. xii, 110; S. i, 315; A. (1814-5), 85; A. (1814-5), 87; A. (1823-4), 83; A. (1824-5), 76; A. (1825-6), 40; A. (1831-2), 47.
1778 (J. Jan. 12, 1778);	Rockbridge;	Augusta and Botetourt; and part of Botetourt;
		H. ix, 420; H. xii, 74; A. (1887-8), 556.

Formed	County	Land formed from	References
1778 (J. Jan. 12, 1778);	Rockingham;	Augusta;	H. ix, 420; H. xii, 637; A. (1830-1), 140.
1778 (J. Jan. 12, 1778);	Shenandoah;	Formerly Dunmore;	H. ix, 424; A. (1830-1), 140; A. (1835-6), 22; A. (1847-8), 43.
1790 (J. Dec. 1, 1789);	Wythe;	Montgomery; and part of Grayson;	H. xiii, 76; H. xiii, 559; S. ii, 217; S. iii, 389; A. (1824-5), 75; A. (1825-6), 40; A. (1831-2), 47; A. (1839), 30; A. (1839-0), 35; A. (1840-1), 62; A. (1861), 45; A. (1861-2), 106; A. (1874-5), 26.

1831 (J. Mar. 30, 1831);	Page;	Rockingham and Shenandoah; A (1830-1), 140.
1832 (J. Feb. 23, 1832);	Smyth;	Washington and Wythe; A (1831-2), 47; A (1874-5), 330.
1836 (J. Mar. 8, 1836);	Clarke;	Frederick; and part of Warren; A (1835-6), 20; A (1859-0), 496.
1836 (J. Mar. 9, 1836);	Warren;	Shenandoah and Frederick; A (1835-6), 22; A (1859-0), 496.
1838 (J. Mar. 30, 1838);	Roanoke;[207]	Botetourt; and part of Montgomery; A (1838), 54; A (1848-9), 28; A (1850-1), 21.
1839 (J. Mar. 30, 1839);	Pulaski;	Montgomery and Wythe;[208] and part of Wythe; A (1839), 30; A (1839-0), 35; A (1841-2), 39; A (1861-2), 106.

[207] See note 17.
[208] See note 64.

TRANS-ALLEGHANY

Formed	County	Land formed from	References
1754 (J. Dec. 13, 1753);	w Hampshire;	Augusta and Frederick; and part of Augusta; and part of Hardy;	H. vi, 376; H. ix, 420; H. xii, 86; H. xii, 597; A. (1819-0), 27; A. (1820-1), 120; A. (1823-4), 83.
1772 (J. Mar. 24, 1772);	w Berkeley;	Frederick;	H. viii, 597; S. ii, 271; A. (1819-0), 27; A. (1862, Wheeling), ?; A. (1865-6), 194; A. (1865-6), 195.
1776 (J. Nov. 6, 1776);	w Monongalia;	Augusta; and part of Augusta; and part of Augusta; and part of Preston;	H. ix, 262; H. x, 114; H. x, 351; H. xi, 366; S. ii, 203; A. (1817-8), 32; A. (1818-9), 141; A. (1840-1), 61; A. (1841-2), 34; A. (1846-7), 57.

1776 (J. Nov. 6, 1776);	w Ohio;	Augusta; and part of Yohogania;	H. ix, 262; H. xii, 114; S. ii, 54; S. iii, 174; A (1814-5), 87; A (1832-3), 48; A (1834-5), 38.
1776 (J. Nov. 6, 1776);	e Yohogania;[209] (1776-1786)[210]	Augusta;	H. ix, 262; H. xii, 114.
1777 (J. Dec. 7, 1776);	e Kentucky;[211] (1777-1780)[212]	Fincastle;	H. ix, 257; H. x, 315.
1778 (J. Jan. 12, 1778);	w Greenbrier;	Botetourt and Montgomery; and part of Monroe; and part of Fayette; and part of Fayette;	H. ix, 420; H. xii, 670; H. xiii, 165; S. i, 388; S. ii, 168; A (1817-8), 34; A (1824-5), 73; A (1826-7), 41; A (1830-1), 134; A (1830-1), 136; A (1832-3), 47.

[209] See note 86. [210] See note 87. [211] See note 36. [212] See note 37.

Formed	County	Land formed from	References
1778 (J. Dec. 9, 1778);	e Illinois;[213] (1778-1784)[214]	"on the western side of the Ohio River" [Augusta]	H. ix, 552; H. x, 303; "Journals of Congress," 1823, iii, 516-7; H. x, 564; H. xi, 571-5; "Journals of Congress," 1823, iv, 341-4.
1780 (J. June 30, 1780);	k Fayette;	Kentucky;	H. x, 315; H. xii, 89; H. xii, 663.
1780 (J. June 30, 1780);	k Jefferson;	Kentucky;	H. x, 315; H. xi, 469.
1780 (J. June 30, 1780);	k Lincoln;	Kentucky;	H. x, 315; H. xii, 118.

[213] See note 32.
[214] See note 33.

1784 (J. June 4, 1784);	w Harrison;	Monongalla;	H. xi, 366;
			H. xii, 393;
		and part of Monongalia;	S. ii, 170;
		and part of Randolph;	S. ii, 203;
		and part of Ohio;	S. ii, 345;
			S. iii, 174;
			A. (1816-7), 152;
			A. (1816-7), 154;
			A. (1818-9), 142;
			A. (1841-2), 34;
			A. (1842-3), 35;
			A. (1842-3), 37;
			A. (1843-4), 34;
			A. (1844-5), 42;
			A. (1849-0), 33.
1785 (J. Nov. 29, 1784);	k Nelson;	Jefferson;	H. xi, 469.
1786 (J. Dec. 10, 1785);	w Hardy;	Hampshire;	H. xii, 86;
			H. xii, 597;
			H. xii, 637;
			A. (1823-4), 83.
1786 (J. Dec. 15, 1785);	k Madison;	Lincoln;	H. xii, 118.
1786 (J. Dec. 15, 1785);	k Mercer;	Lincoln;	H. xii, 118.
1786 (J. Dec. 29, 1785);	k Bourbon;	Fayette;	H. xii, 89;
			H. xii, 658.

Formed	County	Land formed from	References
1786 (J. Jan. 6, 1786);	Russell;	Washington;	H. xii, 110; H. xiii, 556; S. ii, 217; S. iii, 310; A (1812-3), 110; A (1814-5), 85; A (1814-5), 87; A (1823-4), 83; A (1824-5), 76; A (1834-5), 40; A (1855-6), 87; A (1857-8), 108; A (1879-0), 125.
1787 (J. Nov. 29, 1786);	w Randolph;	Harrison;	H. xii, 393; S. ii, 345; A (1817-8), 34; A (1817-8), 184; A (1821-2), 27; A (1827-8), 53; A (1838), 57; A (1842-3), 37; A (1848-9), 30; A (1850-1), 23; A (1855-6), 95; A (1859-0), 151.

1788 (J. Dec. 4, 1787);	w Pendleton;	Augusta, Hardy and Rockingham; and part of Bath;	H. xii, 637; S. ii, 53; A (1821-2), 27; A (1846-7), 52.
1789 (J. Nov. 5, 1788);	k Mason;	Bourbon;	H. xii, 658.
1789 (J. Nov. 12, 1788);	k Woodford;	Fayette;	H. xii, 663.
1789 (J. Nov. 14, 1788);	w Kanawha;[215]	Greenbrier and Montgomery; and part of Fayette;	H. xii, 670; S. i, 383; S. ii, 263; S. iii, 77; A (1808-9), 44; A (1816-7), 154; A (1817-8), 34; A (1817-8), 135; A (1823-4), 20; A (1823-4), 80; A (1823-4), 81; A (1829-0), 117; A (1830-1), 134; A (1830-1), 138; A (1835-6), 18; A (1839), 33; A (1843-4), 37; A (1844-5), 45; A (1846-7), 49; A (1847-8), 34; A (1849-0), 24; A (1849-0), 25; A (1855-6), 91.

[215] See note 35.

Formed	County	Land formed from	References
1791 (J. Dec. 14, 1790);	Bath;	Augusta, Botetourt and Greenbrier;	H. xiii, 165; S. ii, 53; A. (1821-2), 27; A. (1821-2), 28; A. (1822-3), 38; A. (1846-7), 52; A. (1846-7), 57.
1793 (J. Oct. 25, 1792);	Lee;	Russell; and part of Scott;	H. xiii, 556; A. (1812-3), 110; A. (1814-5), 85; A. (1814-5), 87; A. (1822-3), 90; A. (1836-7), 34; A. (1855-6), 87.
1797 (J. Nov. 30, 1796);[216]	w Brooke;	Ohio;	S. ii, 54; A. (1847-8), 30.
1798 (J. Dec. 22, 1798);[217]	w Wood;	Harrison; and part of Kanawha;	S. ii, 170; S. ii, 263; A. (1830-1), 138; A. (1842-3), 35; A. (1843-4), 34; A. (1847-8), 38; A. (1850-1), 25.

[216] See note 10.

[217] See note 85.

1799 (J. Jan. 15, 1799);[318]	▼Monroe (Munroe);[319]	Greenbrier; and part of Botetourt; S. II, 168; S. II, 345; S. III, 244; A (1821-2), 28; A (1826-7), 41; A (1826-7), 42; A (1828-9), 119; A (1842-3), 40; A (1850-1), 21; A (1852-3), 130; A (1855-6), 97; A (1855-6), 383.
1800 (J. Dec. 2, 1799);[320]	Tazewell;	Wythe and Russell; and part of Russell; and parts of Washington and Wythe; and part of Logan; and part of Russell; S. II, 217; S. III, 310; S. III, 244; A (1823-4), 20; A (1825-6), 39; A (1825-6), 40; A (1827-8), 52; A (1833-4), 73; A (1834-5), 40; A (1835-6), 24; A (1836-7), 31; A (1857-8), 106; A (1857-8), 108; A (1859 0), 169; A (1861), 45.

[318] See note 51. [319] See note 50. [320] See note 75.

Formed	County	Land formed from	References
1801 (J. Jan. 8, 1801);	w Jefferson;	Berkeley;	S. ii, 271; A. (1862, Wheeling), 3; A. (1865-6), 194; A. (1865-6), 195.
1804 (J. Jan. 3, 1804);¹²¹	w Mason;	Kanawha;	S. iii, 77; A. (1816-7), 157; A. (1823-4), 81; A. (1836-1), 138; A. (1847-8), 34.
1806 (J. Jan. 16, 1806);	Giles;¹²²	Montgomery, Monroe and Tazewell; and part of Wythe; and part of Tazewell; and part of Monroe; and part of Tazewell; and part of Mercer; and part of Craig;	S. iii, 244; S. iii, 389; A. (1823-4), 20; A. (1825-6), 39; A. (1826-7), 42; A. (1827-8), 52; A. (1828-9), 119; A. (1835-6), 24; A. (1836-7), 31; A. (1840-1), 61; A. (1857-8), 114; A. (1861), 45; A. (1879-0), 183; A. (1899-00), 665.

¹²¹ See note 48.   ¹²² See note 17.

Virginia Counties

1809 (J. Jan. 2, 1809); w Cabell; Kanawha;
A (1808-9), 44;
A (1817-8), 185;
A (1823-4), 20;
A (1829-0), 117;
A (1841-2), 36;
A (1846-7), 49;
A (1847-8), 34;
A (1849-0), 24.

1814 (J. Nov. 24, 1814);[228] Scott; Lee, Russell and Washington;
A (1814-5), 85;
A (1814-5), 87;
A (1822-3), 90;
A (1836-7), 34;
A (1855-6), 87.

1814 (J. Dec. 3, 1814);[224] w Tyler; Ohio;
A (1814-5), 87;
A (1815-6), 154;
A (1832-3), 48;
A (1844-5), 42;
A (1845-6), 51;
A (1849-0), 33;
A (1850-1), 25.

[223] See note 70.   [224] See note 76.

Formed	County	Land formed from	References
1816 (J. Dec. 18, 1816);	w Lewis;	Harrison; and part of Randolph;	A (1816-7), 152; A (1817-8), 184; A (1818-9), 142; A (1835-6), 18; A (1842-3), 35; A (1843-4), 37; A (1844-5), 42; A (1844-5), 45; A (1846-7), 58; A (1849-0), 33; A (1850-1), 23.
1818 (J. Jan. 19, 1818);	w Preston;	Monongalia; and part of Randolph; and part of Randolph; and part of Monongalia;	A (1817-8), 32; A (1818-9), 141; A (1827-8), 53; A (1838), 57; A (1840-1), 61.
1818 (J. Jan. 30, 1818);	w Nicholas;	Greenbrier, Kanawha and Randolph; and part of Kanawha;	A (1817-8), 34; A (1818-9), 72; A (1819-0), 91; A (1823-4), 80; A (1830-1), 134; A (1835-6), 18; A (1843-4), 37; A (1857-8), 111; A (1859-0), 151.

1820 (J. Feb. 9, 1820);	w Morgan;	Berkeley and Hampshire;	A (1819-0), 27; A (1820-1), 120; A (1827-8), 51.
1821 (J. Dec. 21, 1821);	w Pocahontas;	Bath, Pendleton and Randolph; and part of Greenbrier;	A (1821-2), 27; A (1824-5), 73.
1822 (J. Jan. 5, 1822);	Alleghany;	Bath, Botetourt and Monroe; and part of Monroe; and part of Bath;	A (1821-2), 28; A (1822-3), 88; A (1842-3), 40; A (1846-7), 57; A (1855-6), 97; A (1885-6), 383.
1824 (J. Jan. 12, 1824);	w Logan;²⁵	Giles, Cabell, Tazewell and Kanawha; and parts of Kanawha and Cabell;	A (1823-4), 20; A (1829-0), 117; A (1830-1), 134; A (1833-4), 33; A (1846-7), 49; A (1849-0), 21.
1831 (J. Feb. 28, 1831);	w Fayette;	Logan, Greenbrier, Nicholas and Kanawha; and part of Kanawha;	A (1830-1), 134; A (1830-1), 136; A (1832-3), 47; A (1839), 33; A (1849-0), 19; A (1849-0), 25; A (1850-1), 26.

Formed	County	Land formed from	References
1831 (J. Mar. 1, 1831);	w Jackson;	Mason, Kanawha and Wood; and part of Wirt;	A (1830-1), 138; A (1847-8), 38; A (1852-3), 130; A (1855-6), 91.
1835 (J. Mar. 12, 1835);	w Marshall;[226]	Ohio;	A (1834-5), 38.
1836 (J. Jan. 15, 1836);	w Braxton;	Lewis, Kanawha and Nicholas; and part of Randolph;	A (1835-6), 18; A (1843-4), 37; A (1848-9), 30; A (1857-8), 111. A (1859-0), 151.
1837 (J. Mar. 17, 1837);	w Mercer;	Giles and Tazewell;	A (1836-7), 31; A (1840-1), 61; A (1846-7), 57.
1842 (J. Jan. 14, 1842);	w Marion;[227]	Monongalia and Harrison; and part of Monongalia;	A (1841-2), 34; A (1842-3), 40; A (1843-4), 34; A (1846-7), 57; A (1855-6), 98.
1842 (J. Jan. 18, 1842);	w Wayne;	Cabell;	A (1841-2), 36.

[225] See note 35. [226] See note 47. [227] See note 50.

1843 (J. Feb. 18, 1843);	w Ritchie;	Harrison, Lewis and Wood;	A (1842-3), 35; A (1843-4), 34; A (1844-5), 42; A (1849-0), 33; A (1850-1), 25.
1843 (J. Mar. 3, 1843);	w Barbour;	Harrison, Lewis and Randolph;	A (1842-3), 37; A (1843-4), 34; A (1850-1), 23.
1844 (J. Jan. 19, 1844);	w Taylor;[228]	Harrison, Barbour and Marion; and part of Marion;	A (1843-4), 34; A (1855-6), 98.
1845 (J. Feb. 3, 1845);	w Gilmer;	Lewis and Kanawha;	A (1844-5), 45; A (1846-7), 58; A (1855-6), 90; A (1855-6), 91.
1845 (J. Feb. 4, 1845);	w Doddridge;	Harrison, Tyler, Ritchie and Lewis;	A (1844-5), 42; A (1849-0), 33.
1846 (J. Jan. 10, 1846);	w Wetzel;[229]	Tyler;	A (1845-6), 51.
1847 (J. Mar. 11, 1847);	w Boone;	Kanawha, Cabell and Logan;	A (1846-7), 49.
1847 (J. Mar. 19, 1847);	Highland;	Pendleton and Bath;	A (1846-7), 52.
1848 (J. Jan. 15, 1848);	w Hancock;	Brooke;	A (1847-8), 30.

[228] See note 50.
[229] See note 84.

Formed	County	Land formed from	References
1848 (J. Jan. 19, 1848);	w Wirt;	Wood and Jackson;	A (1847-8), 38; A (1852-3), 130.
1848 (J. Mar. 11, 1848);	w Putnam;	Kanawha, Cabell and Mason; and parts of Cabell and Kanawha;	A (1847-8), 34; A (1849-0), 24.
1850 (J. Jan. 23, 1850);	w Raleigh;	Fayette;	A (1849-0), 19. A (1850-1), 26.
1850 (J. Jan. 26, 1850);	w Wyoming;	Logan;	A (1849-0), 21.
1851 (J. Mar. 21, 1851);	Craig;	Botetourt, Roanoke, Giles and Monroe;[280] and part of Monroe; and part of Montgomery; and part of Alleghany; and part of Monroe; and part of Giles;	A (1850-1), 21; A (1852-3), 130; A (1852-3), 130; A (1855-6), 97; A (1855-6), 97; A (1857-8), 114; A (1879-0), 183.
1851 (J. Mar. 27, 1851);[281]	w Upshur;	Randolph, Barbour and Lewis;	A (1850-1), 23.
1851 (J. Mar. 29, 1851);	w Pleasants;	Wood, Tyler and Ritchie;	A (1850-1), 25.

[280] See note 17.
[281] See note 78.

Virginia Counties 159

1856 (J. Feb. 16, 1856);	Wise;	Lee, Scott and Russell;	A (1855-6), 87; A (1879-0), 125.
1856 (J. Mar. 5, 1856);	w Calhoun;	Gilmer;	A (1855-6), 90.
1856 (J. Mar. 7, 1856);	w Tucker;	Randolph;	A (1855-6), 95.
1856 (J. Mar. 11, 1856);	w Roane;	Kanawha, Jackson and Gilmer;	A (1855-6), 91.
1858 (J. Feb. 16, 1858);[232]	Buchanan;	Tazewell and Russell;	A (1857-8), 108; A (1879-0), 125.
1858 (J. Feb. 20, 1858);	w McDowell;	Tazewell;	A (1857-8), 106; A (1859-0), 169.
1858 (J. Mar. 29, 1858);	w Clay;	Braxton and Nicholas;	A (1857-8), 111.
1860 (J. Jan. 10, 1860);	w Webster;	Nicholas, Braxton and Randolph;	A (1859-0), 151; A (1861), 50.
1861 (J. Mar. 30, 1861);[233]	Bland;	Giles, Wythe and Tazewell; and part of Giles;	A (1861), 45; A (1899-00), 665.
1880 (J. Feb. 27, 1880);[234]	Dickenson;	Russell, Wise and Buchanan;	A (1879-0), 125.

[232] See note 12.   [233] See note 8.   [234] See note 20.

PART IV.

"GENEALOGICAL" ARRANGEMENT

The Notes are assembled in series under Part I, Alphabetical Arrangement.

It is but natural that the eight original shires (or counties: Hening i, 224) and the "original County" of Northumberland (Hening i, 337-8) should be selected as the "immigrant ancestors" of the counties which have resulted from Virginia legislation, with the result that the charts which compose this Part are numbered 1 to 9,—# 9 having four supplemental charts on account of the large number of counties descended through this line. In preparing these "family trees", it soon developed that the lines often crossed from one chart to another, as in the case of Louisa, which came through the Charles River line, and appears on chart # 3, a portion of which was added to Albemarle (Hening vii, 419),—a county which came through the Henrico line and appears on chart # 5. Thus, it was obviously difficult to present clearly the data for all the counties on one chart. The complexity of such a task will be recognized more clearly when one considers the fact that Appomattox, Craig, Doddridge, Fayette and Logan were each initially formed from four counties, one of them (Craig) having as many as five additions to its area, while twenty-six of them were each initially formed from portions of three counties,—to one of which (Giles) there were added six territorial increments.

For these reasons, it was decided to give to each of the "immigrant ancestors" a chart of its own, and to have an individual index for this part of the Bulletin,—chart # 9 having four supplemental charts on account of the large number of counties which descend through the Northumberland line,—one hundred and sixteen in number.

The number of counties "descended" from each of the "immigrant ancestors" is as follows:

```
1634,—Accawmack, .................................................  3;
       Charles City, ..............................................  18;
       Charles River, .............................................  9;
       Elizabeth City, ............................................  7;
       Henrico, ...................................................  11;
       James City, ................................................  3;
       Warrosquyoake, .............................................  3;
       Warwick River, .............................................  2;
1648,—Northumberland, ............................................30;
              Augusta,........................20;
              Monongalia,................18;
              Botetourt,.................39;
                     Kentucky,........ 9;   116;
                                             ——
              Counties here listed,............172.
```

The horizontal lines on each chart have no significance, other than the adjustment and balance of each individual chart, except, of course, that the earliest county from each parent-county appears at the left, while the vertical lines indicate in an approximately correct degree the chronological descent,—the "scale" being uniform on each chart, but not the same for all,—and where two or more counties come into existence in the same year, they appear at the same distance below the parent-county; or, if formed from different parent-counties, at the same distance below the "immigrant ancestor". If they be from the same parent-county, they are in alphabetical order from left to right, as can be seen by reference to chart # 9, where it appears that Essex and Richmond were formed from Rappahannock in 1692; that Berkeley and Dunmore were formed from Frederick in 1772; and that Warren and Clarke, formed from different parent-counties, are on the same chronological line, though not in alphabetical order for reasons which have been given.

In naming the parent-county in cases where portions of several counties were initially utilized to form the new county, only the name of the first county mentioned in the title if the Act has been used, as where Appomattox was formed from Buckingham, Prince Edward, Charlotte and Campbell, in which case the chart (# 5) shows only that Appomattox was formed from Buckingham, but in each of these cases an asterisk refers to a note which says, "Initially formed from portions of more than one county,— the parent-county here shown being the first one mentioned in the title of the Act of Assembly forming this county: for other counties, portions of which were utilized in the formation of this county, see Part I, Alphabetical Arrangement". Some such arbitrary treatment was necessary in order to avoid the alternative of a confused tangle of crossing lines; and the plan adopted gives a direct and unconfused "line of descent" for each of one hundred and twenty-three counties which were initially formed from but one county (which include the eight original shires; Northumberland, an "original county", which was formed from an indeterminate area called "Chickacoan"; Brunswick which was formed from an area not named [Prince George]; and Illinois which was formed from territory "on the western side of the Ohio River" [Augusta], while the twenty-one counties which were initially formed from portions of two counties, the twenty-three which were initially formed from portions of three counties, and the five which were initially formed from portions of four counties are just as clearly set forth, with an asterisk, and the corresponding note which explains that there were more than one parent-county and refers to direct data as to these additional parent-counties.

It is a source of the greatest regret to the compiler that the financial condition of the Library prevented the adoption of his suggestion that all these charts be assembled in one chart originating from "Virginia, 1607", which he considered as necessary to a proper presentation of the relativity of the counties, as is a map of the United States to the same status concerning the several states.

The following abbreviations are used in this Part:

E (superior): resulted from Virginia legislation, but now extinct, as shown by accompanying dates.
K (superior): resulted from Virginia legislation, but now in Kentucky.
W (superior): resulted from Virginia legislation, but now in West Virginia.

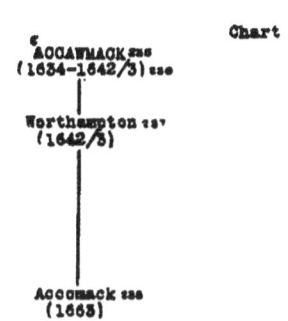

Chart 1

---

235 See note 1.
236 See note 2.
237 See note 58.
238 See note 3.

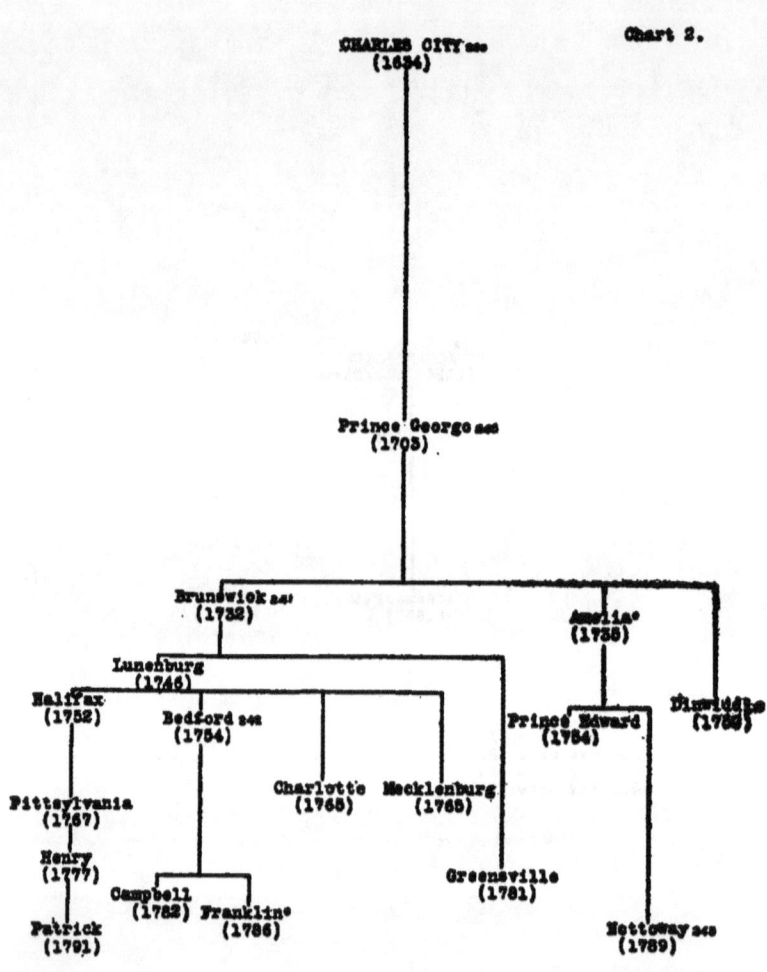

Chart 2.

239 See note 1.
240 See note 62.
241 See notes 11 and 11, a.
242 See note 7.
243 See note 61.

* Initially formed from portions of more than one county,— the parent-county here shown being the first mentioned in the title of the Act of Assembly forming this county; for other counties, portions of which were utilized in the formation of this county, see Part 1, Alphabetical Arrangement.

Virginia Counties 165

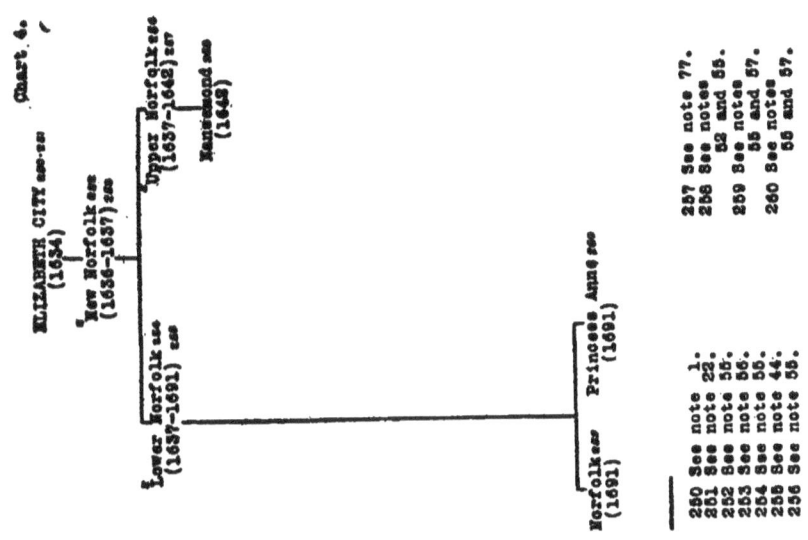

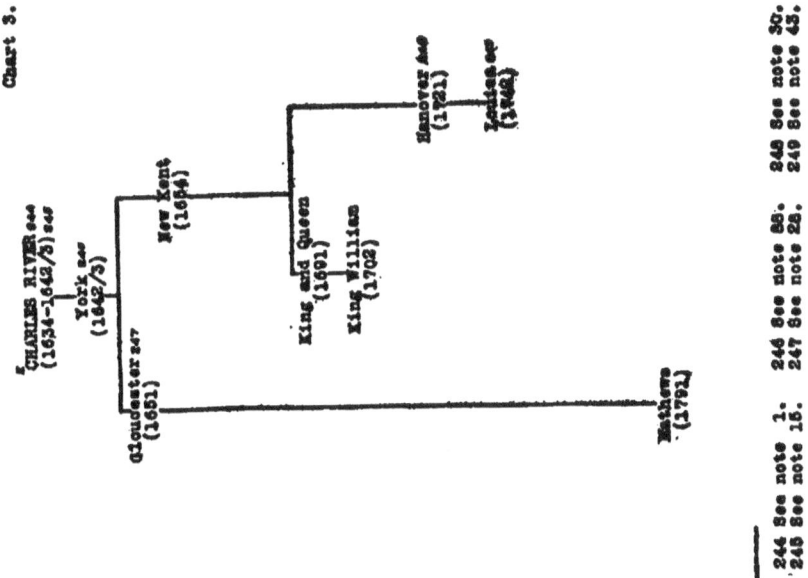

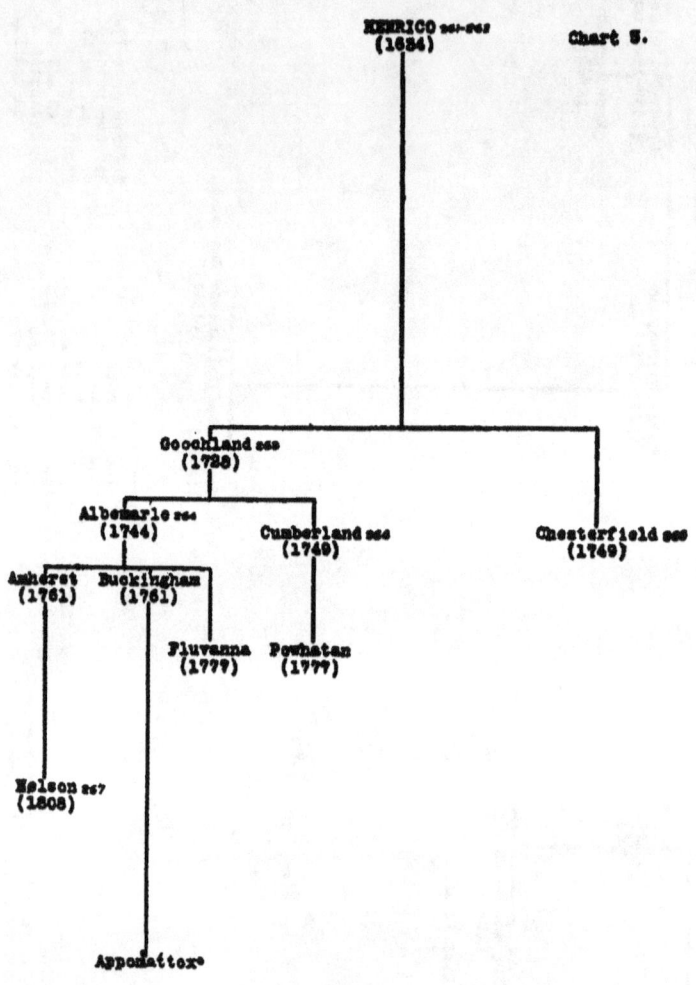

261 See note 1.   264 See note 4.   267 See note 52.
262 See note 31. 265 See note 16.
263 See note 29. 266 See note 19.

* Initially formed from portions of more than one county,— the parent-county here shown being the first mentioned in the title of the Act of Assembly forming this county; for other counties, portions of which were utilized in the formation of this county, see Part I, Alphabetical Arrangement.

Virginia Counties 167

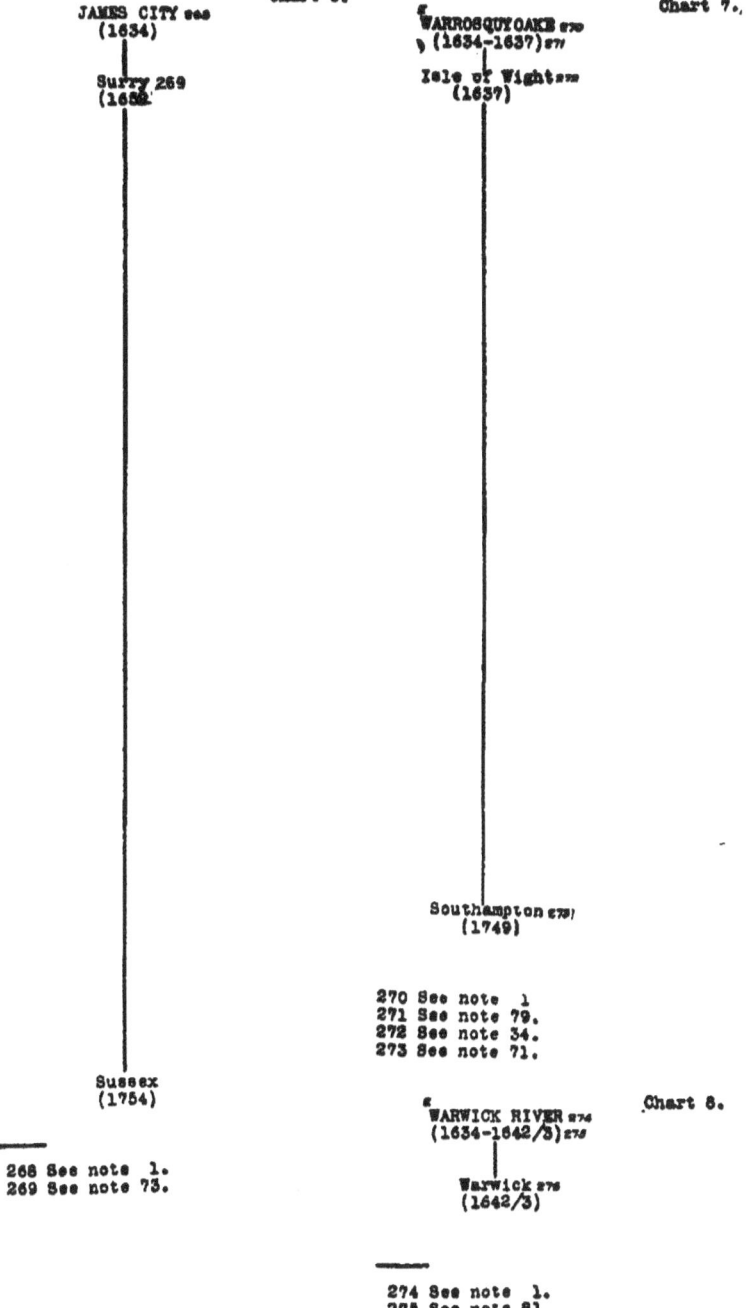

Chart 6.

JAMES CITY [268]
(1634)

Surry [269]
(1652)

Sussex
(1754)

268 See note 1.
269 See note 73.

Chart 7.

WARROSQUYOAKE [270]
(1634-1637) [271]

Isle of Wight [272]
(1637)

Southampton [273]
(1749)

270 See note 1
271 See note 79.
272 See note 34.
273 See note 71.

Chart 8.

WARWICK RIVER [274]
(1634-1642/3) [275]

Warwick [276]
(1642/3)

274 See note 1.
275 See note 81.
276 See note 80.

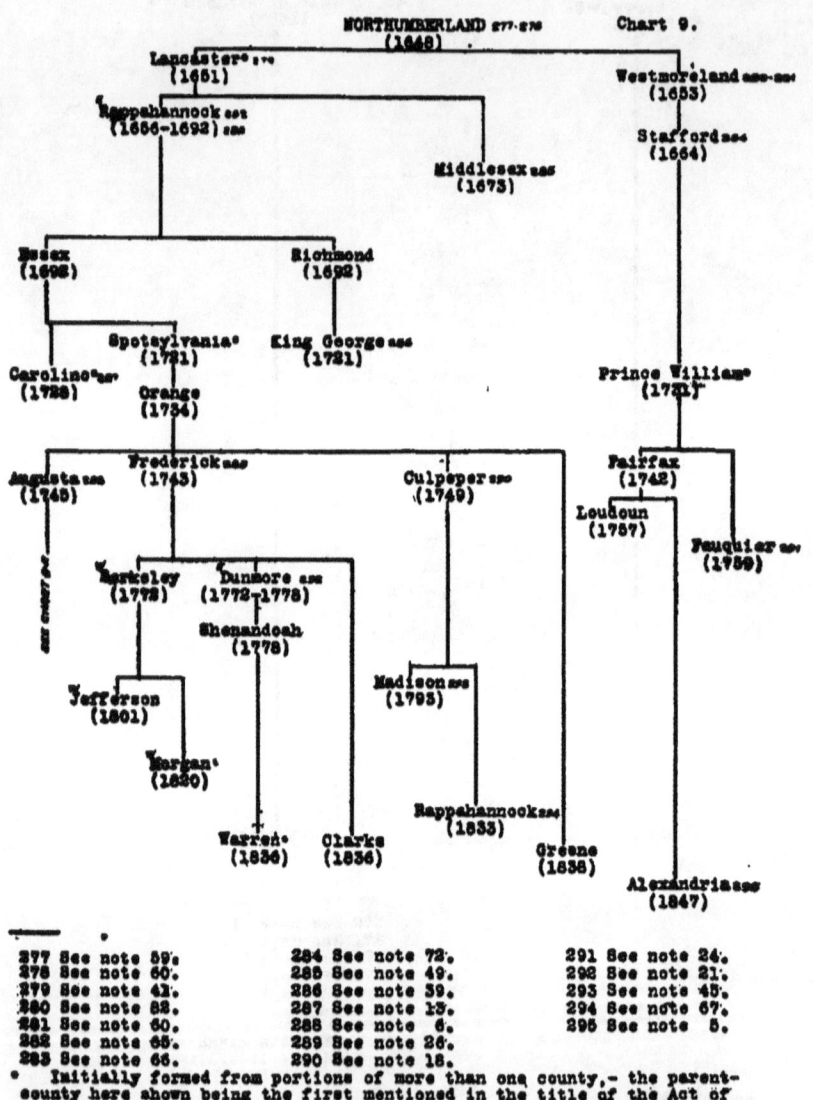

Chart 9.

277 See note 59.
278 See note 60.
279 See note 41.
280 See note 82.
281 See note 60.
282 See note 65.
283 See note 66.
284 See note 72.
285 See note 49.
286 See note 39.
287 See note 13.
288 See note 6.
289 See note 26.
290 See note 18.
291 See note 24.
292 See note 21.
293 See note 45.
294 See note 67.
295 See note 5.

* Initially formed from portions of more than one county,— the parent-county here shown being the first mentioned in the title of the Act of Assembly forming this county: for other counties, portions of which were utilized in the formation of this county, see Part I, Alphabetical Arrangement.

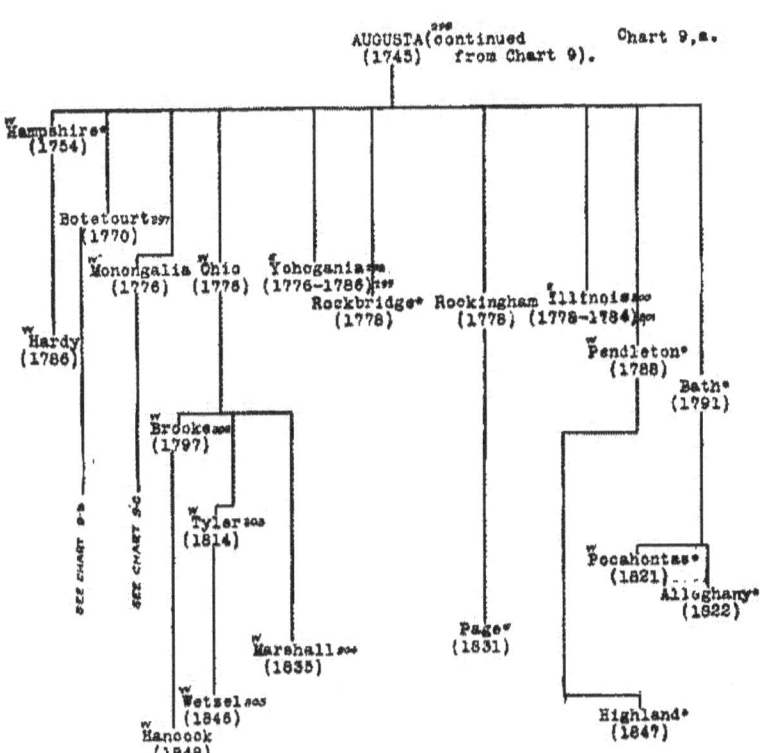

Chart 9,a.

296 See note 6.
297 See note 17.
298 See note 86.
299 See note 87.
300 See note 32.
301 See note 33.
302 See note 10.
303 See note 76.
304 See note 47.
305 See note 84.

* Initially formed from portions of more than one county,- the parent-county here shown being the first mentioned in the title of the Act of Assembly forming this county; for other counties, portions of which were utilized in the formation of this county, see Part I, Alphabetical Arrangement.

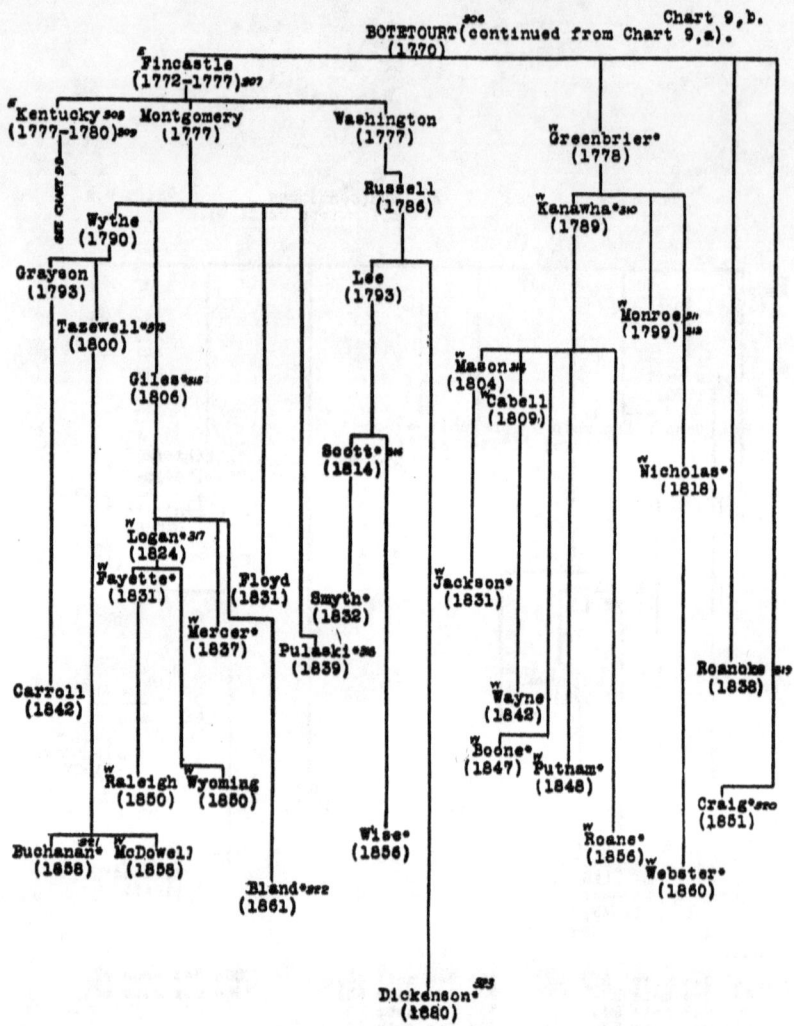

306 See note 17.
307 See note 25.
308 See note 36.
309 See note 37.
310 See note 35.
311 See note 17.
312 See note 51.
313 See note 75.
314 See note 48.
315 See note 17.
316 See note 70.
317 See note 35.
318 See note 64.
319 See note 17.
320 See note 17.
321 See note 12.
322 See note 8.
323 See note 20.

* Initially formed from portions of more than one county,— the parent-county here shown being the first mentioned in the title of the Act of Assembly forming this county: for other counties, portions of which were utilized in the formation of this county, see Part I, Alphabetical Arrangement.

Virginia Counties   171

Chart 9.c.

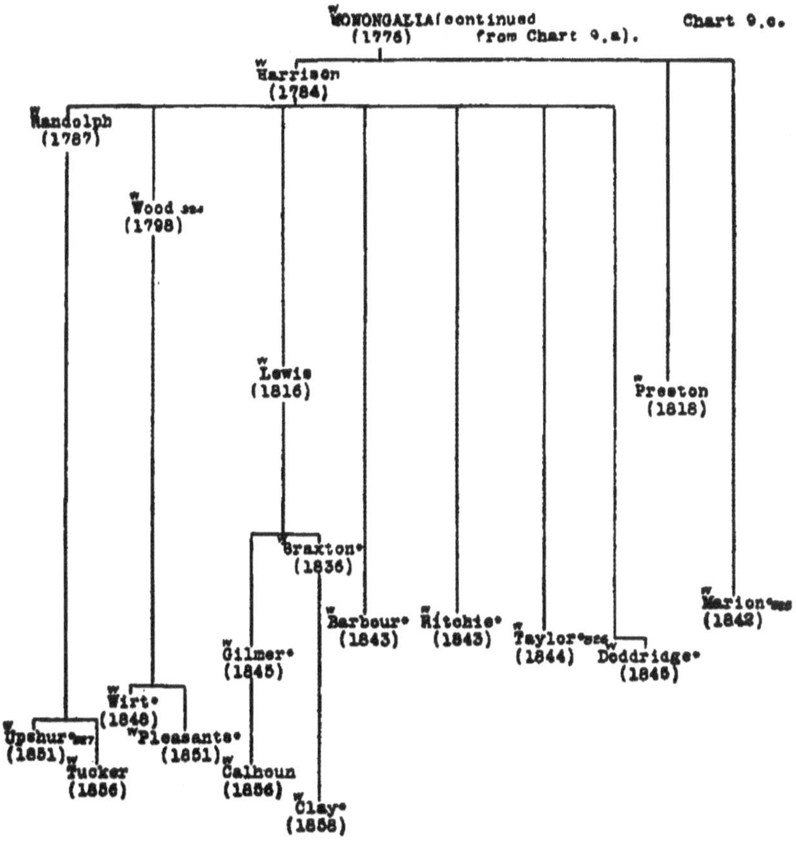

MONONGALIA (continued (1776) from Chart 9.a).

Harrison (1784)

Randolph (1787)

Wood (1798)

Lewis (1816)

Preston (1818)

Braxton* (1836)

Barbour* (1843)   Ritchie* (1843)   Taylor* (1844)   Doddridge* (1845)

Marion (1842)

Gilmer* (1845)

Wirt* (1848)

Upshur (1851)   Pleasants* (1851)

Tucker (1856)   Calhoun (1856)

Clay* (1858)

---

324 See note 85.   326 See note 50.
325 See note 50.   327 See note 78.
* Initially formed from portions of more than one county,— the parent-
county here shown being the first mentioned in the title of the Act of Assembly forming this county; for other counties, portions of which were u-
tilized in the formation of this county, see Part I, Alphabetical Arrangement.

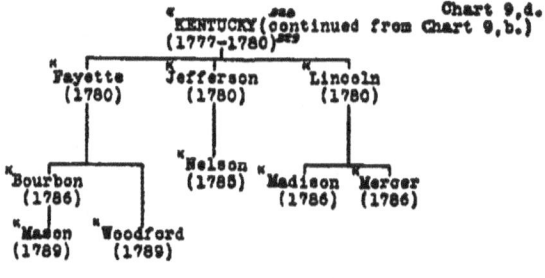

Chart 9.d.

KENTUCKY (continued from Chart 9.b.) (1777-1780)

Fayette (1780)   Jefferson (1780)   Lincoln (1780)

Bourbon (1786)   Nelson (1785)   Madison (1786)   Mercer (1786)

Mason (1789)   Woodford (1789)

---

328 See note 36.
329 See note 37.

INDEX TO CHARTS

Name	Chart
° Accawmack (1634)	1.
Accomack (1663)	1.
Albemarle	5.
Alleghany	9, a.
Alexandria	9.
Amelia	2.
Amherst	5.
Appomattox	5.
Augusta	9 and 9, a.
ʷ Barbour	9, c.
Bath	9, a.
Bedford	2.
ʷ Berkeley	9.
Bland	9, b.
ʷBoone	9, b.
Botetourt	9, a and 9, b.
ᵏ Bourbon	9, d.
ʷ Braxton	9, c.
ʷ Brooke	9, a.
Brunswick	2.
Buchanan	9, b.
Buckingham	5.
ʷ Cabell	9, b.
ʷ Calhoun	9, c.
Campbell	2.
Caroline	9.
Carroll	9, b.
Charles City	2.
° Charles River	3.
Charlotte	2.
Chesterfield	5.
Clarke	9.
ʷ Clay	9, c.
Craig	9, b.
Culpeper	9.
Cumberland	5.
Dickenson	9, b.
Dinwiddie	2.
ʷ Doddridge	9, c.
° Dunmore	9.
Elizabeth City	4.
Essex	9.
Fairfax	9.
Fauquier	9.
ᵏ Fayette (1780)	9, d.
ʷ Fayette (1831)	9, b.
° Fincastle	9, b.
Floyd	9, b.
Fluvanna	5.
Franklin	2.
Frederick	9.
Giles	9, b.
ʷ Gilmer	9, c.
Gloucester	3.
Goochland	5.
Grayson	9, b.
ʷ Greenbrier	9, b.
Greene	9.
Greensville	2.
Halifax	2.
ʷ Hampshire	9, a.
ʷ Hancock	9, a.
Hanover	3.
ʷ Hardy	9, a.
ʷ Harrison	9, c.
Henrico	5.
Henry	2.
Highland	9, a.
° Illinois	9, a.
Isle of Wight	7.
ʷ Jackson	9, b.
James City	6.
ᵏ Jefferson (1780)	9, d.
ʷ Jefferson (1801)	9.
ʷ Kanawha	9, b.
° Kentucky	9, b and 9, d.
King and Queen	3.
King George	9.
King William	3.
Lancaster	9.
Lee	9, b.
ʷ Lewis	9, c.
ᵏ Lincoln	9, d.
ʷ Logan	9, b.
Loudoun	9.
Louisa	3.
° Lower Norfolk	4.
Lunenburg	2.
ʷ McDowell	9, b.
ᵏ Madison (1786)	9, d.
ʷ Madison (1793)	9.
ʷ Marion	9, c.
ʷ Marshall	9, a.
ᵏ Mason (1789)	9, d.
ʷ Mason (1804)	9, b.
Mathews	3.
Mecklenburg	2.
ᵏ Mercer (1786)	9, d.
ʷ Mercer (1837)	9, b.
Middlesex	9.
ʷ Monongalia	9, a and 9, c.
ʷ Monroe	9, b.
Montgomery	9, b.
ʷ Morgan	9.
Nansemond	4.
ᵏ Nelson (1785)	9, d.
ʷ Nelson (1808)	5.
New Kent	3.
° New Norfolk	4.
ʷ Nicholas	9, b.
Norfolk	4.
Northampton	1.
Northumberland	9.
Nottoway	2.
ʷ Ohio	9, a.
Orange	9.
Page	9, a.
Patrick	2.
ʷ Pendleton	9, a.
Pittsylvania	2.
ʷ Pleasants	9, c.
ʷ Pocahontas	9, a.
Powhatan	5.
ʷ Preston	9, c.
Prince Edward	2.
Prince George	2.
Prince William	9.
Princess Anne	4.
Pulaski	9, b.
ʷ Putnam	9, b.
ʷ Raleigh	9, b.
ʷ Randolph	9, c.
° Rappahannock (1656)	9.
Rappahannock (1833)	9.
Richmond	9.
ʷ Ritchie	9, c.
Roanoke	9, b.
ʷ Roane	9, b.
Rockbridge	9, a.
Rockingham	9, a.
Russell	9, b.
Scott	9, b.
Shenandoah	9.
Smyth	9, b.
Southampton	7.
Spotsylvania	9.
Stafford	9.
Surry	6.
Sussex	6.
ʷ Taylor	9, c.
Tazewell	9, b.
Tucker	9, c.
ʷ Tyler	9, a.
° Upper Norfolk	4.
ʷ Upshur	9, c.
Warren	9.
° Warrosquyoake	7.
Warwick	8.
° Warwick River	8.
Washington	9, b.
ʷ Wayne	9, b.
ʷ Webster	9, b.
Westmoreland	9.
ʷ Wetzel	9, a.
ʷ Wirt	9, c.
Wise	9, b.
ʷ Wood	9, c.
ᵏ Woodford	9, d.
ʷ Wyoming	9, b.
Wythe	9, b.
° Yohogania	9, a.
York	3.

PART V.

ORIGIN OF COUNTY NAMES

In the preparation of Part V, no account has been taken of conflicting county traditions, nor has an attempt been made to harmonize such traditions with apparently correct interpretations, but an effort has been made to assemble, under an alphabetical arrangement of the county names, the most reliable and concise quotations bearing upon this phase of the subject.

Each quotation is immediately followed by a citation of the authority quoted, while additional references,—in alphabetical order,—furnish corroborative and cumulative evidence in support of the quotation actually offered.

In cases of widely varying interpretations, these several interpretations have been given,—each with its own citation,—with a view to offering the student the larger scope in connection with those cases; but, where the Acts of Assembly are quoted as authority for the origin of the name, no corroborative or other evidence is offered, as there is no appeal from such authority.

For re-capitulation of sources of names, see end of this Part.

The following abbreviations are used in this Part:

A.: Acts of the General Assembly of Virginia, for the session indicated.
Brock: Robert A. Brock's "Virginia and Virginians".
Collins: R. H. Collins's "History of Kentucky" (1878).
E (superior): resulted from Virginia legislation, but now extinct, as shown by accompanying dates.
Green: B. W. Green's "Word Book of Virginia Folk Speech" (1912).
H.: Hening's "Statutes at Large".
H. A. I.: "Handbook of American Indians" (Bureau of American Ethnology, Bulletin 30: 1907).
H. B.: "Journals of the House of Burgesses", 1619-1776 (Virginia State Library: 1905-1915).
K (superior): resulted from Virginia legislation, but now in Kentucky.
Lewis: Virgil A. Lewis's "History of West Virginia" (1889).
Long: Charles M. Long's "Virginia County Names" (1908).
U. S.: United States Geological Survey, Bulletin 258 (1905).
W (superior): resulted from Virginia legislation, but now in West Virginia.

* ACCAWMACK:
 (1634-42/3)   Named after the Accomack Indians, "A tribe of the Powha-
 and   tan Confederacy that formerly lived in Accomac and North-
 (1663)   ampton Counties." (H. A. I.; Long, 163, 165). The word means "on-the-other-side-of-water place". For etymology, meanings, and variants, see H. A. I.

ALBEMARLE:
 (1744)   "the name of Albemarle was given to the new county from the title of William Anne Keppel, Second Earl of Albemarle, at that time [1737-1754] Governor General of the Colony." (Wood's "History of Albemarle County", 8; Long, 70).

ALEXANDRIA:
(1847) "the said county shall contain that part of said District [of Columbia], which lies on the west side of said [Potomac] River, and shall be called the County of Alexandria" (U. S. Stats. II, 105).

Named from Alexandria (City), which was organized in 1748 and was built on a part of "the whole of the domain from Great Hunting Creek to the Falls of the Potomac extending miles inland and embracing six thousand acres [which] had been purchased by John Alexander in 1669 of Capt. Robert Howsen, for 6600 pounds of tobacco. Howsen had secured his right to it by a Royal Patent granted to him in 1688 [1669] by Governor Berkeley for having brought to Virginia a certain number of immigrants. The nucleus of the town was first formed somewhere near the site of the gas works, and was called Belle Haven." (Snowden's "Some Old Historic Landmarks", 13).

ALLEGHANY:
(1822) "A corruption of the Delaware Indian name for the Allegheny and Ohio Rivers, the meaning of the name being 'lost.'" (U. S., 21; Long, 168). For etymology, meanings and variants, see H. A. I.

AMELIA:
(1735) "named for the Princess Amelia [Sophia], the youngest daughter of George II. of England." (U. S., 23; Long, 50).

AMHERST:
(1761) "named after the hero of Ticonderoga [Major General (Sir) Jeffrey Amherst], the most successful as well as the most popular of all the English Colonial Governors-General. [1763-1768]." ("Facts of interest about Amherst County", 5; Long, 71).

APPOMATTOX:
(1845) "Indian names for places are apt to be descriptive of the places. These Indians were Algonquins, in whose language 'apamu-tiku' means 'a sinuous tidal estuary'. Their chief town in 1607 was in, or rather just below, the present 'Turkey Island bend', and the name was applicable rather to the James than to the Appomattox; but the English had previously named that river for their king. In the course of time the 'apamu-tiku' country of the Indian came to be called 'the curls of the river' by the English". (Brown's "First Republic", p. 195; Tyler's "Cradle of the Republic", p. 14).

"An Indian word meaning 'tobacco plant country'". (U. S., 27; Long, 166). For etymology, meanings and variants, see H. A. I.

AUGUSTA:
(1745) "named in honor of Princess Augusta [of Saxe-Gotha], wife of Frederick, Prince of Wales, Father of George III." (Waddell's "Annals of Augusta County" (1902), 36; Long, 51).

w BARBOUR:
(1843) "shall form one distinct and new county, and be called and known by the name of Barbour County, in honour to and in memory of Philip P. Barbour of Virginia." (A., 1842-3, p. 37).

BATH:
(1791) "so called because of the medical springs." (U. S., p. 38; Long, 175).

BEDFORD:
(1754) "was named in honor of John Russell, the Fourth Duke of Bedford, who was Secretary of State of Great Britain from February 13th, 1748, to June 26th, 1757." ("Historical Sketch of Bedford County", p. 4; Long, 90).

w BERKELEY:
(1772) "named Berkeley, in honor of Norborne Berkeley, Baron de Botetourt, 'the good Governor of Virginia [1768-1770]', as he was called, under George III." (Norris's "History of the Lower Shenandoah Valley", p. 220; Long, 139).

BLAND:
(1861) "said to have been named after Richard Bland, of Revolutionary fame." (U. S., p. 49; Long, 101).

w BOONE:
(1847) "shall form distinct and new county, and be called and known by the name of Boone County, in honour to and in memory of Daniel Boone, the well known pioneer of the western frontier settlements." (A., 1846-7, p. 49.)

BOTETOURT:
(1770) "was named in honor of Norborne Berkeley, Lord Botetourt, who was Governor of Virginia in 1768-[1770]." (Waddell's "Annals of Augusta County" (1902), p. 216; Long, 138).

k BOURBON:
(1786) "was named in compliment to the Bourbon Family of France,— a prince of that family, then upon the throne, having rendered the American Colonies aid, in men and money, in the struggle for independence." (Collins's "History of Kentucky", ii, p. 66).

w BRAXTON:
(1836) "named in honor of Carter Braxton, one of Virginia's signers of the Declaration of Independence." (Lewis, p. 673).

w BROOKE:
: (1797) "named in honor of Robert Brooke [Governor of Virginia, 1794-1796], a grandson of Robert Brooke, who in company with Robert Beverly the historian accompanied Governor Spottswood to Virginia in 1710." (Lewis, p. 578).

BRUNSWICK:
: (1732) "named for the Duchy [of Brunswick] in Germany." (U. S., 59; Long, 48).

BUCHANAN:
: (1858) "named for President James Buchanan [1857-1861]." (U. S., 59; Long, 155).

BUCKINGHAM:
: (1761) Most probably named after the Duke of Buckingham; but an Act concerning lands of Archibald Cary (H. vii, 440), finally passed by the House of Burgesses on April 1, 1761 (H. B. 1758-1761, 243), says, "lying and being on the west side and on the branches of Buck river, otherwise called Willis's Creek, in the county of Goochland, commonly called and known by the name of Buckingham": and we also have the petition of Archibald Cary (at that time a member of the House of Burgesses from Chesterfield), under date of March 16, 1761 (H. B., 1758-1761, 214), which says that he "is also seized of a Tract of Land called Buckingham in Albemarle in Fee Simple", which is in harmony with the Act forming Buckingham County from Albemarle (H. vii, 419), which finally passed the House of Burgesses on April 7, 1761 (H. B., 1758-1761, 251).

w CABELL:
: (1809) "William H. Cabell, in honor of whom the county was named, * * *, was elected Governor of Virginia (in 1805), a position which he held until 1808, when he was chosen a judge of the General Court [1808-1811]." (Lewis, p. 626).

w CALHOUN:
: (1856) "was named in honor of John C. Calhoun, so distinguished in American politics." (Lewis, p. 721).

CAMPBELL:
: (1782) "General William Campbell, the hero of King's Mountain (after whom the County of Campbell, formed in 1784, was named) was born in 1745, and was killed in 1781." (Brock, i, p. 176; Long, 104).

CAROLINE:
: (1728) "named after Queen Caroline, wife of George II." (Green, p. 50; Long, 48; U. S., p. 70).

CARROLL:
(1842) "shall form one distinct and new county, and be called and known by the name of Carroll County, in memory of Charles Carroll of Carrollton." (A., 1841-2, p. 32).

CHARLES CITY:
(1634) "another [town] (established soon after) was called after his second son, Charles, afterwards King Charles the First." (Green's "Genesis of Counties", 118).

"As 'Charles City', so 'Henrico' came soon to signify much more than the mere town or site for it, and extended over a large tract of country, till it, too, became the name of an original shire or county formed in 1634." (Green's "Genesis of Counties", p. 115; Long, 32).

• CHARLES RIVER:
(1634-1642/3) "so called after the river named by the colonists in honor of King Charles." (Scott's "History of Orange County, Virginia", p. 17).

CHARLOTTE:
(1765) "named the new county after the young Queen of George III., the Princess Charlotte [Sophia] of Mecklenberg." (Gaines's "Handbook of Charlotte County", p. 7; U. S., p. 76; Long, 54).

CHESTERFIELD:
(1749) "Named after Philip Dormer Stanhope, [Fourth Earl of Chesterfield], the celebrated Lord Chesterfield". (Green, 50; Long, 73).

CLARKE:*:
(1836) "Named after General George Rogers Clark. The name should be spelt 'Clark', without the final 'e'." (Green, p. 50; Long, 107).

w CLAY:
(1858) "named in honor of Henry Clay." (Lewis, p. 724).

CRAIG:
(1851) "Named after Robert Craig, member of Congress [from Virginia, 1829-1834, 1835-1841]." (Green, p. 50; Long, 176).

CULPEPER:
(1749) "Probably named after Lord Culpeper, Governor of Virginia [1680-1683], as a compliment to Lord Fairfax, who had inherited from him the ownership of the Northern Neck." (Green, p. 51; Long, 136).

---

* The enrolled bill and the text of the Act of Assembly forming this county contain only the name Clarke (with the final "e"), although the county was named after George Rogers Clark (without the final "e").

CUMBERLAND:
(1749) "Named after William Augustus, Duke of Cumberland, the victor of Culloden [in 1746]." (Green, p. 51; Long, 49).

DICKENSON:
(1880) "Named after W[illiam] J. Dickenson, a prominent member of the dominant, Readjuster Party, when the county was formed." (Green, p. 51; U. S., p. 106).

DINWIDDIE:
(1752) "named for Robert Dinwiddie, lieutenant-governor of the Colony [1751-1758]." (U. S., p. 106; Green, p. 51; Long, 138).

▼ DODDRIDGE:
(1845) "named in honor of the distinguished Philip Doddridge [member of Congress from Virginia, 1829-32, when he died]". (Lewis, p. 685).

● DUNMORE:
(1772-1778) "It had been named after and in honor of Lord Dunmore, the then Governor [1771-1776] under the royal government." (Kercheval's "History of the Valley" (1850), p. 154).
"So odious did the name of Dunmore become that a county named for him, once in the domain of Orange, lost its identity under that name, and was re-christened 'Shenandoah'". (Scott's "History of Orange County, Virginia", p. 63).

ELIZABETH CITY:
(1634) "* * * and Kiccowtan (which hereafter [in reply to the 6th petition of their General Assembly of August 1619] shall be called Elizabeth City, by the name of his Majesties most vertuous and renowned Daughter) * * *" (Brown's "First Republic", p. 377).
"At which (Assembly) [1619], divers petitions were made to the Treasurer, Council and Company (in England), whereof 'the sixte and laste' was, 'That they' would 'be pleased to change the savage name of Kiccowtan and to give that incorporation a newe name'. 1 McDon. Papers, p. 16 [Virginia State Library]. And I think there is demonstrative proof that this change was authoritatively made within a short time thereafter, and that the place, by which I mean the site of the Indian village aforesaid, was re-named 'Elizabeth City', not after Queen Elizabeth of England, but after King James's daughter, the Princess Elizabeth, who, on Valentine's Day, 14th February, 1612-'13, had married Frederick, Elector Palatine. But nevertheless the first name, though not afterwards used as the legal designation, was long continued as the popular designation, and often employed by writers on Virginian affairs,—a thing by no means uncommon as to places existing and flourishing in this State and elsewhere.

[References omitted]." (Green's "Genesis of Counties", p. 117-18 —in Slaughter's "Brief Sketch of the Life of William Green, LL. D."; Brown's "First Republic", 377; Long, 32).

ESSEX:
(1692) "named for the English County of Essex." (U. S., p. 121; Long, 91).
"Probably named after the Earl of Essex." (Green, p. 51).

FAIRFAX:
(1742) "was named for that most faithful of all Tories,—[Thomas] Lord Fairfax." (Choat's "History of Fairfax County", 8; Long, 69).

FAUQUIER:
(1759) "was named in his [Francis Fauquier's] honor." He was lieutenant-governor of Virginia, 1758-1768. (Brock, 1, 555; Long, 138).

★ FAYETTE:
(1780) "received its name as a testimonial of gratitude to Gen. Gilbert Mortimer de La Fayette,—the gallant and generous Frenchman, who volunteered as the Champion of Liberty of this side of the Atlantic." (Collins, ii, 169).

▼ FAYETTE:
(1831) "named in honor of General Lafayette." (Lewis, 662).

• FINCASTLE:
(1772-1777) "named after George Lord Fincastle, son of Lord Dunmore, who was governor at the time". (Campbell's "History of Virginia", 572.)
"named after the Town of Fincastle, which 'was established by law in 1772, and called after Lord Botetourt's country seat in England.'" (Waddell's "Annals of Augusta County, Virginia", ed., 1902, p. 216).

FLOYD:
(1831) "Floyd County, formed in 1831, from Montgomery County, was named in his (John Floyd's) honor. [He was Governor of Virginia, 1830-1834]." (Brock, 1, 163; Long, 148).

FLUVANNA:
(1777) "Queen Ann's name and reign are perpetuated in Rapidan, North and South Anna, Fluvanna, Rivanna, Germana, &c." (Slaughter's "St. Mark's Parish," 27; Long, 86).

FRANKLIN:
(1786) "Named after Benjamin Franklin." (Green, 52).

FREDERICK:
(1743)   "named in honor of Frederick, Prince of Wales, son of George II., and father of George III." (Waddell's "Annals of Augusta County, Virginia", ed., 1902, 36; Long, 51).

GILES:
(1806)   "Giles County, Virginia, formed in 1806, from the counties of Monroe and Tazewell, was named in his [William Branch Giles's] honor." He was Governor of Virginia, 1827-1830. (Brock, i, p. 156; Long, 147).

wGILMER:
(1845)   "Named for Thomas Walker Gilmer, * * *, elected Governor of Virginia, February 14, 1840, but a few months later resigned to take a seat in Congress, * * *." (Lewis, p. 686).

GLOUCESTER:
(1651)   "Named after Henry, Duke of Gloucester (b. 1640, d. 1660), third son of Charles I." (Green, p. 52; Long, 34).

GOOCHLAND:
(1728)   "named for William Gooch, Lieutenant-Governor of Virginia, in 1727-1749". (U. S., p. 139; Long, 137).

GRAYSON:
(1793)   "Named after [Colonel] William Grayson, United States Senator [from Virginia, 1789 to his death (March 12, 1790)]." (U. S., p. 142).

wGREENBRIER:
(1778)   "Named from its principal river." (Myers, "History of West Virginia", ii, p. 21.
"This is one of the prettiest mountain rivers in America. * * * The Miami Indians knew it as 'We-o-to-we' and the Delawares called it 'O-ne-pa-ke'. Whence comes the present name, that of Greenbrier? The French knew the stream as the 'Ronceverte' ('Ronce',—brier or bramble, and 'verte', or 'verd', green or verdant), the greenbrier. This the Virginians Saxonized and called the stream Greenbrier River. The old French name is preserved in that of the progressive Town of Ronceverte, on its banks, in Greenbrier County." (Lewis, "First Biennial Report (1906) Department of Archives and History of West Virginia," p. 256).

GREENE:
(1838)   "shall form one distinct and new county, and be called and known by the name of Greene County, in memory of General Nathaniel Greene, who served his country in the Revolutionary War." (A., 1838, p. 52; Long, 113).

GREENSVILLE:
(1781) "Also named after Gen. Greene, who after the Battle of Guildford C. H., marched into this County" (Lyon G. Tyler).

HALIFAX:
(1752) "was named for [George Montagu Dunk], the [Second] Earl of Halifax, one of the distinguished Family of Montagu, who was First Lord of the Board of Trade about that time [1752] and as such greatly interested himself in the trade of the Colonies." (Morrison's "Halifax County, Virginia", p. 66; Long, 73).

w HAMPSHIRE:
(1754) "named for the county in England." (U. S., p. 148).

w HANCOCK:
(1848) "named in honor of John Hancock, President of the Continental Congress, and first signer of the Declaration of Independence." (Lewis, p. 701).

HANOVER:
(1721) "named for the Duke of Hanover, afterwards George I. of England, or from the Prussian province and city belonging to him." (U. S., p. 149; Green, p. 53; Long, 48).

w HARDY:
(1786) "Samuel Hardy, in honor of whom the county was named, was long a resident of Isle of Wight County, Virginia, * * *, [and one of the number who signed the Deed of Cession which transferred the Northwest Territory to the General Government]." (Lewis, p. 555).

w HARRISON:
(1784) "Benjamin Harrison, in honor of whom the county was named, was a native of Charles City County, Virginia, * * *, one of the signers of the Declaration of Independence [and] Governor of Virginia from 1781 to 1784." (Lewis, p. 543).

HENRICO:
(1634) "and being arrived at the Place, he environed it with a Palisade, and in honor of Prince Henry [son of King James], called it 'Henrico'". (Stith's "History of Virginia", p. 123-4).
"another [town] (the second one of the colonists' building) was called after his [James I's] son Henry, then Prince of Wales." (p. 118). "As 'James City' and 'Charles City', so 'Henrico' came soon to signify much more than the mere town or site for it, and extended over a large tract of country, till it, too, became the name of an original shire or county formed in 1634, at which time it took in, on the north side of James River, all land westward from Charles City, between that river and the

Chickahominy, and still further west along the James till Goochland was created from it in 1727 ('4 Hen. Stat., 240') and, on the south side of James River, all the land westward from the Appomattox (which divided it on that side, originally from Charles City, afterwards from Prince George,) till 1727, when its more western part was made part of Goochland and 1748, when the portion of it left between Goochland and the Appomattox was formed into the County of Chesterfield." (p. 115). (Green's "Genesis of Counties," pp. 115 and 118; Long, 32).

HENRY:
(1777) "[Patrick Henry] purchased about ten thousand acres of land in Henry County, formed in 1776 from Pittsylvania County and named in his honor, as was subsequently the neighboring County of Patrick carved from Henry County in 1791." (Brock, 1, p. 72; Long, 141).

HIGHLAND:
(1847) "In view of the exceptionally high altitude of the county, the name selected is very appropriate, * * *, as to who is responsible for the choice, there is some dispute." (Morton's "History of Highland County, Virginia", p. 115; Long, 175).

•ILLINOIS:
(1778-1784) "Named from the Illini Indians, who inhabited the region, the name meaning 'men'". (U. S., p. 165).
"In 1721 the Company of the Indies divided Louisiana into nine districts, one of which was known as the Illinois District, extending east and west of the Mississippi River between the Arkansas and Illinois Rivers." (Turner's "Great Britain and the Illinois Country", p. 6). For etymology, variants and meanings, see H. A. I.

ISLE OF WIGHT:
(1637) "Named after the Isle of Wight in England. At a very early date a settlement was made within the limits of this county by a company, several of whose members lived in Isle of Wight ['at least one of the principal patentees was certainly from Isle of Wight, Sir Richard Worsley, who came over in 1608' (Morrison's "Isle of Wight County", p. 50)]; and which was called 'The Isle of Wight Plantation'. The Isle of Wight is an island in the English Channel. 'Wight' means a 'Channel', or 'passage'. The name means 'island of the channel' ". (Green, p. 53; Long, 95).

w JACKSON:
(1831) "named in honor of Andrew Jackson, then [1829-1837] President of the United States." (Lewis, p. 657).

JAMES CITY:
(1634) "Having pitched upon a Place to settle, they called it Jamestown, in Honour of his Majesty then reigning, and every Man fell to work." (Stith's "History of Virginia", p. 46).
"one town (the first) in Virginia, was called after King James" (p. 118). "As 'James City' and 'Charles City', so 'Henrico' came soon to signify much more than the mere town or site for it, and extended over a large tract of country, till it, too, became the name of an original shire or county formed in 1634." (Green's "Genesis of Counties", pp. 115 and 118; Long, 31).

k JEFFERSON:
(1780) "named in honor of Thomas Jefferson, the Governor of the State [1779-1781]." (Collins, ii, p. 355).

w JEFFERSON:
(1801) "named in honor of President Jefferson [1801-1809]." (Lewis, p. 613).

w KANAWHA:
(1789) "named from its principal river." (Lewis, p. 570).
"This river derives its name from a small tribe of Indians which dwelt upon its sources long ago. * * *. Their tribal name has been spelled many ways as Conoys, Conois, Conoways, * * *, Kanhawas, Kanhaway, and Kanawhas, the last having been adopted by the Virginians." (Lewis, "First Bienniel Report (1906) of the Department of Archives and History of the State of West Virginia", p. 255). For etymology, variants and meanings, see H. A. I.

• KENTUCKY:
(1777-1780) "General Clark says (vide Dr. Campbell) that Kentuck-e [the name the Indians gave to this section of the country], in the language of the Indians, signifies 'the river of blood' ". (Collins, ii, p. 382).

KING AND QUEEN:
(1691) "It [the Battle of the Boyne] resulted in a victory for the latter [William III., Prince of Orange], and William and Mary became joint sovereigns of the realm [1688-1694]. The new county being organized in the following year, was named for these illustrious personages, King and Queen." (Bagby's "King and Queen County, Virginia", p. 25; Long, 41).

KING GEORGE:
(1721) "named for King George I. of England [1714-1727]." (U. S., p. 175; Long, 48).

KING WILLIAM:
  (1702) "Named after William of Orange, King of England [with Mary, 1688-1694; alone, 1694-1702]." (Green, p. 54; Long, 41).

LANCASTER:
  (1651) "Named probably from the County of Lancaster in England. As that is one of the northern shires of England, so this Lancaster is one of the northern Counties of Virginia." (Green, p. 54; Long, 91; U. S., p. 180).

LEE:
  (1793) "Lee County, formed in 1792 from Russell, was named in honor of General [Henry] Lee [who was Governor of Virginia, 1791-1794]". (Brock, i, p. 88; Long, 145).

w LEWIS:
  (1816) "named in memory of Colonel Charles Lewis, who was killed at the battle of Point Pleasant." (Lewis, p. 636).

k LINCOLN:
  (1780) "named in honor of General Benjamin Lincoln, a distinguished officer of the Revolutionary Army." (Collins, ii, p. 468).

w LOGAN:
  (1824) "derived its name from Logan, the famous Mingo chief." (Lewis, p. 656).

LOUDOUN:
  (1757) "Named after John Campbell, Fourth Earl of Loudoun, Commander-in-Chief of British forces in North America during the latter part of the French and Indian War [and Governor-General of all the American Colonies, 1756-1763]." (Green, p. 54; Long, 71; U. S., p. 190).

LOUISA:
  (1742) "Named after [the Princess] Louisa, daughter of George II. and wife of Frederick V., King of Denmark." (Green, p. 54; U. S., p. 191; Long, 50).

• LOWER NORFOLK:
  (1637-1691) the lower portion of "New Norfolk", q. v.

LUNENBURG:
  (1746) "The Anglicised form of Luneburg, which was one of the titles of George I., as Duke of Brunswick-Luneburg." (U. S., p. 192; Green, p. 54; Long, 50).

w McDOWELL:
  (1858) "named in honor of James McDowell, * * *, elected Governor of Virginia, 1841 [1843-1846]." (Lewis, p. 728).

k MADISON:
(1786) "named in honor of James Madison, afterward[s] President of the United States [1809-1817]." (Collins, ii, p. 493).

MADISON:
(1793) "and named for James Madison." (Scott's "History of Orange County, Virginia", p. 18; Long, 155).

w MARION:
(1842) "shall form one distinct and new county, and be called and known by the name of Marion County, in honour to, and in memory of General Francis Marion, who served his country in the War of the Revolution." (A., 1841-2, p. 34).

w MARSHALL:
(1835) "was named in honor of John Marshall, Chief Justice of the United States [1801-1835]." (Lewis, p. 664).

k MASON:
(1789) "named after George Mason, one of her [Virginia's] distinguished lawyers and statesmen." (Collins, ii, p. 545).

w MASON:
(1804) "named in honor of the celebrated George Mason, one of the prominent actors on the theatre of the Revolution." (Lewis, p. 616).

MATHEWS:
(1791) "Named after Major Thomas Mathews, of the Revolution, afterwards prominent in the legislature [in the House, from Borough of Norfolk, 1785-1794]." (Green, p. 55; Long, 106).

MECKLENBURG:
(1765) "named after the Queen of George III., Charlotte of Mecklenburg-Strelitz." (Green, p. 55; Long, 54; U. S., p. 204).

k MERCER:
(1786) "named in honor of General Hugh Mercer." (Collins, ii, p. 602).

w MERCER:
(1837) "shall form one distinct and new county, and be called and known by the name of Mercer County, in memory of General Hugh Mercer who fell at Princeton." (A., 1836-7, p. 32).

MIDDLESEX:
(1673/4) "Named probably after the English county. The country of the Middle Saxons." (Green, p. 55; Long, 91).

w MONONGALIA:
(1776) "The name was received from the river Monongahela, which in the Indian language signifies 'River of caving or crumbling banks'". (Lewis, p. 506).
"A Latinized form of the Indian word 'monongahela' [a corruption of the Delaware Indian word 'menaungehilla', meaning 'river with the sliding banks'], meaning 'falling in river bank'." (U. S., p. 212). For etymology, meanings and variants, see H. A. I.

w MONROE:
(1799) "was named in honor of the President of the United States [1817-1825]". (Lewis, p. 594).

MONTGOMERY:
(1777) "Named after General Richard Montgomery [an American Revolutionary officer, who was killed before Quebec, December 31, 1775]". (Green, p. 55; Long, 110).

w MORGAN:
(1820) "was named in honor of General Daniel Morgan of the Revolution." (Lewis, p. 644).

NANSEMOND:
(1642) "The Indian word 'Nansemond' means 'fishing-point or angle' and was the name given by the Indians to their town which was situated in the angle made by the junction of the Western Branch with the main stream of the river (Nansemond)". (Dunn's "History of Nansemond County, Virginia", 14; Long, 164). For etymology, meanings and variants, see H. A. I.

k NELSON:
(1785) "named in honor of ex-Governor [Thomas] Nelson of Virginia [1781]". (Collins, ii, 602).

NELSON:
(1808) "was named * * * in honor of General Nelson [Thomas Nelson, Jr., Governor of Virginia, 1781 (third Governor under the State Government)]". (Brock, i, 80; Long, 144).

NEW KENT:
(1654) "I think this county was named by Col. William Claiborn after Kent Island, from which he was driven by Lord Baltimore". (Lyon G. Tyler).
"Named after the English Kent". (Green, 55; Long, 86; U. S., 223).

• NEW NORFOLK:
(1636-1637) "Jefferson's Notes in 1792 says that the county was named for the Duke of Norfolk, but as it was first called 'New Nor-

folk', it is reasonable to presume that it was called for Norfolk in England [which is also on the water]". (Stewart's "History of Norfolk County", 16).

⋆ NICHOLAS:
(1818) "derives its name from Wilson Cary Nicholas, * * * [who] became Governor of Virginia [1814-1816]". (Lewis, 641).

NORFOLK:
(1691) "the remaining portion of Lower Norfolk County, after Princess Anne County was cut off". See "New Norfolk"; also see Long, 188).

NORTHAMPTON:
(1642/3) "Said to have been named after the English County as a compliment to [Colonel] Obedience Robins, a Burgess for the Virginia County [of Accomacke], and a native of Northamptonshire, England." (Green, 56).
"named after an English earl killed in fighting for King Charles I." (Long, 63, 64).
"named from the county in England". (U. S., 226).

NORTHUMBERLAND:
(1648) "Probably named after the English County". (Green, 56).
"named from the county in England". (U. S., 227).

NOTTOWAY:
(1789) "named for the Indian tribe, the word meaning a 'snake', that is, an enemy." (U. S., 227; Long, 166).
"Indian: named after tribe and river. Means 'adders', or enemies." (Green, 56).
For etymology, meanings and variants, see H. A. I.

⋆ OHIO:
(1776) "named from the river of that name" (Myers, "History of West Virginia," ii, p. 9), on which (then including the present counties of Brooke, Hancock and Marshall) it bordered its whole length. 'The Miamis called it (the river) 'Cau-si-sip-i-on-e'; the Delawares knew it as the 'O-h-i-o-ple', the 'River of White Caps'; the Shawnees bestowed upon it a name signifying 'Eagle River'; the Wyandots knew it as the 'Ki-to-no'. When La Salle discovered it in 1669, the Iriquois nations called it the 'O-li-gen-si-pen', meaning the 'Beautiful River'. When the French came to behold it and to admire its enchanting vistas presented by the banks, as scene after scene opened up to view like scrolls of a beautiful panorama, they literally translated the Iriquois name and called it 'La Belle Riviere',—the 'Beautiful River', or 'How Beautiful the Scene'. The English contracted the Delaware name to 'Oyo', now Ohio, by which this noble river is now known all over the world." (Lewis, "First Biennial Report (1906) of the

Department of Archives and History of the State of West Virginia," p. 259).

ORANGE:
(1734) "was named * * * for William, Prince of Orange, one of Engalnd's most worthy kings". (Scott's "History of Orange County, Virginia", p. 22; Long, 42).

PAGE:
(1831) "The County of Page, formed from those of Rockingham and Shenandoah in 1831, was named in honor of Governor [John] Page [1802-1805]." (Brock, 1, p. 97; Long, 147).

PATRICK:
(1791) See "Henry".

w PENDLETON:
(1788) "Edmund Pendleton, in honor of whom the county was named, was President of the Virginia Convention of 1775, * * *, twice a member of the Continental Congress [1774-1775], and long President of the Virginia Court of Appeals [1788-1803]." (Lewis, p. 565).

PITTSYLVANIA:
(1767) "Named for Sir William Pitt, Earl of Chatham, the celebrated English statesman." (U. S., p. 247; Green, p. 56; Long, 74).

w PLEASANTS:
(1851) "named in memory of James Pleasants, * * *, elected Governor of Virginia, December 1, 1822, and by successive re-elections served until 1825". (Lewis, p. 719).

w POCAHONTAS:
(1821) "Pocahontas, the Indian princess for whom the county was named, was a daughter of Powhatan, the King of the Confederated Tribes of Atlantic Virginia." (Lewis, p. 647). For etymology, meanings and variants, see H. A. I.

POWHATAN:
(1777) "named for the celebrated Indian chief." (U. S., p. 252; Green, p. 56; Long, 167). For etymology, meanings and variants, see H. A. I.

w PRESTON:
(1818) "More than half of the counties of West Virginia are named for public men of the Old Dominion. Following this custom, the legislature sitting in 1818 gave the county the name of the honored citizen [James Patton Preston] who was then filling the governor's seat [1816-1819]." (Morton's "History of Preston County, West Virginia", p. 96).

PRINCE EDWARD:
(1754) "named for Edward [Augustus], a son of Frederick, Prince of Wales." (U. S., p. 254; Green, p. 56; Long, 52).

PRINCE GEORGE:
(1703) "called after Prince George (of Denmark), the husband of the Queen (Anne), who was then [1702] on the throne". (Green's "Genesis of Counties", p. 112; Long, 38).

PRINCE WILLIAM:
(1731) 'named for William [Augustus], Duke of Cumberland, in 1730." (U. S., p. 254; Green, p. 56; Long, 49).

PRINCESS ANNE:
(1691) "named for Princess, afterwards Queen, Anne of England [1702-1714]." (U. S., p. 254; Green, p. 57; Long, 35).

PULASKI:
(1839) "Named for the Polish patriot, Count Casimir Pulaski, friend of the Americans in the Revolutionary War." (U. S., p. 255; Green, p. 57; Long, 110).

w PUTNAM:
(1848) "named for General Israel Putnam, distinguished in the Revolutionary War." (U. S., p. 255).

w RALEIGH:
(1850) "shall form one distinct and new county, and be called and known by the name of Raleigh County, in memory of Sir Walter Raleigh, who made the earliest effort to colonize Virginia." (A., 1849-50, p. 19).

w RANDOLPH:
(1787) "Edmund Randolph, in honor of whom the county was named, was appointed first Attorney-General of the Commonwealth, and in 1779, * * *, he was elected a member of the Continental Congress, * * *." (Lewis, p. 560).

• RAPPAHANNOCK:
(1656-1692) Named from "the Indian tribe of the Powhatan Confederacy, formerly living on the Rappahannock River,"—the word meaning "the people of the alternating (ebb and flow) stream." (H. A. I.; Long, 166). For etymology, meanings and variants, see H. A. I.

RAPPAHANNOCK:
(1833) "Indian name from the Rappahannock River [which rises within the bounds of this county]." (Green, p. 57; Long, 166; U. S., p. 258). For etymology, meanings and variants, see H. A. I.

RICHMOND:
(1692) "Name uncertain" (Green, p. 57). U. S., p. 262, says, "so named on account of resemblance to Richmond, County Surry, England." Long's "Virginia County Names", p. 67, says, "There remains the possibility that the county may take the name of some English Earl or Duke of Richmond, living, or in public remembrance, at the time the county was named." (Also see Long, 63, 67).

w RITCHIE:
(1843) "Thomas Ritchie, from whom the county derives its name, was Virginia's most famous journalist." (Lewis, p. 683).

w ROANE:
(1856) "its own name, and that of its seat of justice, Spencer, commemorate that of him [Spencer Roane] whose life and public services added lustre to the annals of Virginia jurisprudence [as judge of the Supreme Bench from 1794 to 1822]." (Lewis, p. 725).

ROANOKE:
(1838) "A name applied, with several variants, by the Virginia colonists, to the shell-beads employed by the neighboring Indians as articles of personal adornment or media of exchange; a case of substitution of a familiar word for one that was ill understood and probably more difficult to pronounce." (H. A. I.; Long, 169). For etymology, meanings and variants, see H. A. I.

ROCKBRIDGE:
(1778) "was so called from the celebrated Natural Bridge in the southeast part of the county." (Waddell's "Annals of Augusta County, Virginia" (1909), 255; Long, 174).

ROCKINGHAM:
(1778) "It is presumed that Rockingham County was named in honor of the Marquis of Rockingham, Prime Minister of England in 1765-'6. During his administration, the Stamp Act was repealed by Parliament, which caused great rejoicing in America, and the Minister received more credit for the repeal than he perhaps deserved." (Waddell's "Annals of Augusta County, Virginia" (1902), 255; Long, 77).

RUSSELL:
(1786) "named for Gen. William Russell [an officer of the American Revolution, who distinguished himself at the Battle of King's Mountain]". (U. S., 268; Green, 57; Long, 105).

SCOTT:
(1814) "named for Gen. Wingfield Scott." (U. S., p. 278; Green, 57).

SHENANDOAH:
(1778) "An Indian word said to mean 'sprucy stream'" (U. S., p. 281; Green, p. 59). Peyton's "History of Augusta County, Virginia", p. 1, (Long, 168) says, "Sherrando, or Shenandoah, signifies, in the Indian tongue, 'Beautiful Daughter of the Stars'."
"This river drains the beautiful and fertile Shenandoah Valley to which [as well as to the county] it gives a name, * * *. From the summit of the Blue Ridge, Governor Spotswood and party in 1716, descended to its banks, and bestowed upon it the name of 'Euphrates'. But this was not to last. The Indian name was 'Shen-an-do-ah', meaning 'River of the Stars'. From the crest of the mountain barrier, at whose base it flows, the Red Men looked down and in its transparent waters, saw reflected the twinkling stars overhead. Hence the name with its pretty signification." (Lewis, "First Biennial Report (1906) of the Department of Archives and History of the State of West Virginia", p. 261). For etymology, meanings and variants, see H. A. I.

SMYTH:
(1832) "named for Gen. Alexander Smyth [Inspector-General of the Army in 1812], Member of Congress [1817-25; 1827-'30]." (U. S., p. 286; Green, p. 59).

SOUTHAMPTON:
(1749) "Named after Henry Wriothesley, Second Earl of Southampton, the friend of Shakespeare and a leading member of the Virginia Company." (Green, p. 59; Long, 64; U. S., p. 287).

SPOTSYLVANIA:
(1721) "The County of Spotsylvania was named after [Lieutenant-] Governor Spotswood, [1710-1722] who resided in it for some time." (Slaughter's "St. George's Parish", p. 1; Long, 136).

STAFFORD:
(1664) "The County of Stafford and Parish of Overwharton derive their names from the corresponding ones in England." (Boogher's "Overwharton Parish Register", p. v; Long, 91).

SURRY:
(1652) "named from the county in England." (U. S., p. 294; Green, p. 59; Long, 87).

SUSSEX:
(1754) "named from the county in England." (U. S., p. 294; Green, p. 59; Long, 89).

▼TAYLOR:
(1844) "named in honor of General Zachary Taylor." (Lewis, 684).

TAZEWELL:
(1800) "The County of Tazewell, formed in 1799 from Russell and

Wythe, was named in his [United States Senator (1794-1799) Henry Tazewell's honor]." (Brock, i, 166).

w TUCKER:
(1856) "named in honor of St. George Tucker, the eminent Virginia jurist, while the seat of justice derives its name from St. George Tucker, who was Clerk of the House of Delegates at the time the county was formed." (Lewis, 727).

w TYLER:
(1814) "The County of Tyler, formed in 1814, from Ohio County, commemorates the name of Governor [John] Tyler [1808-1811] [the father of President John Tyler]". (Brock, i, 108).

• UPPER NORFOLK:
(1637-1642) The upper portion of "New Norfolk", q. v.

w UPSHUR:
(1851) "named in honor of the lamented Abel P[arker] Upshur, * * *, one of the judges of the General Court [1826-1841], and served as a member of the Constitutional Convention of 1829-30, [and Secretary of State under Tyler]". (Lewis, 719).

WARREN:
(1836) "named for [Major-General] Joseph Warren, who fell in the Battle of Bunker Hill." (U. S., 315; Green, 60; Long, 111).

• WARROSQUYOAKE:
(1634-1637) "A tribe of the former Powhatan Confederacy, living on the south bank of James river in [the limits of the present] Isle of Wight County, Va." The word means "swamp in a depression of land". (H. A. I.) For etymology, meanings and variants, see H. A. I.

WARWICK:
(1642/3) "Named after Robert Rich, Earl of Warwick, a prominent member of the Virginia Company." (Green, 60; Brown's "First Republic," 313; Long, 64; U. S., 316).

• WARWICK RIVER:
(1634-1642/3) See "Warwick", although this county was first so named.

WASHINGTON:
(1777) "it is a fact that this is the first locality in the United States that was honored with the name of the 'Father of Our Country' ". (Summers, "History of Southwest Virginia", 226; Long, 156).

w WAYNE:
(1842) "shall form one distinct and new county, and be called and known by the name of Wayne County, in memory and in honor of General Anthony Wayne." (A., 1841-42, 37).

w WEBSTER:
(1860) "named in honor of Daniel Webster." (Lewis, 729).

WESTMORELAND:
(1653) "named from the county in England." (U. S., 321; Long, 91). "Uncertainty as to its naming." (Green, 60).

w WETZEL:
(1846) "named in honor of Louis Wetzel, the distinguished frontiersman and Indian scout,—the Boone of Northwestern Virginia." (Lewis, 687).

w WIRT:
(1848) "named in honor of the distinguished William Wirt." (Lewis, 697).

WISE:
(1856) "A county of Virginia was named in honor of Governor [Henry Alexander] Wise [1856-1860]." (Brock, i, p. 230; Long, 149).

w WOOD:
(1798) "The county was named in honor of James Wood, the son of Colonel James Wood, the founder of Winchester, Virginia, * * *. He was elected Governor of the State, December 1, 1796, and served until December 1, 1799." (Lewis, p. 585).

kWOODFORD:
(1789) "Gen. William Woodford, in honor of whom this county received its name, a Revolutionary officer of high merit, was born in Caroline County, Virginia. He early distinguished himself in the French and Indian War." (Collins, ii, p. 769).

w WYOMING:
(1850) "The origin of the name [as applied to this county] is involved in obscurity." (Lewis, p. 713). For etymology, meanings and variants, see H. A. I.

WYTHE:
(1790) "named after George Wythe, a signer of the declaration of Independence." (U. S., p. 331; Heuser's "Wythe County", p. 1).

• YOHOGANIA:
(1776-1786) "An Indian word [Youghhiogheny] meaning 'stream flowing in an opposite direction'", of which the name of the county is obviously a variant. (U. S., p. 333). For etymology, meanings and variants, see H. A. I.

YORK:
(1842/3) "Was named after Charles, Duke of York, afterwards Prince of Wales, and Charles I. Charles was King when the county

received its name, but 'York Plantation', the nucleus of the county, had existed a number of years." (Green, p. 60; U. S., p. 333; Long, 34).

"It was named in honor of James, then Duke of York, afterwards James II. He was created Duke of York in 1642/3, the same year Charles River County in Virginia was changed to York". (Lyon G. Tyler).

Of the one hundred and seventy-two counties thus named, seventy-two were formed by the Colony, and we find that the loyalty of the colonists to the Mother Country was strikingly reflected in these names, the sources of which seem to have been (for names of the counties in each group, see below):

> Reigning house in England, and members thereof,.................. 25;
> Localities,—former English homes of the colonists,................ 19;
> Governors appointed by the Crown,............................. 12;
> Englishmen of prominence who had befriended the Colony,......... 8;
> Indian tribes which had owned the areas of these counties,....... 8.
>
> Counties named by the Colony,......................... 72.

Of the remaining one hundred counties, which were named by the State, the sources of the names seem to have been (for names of the counties in each group, see below):

> Soldiers(chiefly Revolutionary), ... 23;
> Governors, ... 19;
> Revolutionary patriots, statesmen, etc., ... 14;
> Indian tribes and personages, ... 14;
> Virginians of prominence (jurists, senators, officials, etc.),........ 11;
> Presidents of the United States, ... 5;
> American statesmen, ... 3;
> Natural features, ... 3;
> Englishmen of prominence, connected with colonial affairs,........ 2;
> Frontiersmen and hunters, ... 2;
> English queen, ... 1;
> Land-owner's family 1;
> Re-adjuster legislator, ... 1;
> Royal family of France .... 1.
>
> Counties named by the State,......................... 100.

Counties resulting from Virginia legislation,................172.

NAMED BY THE COLONY IN HONOR OF:

KINGS AND QUEENS,—

Amelia,	Elizabeth City,	King William,
Augusta,	Frederick,	Louisa,
Brunswick,	Gloucester,	Lunenburg,
Caroline,	Hanover,	Mecklenburg,
Charles City,	Henrico,	Orange,
Charles River,	James City,	Princess Anne,
Charlotte,	King and Queen,	Prince Edward,
Cumberland,	King George,	Prince George,
		Prince William,.....25;

Virginia Counties

LOCALITIES,—

Bedford,	Lower Norfolk,	Northumberland,
Buckingham(?),	Middlesex,	Stafford,
Essex,	New Kent,	Surry,
Hampshire,	New Norfolk,	Sussex,
Isle of Wight,	Norfolk,	Upper Norfolk,
Lancaster,	Northampton,	Westmoreland,
		York, ...19;

GOVERNORS,—

Albemarle,	Culpeper	Fincastle,
Amherst,	Dinwiddie,	Goochland,
Berkeley,	Dunmore.	Loudoun,
Botetourt,	Fauquier.	Spotsylvania, ...12;

ENGLISHMEN,—

Chesterfield,	Pittsylvania,	Warwick.
Fairfax,	Richmond,	Warwick River,..... 8;
Halifax,	Southampton,	

INDIANS (or with Indian words),—

Accawmack (1634),	Nansemond,	Warrosquyoake,
Accomack (1663),	Ohio,	Yohogania, ... 8;
Monongalia,	Rappahannock (1656),	

72.

NAMED BY THE STATE IN HONOR OF:

SOLDIERS,—

Campbell,	Lincoln,	Russell,
Clarke,	Marion,	Scott,
Fayette (1780),	Mercer (1786),	Smyth,
Fayette (1831),	Mercer (1837),	Taylor,
Grayson,	Montgomery,	Warren,
Greene,	Morgan,	Wayne,
Greensville,	Pulaski,	Woodford, ...23;
Lewis,	Putnam,	

GOVERNORS,—

Brooke,	Henry,	Nicholas,
Cabell,	Jefferson,	Page,
Floyd,	Lee,	Pleasants,
Giles,	McDowell,	Preston,
Gilmer,	Nelson (1786),	Tyler,
Harrison,	Nelson (1808),	Wise,
		Wood, ...19;

REVOLUTIONARY PATRIOTS,—

Bland,	Hardy,	Patrick,
Braxton,	Mason (1789),	Pendleton,
Carroll,	Mason (1804),	Randolph,
Franklin,	Marshall,	Wythe, ...14;
Hancock,	Mathews,	

INDIANS (or with Indian words),—

Alleghany,	Kentucky,	Rappahannock (1833),
Appomattox,	Logan,	Roanoke,
Greenbrier,	Nottoway,	Shenandoah,
Illinois,	Pocahontas,	Wyoming 14;
Kanawha,	Powhatan,	

VIRGINIANS OF PROMINENCE,—

Barbour,	Madison, (1793),	Tucker,
Craig,	Ritchie,	Upshur,
Doddridge,	Roane,	Wirt, ...11;
Madison, (1786),	Tazewell.	

PRESIDENTS OF U. S.,—

Buchanan,	Jefferson,	Washington, ...5;
Jackson,	Monroe,	

AMERICAN STATESMEN,—

Calhoun,	Clay,	Webster, ... 3;

NATURAL FEATURES,—

Bath,	Highland,	Rockbridge, ... 3;

ENGLISHMEN,—

Raleigh,	Rockingham, ... 2;

FRONTIERSMEN,—

Boone,	Wetzel, ... 2;

ENGLISH QUEEN,—

Fluvanna, ... 1;

LAND-OWNER'S FAMILY,—

Alexandria, ... 1;

RE-ADJUSTER LEGISLATOR,—

Dickenson, ... 1;

ROYAL FAMILY OF FRANCE,—

Bourbon, ... 1;

                                                                100.

Counties resulting from Virginia legislation,....................172.

PART VI.

TEXTS OF ACTS OF ASSEMBLY (CONCERNING COUNTIES) WHICH DO NOT APPEAR IN HENING

On April 20th, 1916, Mr. Earl G. Swem, Assistant State Librarian, discovered in the Library a full-text copy of the Acts passed "at a Grand Assembly summoned the 6th January 1639", which Acts appear in Hening (1, 224) only in the most abridged form,—one of which (see Chap. 1, below) defines the bounds of Isle of Wight, Upper Norfolk and Lower Norfolk Counties; while An Act [Concerning the Bounds of the Countyes of Nancemund and the Isle of Wight] "passed at the sessions of 1643-1646" is quoted from the "Virginia Magazine of History and Biography", xxiii (July, 1915), 254-5.

The Library had before also been fortunate enough to locate in the Public Record Office in London original manuscript copies of nine Acts of Assembly (forming counties) which do not appear in Hening, copies of which are here printed in full (Chaps. iii to xi, below) for the first time, so far as we have been able to ascertain. Certain it is that those forming these counties appear in Hening by title only, under the references cited:

>   Prince George, passed August 25, 1702 (Hening iii, 223);
>   King George, passed November 24, 1720 (Hening iv, 95);
>   Hanover, passed November 26, 1720 (Hening iv, 95);
>   Goochland, passed March 6, 1727 (Hening iv, 240);
>   Caroline, passed March 15, 1727 (Hening iv, 240);—

> while the following are not even mentioned by title in Hening (vols. 6 and 7):

>   Culpeper, passed March 23, 1748;
>   Cumberland, passed March 23, 1748;
>   Southampton, passed April 30, 1749;
>   Chesterfield, passed May 1, 1749.

The notes appended to the titles of these Acts (Chaps. iii to xi) carry the references current in the Public Record Office in London.

It is hoped that these full-text copies will be of interest to those who are preparing histories of the counties referred to.

CHAP. I.

[An Act Concerning the Bounds of Isle of Wight, Upper Norfolk and Lower Norfolk Counties]*

[Passed at session of January 1639/40.]

It is thought fitt and enacted for a finall Determination of all differences between the Isle of Wight county and the Upper and Lower Norfolk counties that the Isle of Wight county shall begin at Lawnes creek and from thence to extend down along the main River unto the plantation of Richard haies formerly belonging unto John Seward including the s^d plantation & famelies and from thence to extend from the main River into the Woods Southerly unto the plantation of William Nowell and M^r. Robt. Pitt including likewise the s^d plantation and families and from thence Southerly as afores^d. And the Upper county of New Norfolk to begin at the afores^d. plantation of Rich^d. Haies and from thence into the Woods Southerly as aforesaid and by the main River from thence to extend down by the main River unto the creek near the plantation of Francis Bullock being the first creek to the Westward of Cranye Point including the plantation of the s^d Francis Bullock and no ways intrenching upon the Western branch of Elizabeth river nor the creek thereof wch do belong to the county of Lower Norfolk. These bounds being sett and Limitted by the consent and agreem^t of the Burgesses for the s^d counties. And it is further thought fitt that these bounds be as well for the s^d parishes as the counties and that all former Acts of assembly concerning the same by virtue of this Act be repealed and made void.

---

* On April 20th, 1916, Mr. Earl G. Swem, Assistant State Librarian, discovered in the Library a full-text copy of the Acts passed "at a Grand Assembly summoned the 6th Jany. 1639", which Acts appear in Hening (i, 224) only in the most abridged form. In a letter from Mr. Conway Robinson to Governor Giles, under date of February 20th, 1829, Mr. Robinson states to His Excellency that he had found the original which he used in the General Court Office, and had caused a copy of it to be made, which copy he was enclosing to the Governor with the suggestion that provision be made for its publication.

This Act is XXII of those appearing in the manuscript and corresponds with the abridgement appearing on p. 228 of volume 1 of Hening.

CHAP. II.

[An Act Concerning the Bounds of the Countyes of Nancemund and the Isle of Wight]*

[Passed at Session of November, 1647.]

Whereas many differences have beene and are likely to arise through the uncertaine division of the bounds of the countyes of Nancemund and the Isle of Wight as they are sett downe by Acts of Assembly Ao. 1642: Whereby it was expressed that the bounds of Nancemund should stretch southerly into the woods from the plantacon of Richard Hayes upon the main River, wch bounds through the uncertainty of them have occasioned many disputes and controversies tending to discord and disorder bee it therefore enacted for the better understanding and more certaine knowledge of the westerne bounds of the said County of Nancemund. That the plantacon of Richard Hayes upon the maine River shall bee and remayne in the County of the Isle of Wight according to tenor of the said Act Ao. 1642. That the whole track of land belongeing unto M^r ffantleroy shall bee and remayne in the County of

(Rest of manuscript gone)

---

* From the "Virginia Magazine of History and Biography," xxiii (July, 1915), 254-5.

CHAP. III.

An Act for Dividing Charles City County.*

[Passed August 25, 1702.]

Whereas Sundry & diverse inconveniencies attend the Inhabitants of that part of Charles City County wch lyes on the South side of James river when they have any occasion to prosecute Law Suites in the s^d County Court or to go to any other publick meeting by reason of the Difficulty in passing James River Be it Enacted, by the Govern^r Councill & Burgesses of this present Gener^{ll} Assembly And by the Authority thereof And it is hereby Enacted that on and after the 23^d day of Apr^{ll} wch shall be in the year of our Ld God 1703 the s^d County of Charles City be divided into two distinct Counties so that James River divide ye Same And that, that part of the said County wch is & lyes on the North side of the said James river shall for ever thereafter be called & knowne by the name of Charles City County. And that that part of the s^d County wch is & lyes on the South side of the said river shall remain and for ever thereafter be called & knowne by ye name of Prince George County. & for the due administracon of Justice. Be it further Enacted by the Authority afores^d & it is hereby Enacted y^t after the time afores^d a Court for the said Prince George County be constantly held by the Justices thereof upon the Second Wednesday of every month in such manner as by the Laws of this Country is Provided And shall be by their Commission directed & whereas the towne Land Lying at fflowerdy hund^d was purchased by the intire County of Charles City as then it was all ye charges about the Same being equally Levied upon the whole number of Tithables of the said County Be it Enacted by the Authority aforesaid & it is hereby Enacted that one third of the Tob^o ariseing from the Sailes of the said towne Land to the Several takers up thereof be repaid to the Inhabitants that shall be for the time being on the North side of the s^d James river in Charles City County upon ye takeing up of the said towne Land.

[No Endorsement.]

---

* C. O. 5. 1313. No. 16v.
[From a set of Acts passed in the session beginning August 14, 1702.]

CHAP. IV.

An Act for dividing Richmond County.*

[Passed November 24, 1720.]

WHEREAS diverse and Sundry Inconvenienceys attend the Upper Inhabitants of the Said County by reason of their Great distance from the Court-House and other places usually appointed for publick meetings.
BE it therefore ENACTED by the Lieu^t Govern^r Council and Burgesses

of this present General Assembly And It is hereby Enacted by the Authority thereof That from and Imediately after the Twenty Third day of Aprill which Shall be in the Year of Our Lord One Thousand Seven Hundred and Twenty One The Said County of Richmond be divided into Two distinct Countys and that the Same be divided by Charles Bever dams And from the Head thereof by a North Course to Westmoreland County And that that part of the County lyeing below the Said Dams and Course remain and Shall for Ever thereafter be called and knowne by the Name of Richmond County And that part of the County which is above the Said Dams and Course Shall be called and knowne by the Name of King George County And for the due Administration of Justice

BE it further ENACTED by the Authority aforesaid and it is hereby Enacted That after the Time aforesaid A Court for the said King George County be constantly held by the Justices thereof upon the First Friday of Every Month in Such maner as by the Laws of this Country is provided and shall be by their Comission directed.

ex)   J. Randolph. C H B.

[Endorsed:]

13. Virginia. Virginia Septimo Georgy. 1720. AN ACT For dividing Richmond County. reced wth Col^o Spotwood's Lre of 6th March 1720/1.

Reced 8th May 1721. Sent to Mr West 30 Novr 1723. Reced back 16 Jan^{ry} 1723/4. Read. Reported.

---

* C. O. 5. 1387.
Anno. 1720—

CHAP. V.

An Act For dividing New Kent County.*

[Passed November 26, 1720.]

WHEREAS many Inconveniencys attend the Upper Inhabitants of the said County by reason of their Great distance from the Court house and other places usually appointed for publick meetings.

BE it therefore ENACTED by the Lieu^t Govr Council and Burgesses of this present General Assembly And It is hereby Enacted by the Authority of the Same That from and Imediately after the ffirst day of May next the Said County of New Kent be divided into Two distinct Countys And that that part of the County lyeing below the parish of Saint Paul shall for Ever thereafter be called and knowne by the Name of New Kent County And that that part of the County which lyeth in the parish of St Paul shall be called and knowne by the Name of Hannover County And for the due Administration of Justice

BE it further ENACTED by the Authority aforesaid And it is hereby Enacted That after the Time aforesaid a Court for the said County of Hannover be constantly held by the Justices thereof upon the First Friday of Every Month in Such maner as by the Laws of this Country is provided and Shall be by their Comission directed.

ex) J. Randolph. C H B

[Endorsed:]

15 Virginia. Virginia Septimo Georgy. 1720. An Act For dividing New Kent County. reced wth Col^l Spotswoods Lre of 6th March 1720/1. Reced 8th May 1721. Sent to Mr West 30th Novr 1723. Reced back 16 Jan^{ry} 1723/4. Read. Reported.

* C. O. 5. 1387.
Anno. 1720—
(13)

CHAP. VI.

An Act For dividing the County of Henrico.*

[Passed March 6, 1727.]

WHEREAS many Inconveniencies attend the upper Inhabitants of the County of Henrico by reason of their Great distance from the Court-house and other places usually appointed for Public Meetings

BE IT THEREFORE ENACTED by the Lieutenant Governor Council and Burgesses of this present General Assembly And it is hereby Enacted by the Authority of the same That from and immediately after the First day of May next the said County of Henrico be divided into two distinct Counties—And that the Division be made by a Line on the North side James River beginning at the mouth of Tuckahoe Creek thence up the said Creek to Chumley's Branch thence along a line of marked Trees North Twenty degrees East to Hanover County And on the South side James River begining at the Lower Manachin Creek from thence along a line of marked Trees in a direct course to the mouth of Skinquarter Creek on Appamatox River And that that part of the County lying below the said line shall for ever hereafter be called & known by the name of Henrico County And that that part of the County lying above the said line shall be called & known by by the name of Goochland County And that all that part of the Parish of Henrico lying above the said line shall be included in and be part of the Parish of Saint James And that all that part of the sd Parish of Saint James lying below the said line shall be included in and be part of the Parish of Henrico any Act usage or Custom to the contrary thereof in any wise notwithstanding. And for the Administration of Justice BE IT FURTHER ENACTED by the Authority aforesd and it is hereby Enacted That after the time aforesd a Court for the said County of Goochland be constantly held by the Justices thereof upon the third Tuesday of every Month in such manner as by the Laws of this Country is provided and shall be by their Commission directed.

AND WHEREAS there have been several sums of Tobacco levied by the Court of the said County of Henrico for Wolves heads more than sufficient to satisfie the proportion of the Public Levy due from the same. BE IT THEREFORE ENACTED by the Authority aforesaid And it is hereby Enacted That so much of the Overplus of the said several sums of Tobacco or of the money for which the same have been sold as exceeds the proportion of the Public Levy due from the said County of Henrico and which have not already been expended for the use of the said County and all such other Tobacco as is now due to the said County of Henrico for Wolves heads Be divided and paid between the said Counties of Henrico and Goochland Two thirds thereof to the said County of Henrico and the other third to the said County of Goochland for defraying the charge of Public Buildings in each County.

[Endorsed:]

No 17. Virginia. At a General Assembly Begun and held at Williamsburg the first day of February in the first year of the Reign of Our Soverain Lord George II. By the Grace of God of Great Britain France & Ireland, King Defender of the Faith &c. and in the year of Our Lord MDCCXXVII.

An Act For dividing the County of Henrico. Its Effects Perpetual

Rec^d 30th of July 1728. Sent to Mr Fane Oct^{br} ye 8th
Rec^d ba'k Novemb^r 15th } 1728
Read,
Reported,

* C. O. 5. 1338. p. 101-2.

CHAP. VII.

An Act for erecting a new County on the heads of Essex, King and Queen and King William Counties And for calling the same Caroline County.*

[Passed March 15, 1727.]

WHEREAS divers and sundry Inconveniencies attend the upper Inhabitants of the Counties of Essex, King & Queen and King William by reason of their great distance from their respective Court houses and other places usually appointed for Public Meetings,

BE IT THEREFORE ENACTED by the Lieutenant Governor Council and Burgesses of this present General Assembly And it is hereby Enacted by the Authority of the same That from & immediately after the First day of May MDCCXXVIII all the land lying between the Lower line of Spotsilvania County and a line to be run paralel therewith from the mouth of Portobago Creek on Rappahanock River to Morocosick Creek thence down the said Creek to Mattapony River thence up the said River to Boot Swamp and up the said Swamp to the Fork thereof and thence South West to Pamunkey River be divided from the said Counties of Essex, King & Queen and King William and made a distinct County to be from thenceforth known and called by the name of Caroline County And that all and every the Inhabitants thereof be separated & exempt from the said Counties and from all Dependences Offices and Charges for or in respect thereof and also discharged from all duties whatsoever relating to the same except the charge and duties of clearing the Rivers of Mattapony and Pamunkey respectively Which shall be done and performed by the Inhabitants of that part of the said new County now included in the Counties of King & Queen and King William, respectively in such manner as if this act had never been made. And for the due administration of Justice in the s^d new erected County, BE IT FURTHER ENACTED by the authority afores^d And it is hereby Enacted That after the time aforesaid a Court for the said County of Caroline be constantly held by the Justices thereof upon the second Thursday in every month in such manner as by the Laws of this Country is provided and shall be by their Commission directed.

AND WHEREAS it is suggested to this assembly That the County of King William at the laying the last County Levy did raise a considerable sum of Tobacco for defraying some public charge of the County which is not yet expended,

BE IT ENACTED by the Authority aforesaid That if either of the said Counties have levied any Tobacco for Public uses which is not yet laid out & expended such County respectively shall at the laying the next Levy raise and pay to the Inhabitants taken out of the same County their full proportion of the Tobacco so raised and not yet expended to be applied for lessning the Levy of the said Inhabitants.

AND WHEREAS the said Counties have considerable Claims from the Public for killing of Wolves,

BE IT ALSO ENACTED by the authority afores^d That each of the s^d Counties respectively shall contribute their Proportions of the said Claims to the Inhabitants taken out of the said Counties into the County of Caroline according to their number of Tithables to be applied towards building of a Court house for the said County of Caroline.

[Endorsed:]

No 18. Virginia.

At a general Assembly Begun and held at Williamsburg the first day of February in the first year of the Reign of Our Soverain Lord George II. By the Grace of God of Great Britain France & Ireland King Defender of the Faith &c. And in the year of Our Lord MDCCXXVII.

An Act For erecting a new County on the heads of Essex, King and Queen and King William Counties And for calling the same Caroline County. Perpetual.

Rec^d 30 July 1728. Sent to Mr Fane, Octo^{br} 8th }
Rec^d back, Novem^{br} ye 15th } 1728.
Read,
Reported.

---

* C. O. 5. 1388. P. 103-4.

CHAP. VIII.

An Act for dividing the County of Orange.*

[Passed March 23, 1748.]

FOR the greater Ease and Convenience of the Inhabitants of the County of Orange in attending Courts and other public Meetings Be it Enacted by the Lieutenant Governor Council and Burgesses of this present General Assembly and it is hereby enacted by the Authority of the same that from and immediately after the seventeenth day of May next ensuing the said County of Orange shall be divided into two Counties that is to say all that part of the County lying on the south side of Rappahanock River to the Head of the Conway River shall be one distinct County and retain the Name of Orange County and all that other part thereof on the north side the said Rappahanock and Conway River commonly called the Fork of the Rappahanock River shall be one other distinct County and called and known by the Name of Culpeper County And that for the due Administration of Justice after the said seventeenth day of May a Court for the said County of Orange be constantly held by the Justices thereof upon the fourth Thursday and a Court for the said County of Culpeper be constantly held by the Justices thereof upon the third Thursday in every Month in such Manner as by the Laws of this Colony is provided and shall be by their Commissions directed PROVIDED always that nothing herein contained shall be construed to hinder the Sherif or Collector of the said County of Orange as the same now stands entire and undivided to make Distress for any Levies Fees or Dues which shall be due from the said County of Culpeper after the said seventeenth day of May in such Manner and not otherwise as by Law he might have done if this Act had never been made any Law Custom or Usage to the contrary thereof nothwithstanding.

March 22. 1748. Read the third time & passed the House of Burgesses.
           Peter Randolph C. H. B.
           William Gooch
           John Robinson Speaker

March 23. 1748 Read the 3ᵈ Time & agreed to by the Council.
           N. Walthoe C. G. A.

A Copy Test William Randolph C. H. B.

[Endorsed:]

Virginia. At a General Assembly begun and held at the College in Williamsburg on Thursday the Twenty seventh day of October in the Twenty second year of the Reign of our Sovereign Lord George the Second by the Grace of God of Great Britain France and Ireland King Defender of the Faith &c. And in the year of our Lord 1748. Numʳ 34.

An Act for dividing the County of Orange.

Passed yᵉ 10th of May 1749. Recᵈ with Colᵒ Lee's Letter dated yᵉ 6th Novbʳ 1749.
Recᵈ March yᵉ 19th 1749/50.
Sent to Mʳ Lamb May yᵉ 21ˢᵗ 1750.
Recᵈ back Febʳʸ yᵉ 8th 1750/1.

Exᵈ 34.

No Objection
Great Seal of Virginia
taken off pr. S. G.

*C. O. Class 5. Vol. 1394.

CHAP. IX.

An Act for dividing the County of Goochland.*

[Passed March 23, 1748.]

For the Ease and Convenience of the Inhabitants of the County of Goochland in attending Courts and other public Meetings Be it enacted by the Lieutenant Governor Council and Burgesses of this present General Assembly and (ms. defective) [it is] hereby enacted by the authority of the same That from and immediately after the twentieth day of May next ensuing the said County of Goochland be divided into two Counties that is to say all that part of the said County of Goochland lying on the south side of James River shall be one distinct County and called by the Name of Cumberland County and all that other part of the said County of Goochland on the noth side of James River aforesaid shall be one other distinct County and retain the Name of Goochland County And for the due Administration of Justice after the said twentieth day of May a Court for the said County of Cumberlalnd be constantly held by the Justices thereof upon the fourth Monday and a Court for the said County of Goochland be constantly held by the Justices thereof upon the third Tuesday in every Month in such Manner as by the Laws of this Colony is provided and shall be by their Commissions directed PROVIDED always that nothing herein contained shall be construed to hinder the Sherif or Collector of the said County of Goochland as the same now stands entire and undivided to make Distress for any Levies Fees or Dues which shall be due from the said County of Cumberland after the said twentieth day of May in such Manner and not otherwise as by Law he might have done if this Act had never been made any Law Custom or Usage to the contrary thereof nothwithstanding.

March 22ᵈ 1748. Read 3ᵈ Time & passed the House of Burgesses.

Peter Randolph C. H. B.
William Gooch
John Robinson Speaker

March 23. 1748 Read the third Time & agreed by the Council.

N. Walthoe C G. A.

A Copy William Randolph C. H. B.

[Endorsed:]

Virginia. At a General Assembly begun and held at the College in Williamsburg on Thursday the Twenty seventh day of October in the Twenty second year of the Reign of our Sovereign Lord George the Second by the Grace of God of Great Britain France and Ireland King Defender of the Faith &c. And in the year of our Lord 1748. Num^r 35.

An Act for dividing the County of Goochland Passed ye 10th of May 1749. Rec^d with Col^o Lee's Letter dated ye 6th Nov^{br} 1749.

Rec^d March ye 19th 1749/50.

Sent to Mr Lamb May ye 21st 1750:

Rec^d back Feb^{ry} ye 8th 1750/1.

No Objection
Great Seal of Virginia
taken off pr. S. G.

Ex^d 35.

* C. O. Class 5. Vol. 1394.

CHAP. X.

An Act for dividing the County of Isle of Wight into two distinct Counties and for other purposes therein mentioned.*

[Passed April 30, 1749.]

WHEREAS divers Inconveniencies attend the outer Inhabitants of Isle of Wight County by reason of their great Distance from the Court-house and other places appointed for public Meetings Be it therefore enacted by the Lieutenant Governor Council and Burgesses of this present General Assembly And it is hereby enacted by the Authority of the same That from and immediately after the twentieth day of May next the said County of Isle of Wight be divided into two distinct Counties by the River Black Water and that part of the said County which lies to the east of the said River be erected into one distinct County and retain the Name of Isle of Wight and all that other part thereof to the West of the said River be one other distinct County and called by the Name of the County of Southampton And for the due Administration of Justice Be it further Enacted by the authority aforesaid that after the said Twentieth day of May a Court for the said County of Southampton be constantly held by the Justices thereof on the second Thursday in every Month in such Manner as by the Laws of this Colony is provided and shall be by their Commissions directed PROVIDED always that nothing herein shall be construed to restrain the Sherif of the said County of Isle of Wight as it now stands intire and undivided to make Distress for any Levies Fees or other Dues which shall be due from the Inhabitants of the said County after the said twentieth day of May next in such Manner and not otherwise as by Law he might have done if this Act had never been made any Law Custom or Usage to the Contrary thereof in any wise notwithstanding AND whereas there is now in the Hands of Ethelred Taylor of the said County of Isle of Wight Gentleman about one Hundred and Twelve Pounds Current Money also a Quantity of Tobacco which has been levied by the Court of the said County to defray the Contingent Charges thereof AND whereas by reason of the great Number of Bridges in the said County of Southampton which are now maintained at the Charge of the said County of Isle of Wight the Levies of the Inhabitants of the said County of Southampton by the Division aforesaid will be greatly increased and the Inhabitants of the said County of Isle of Wight as it now stands intire and undivided have mutually agreed that the said Money and Tobacco shall remain to the seperate use of the of the County of Southampton aforesaid Be it therefore further Enacted by the Authority aforesaid That the said Money and Tobacco from and after the aforesaid twentieth day of May, shall be vested in the Justices of the Court of the said County of Southampton and their Successors to and for the use of the said County to be by the said Justices and their Successors applied towards maintaining the aforesaid Bridges and defraying the other contingent Charges of the said County PROVIDED nevertheless that nothing herein contained shall be construed deemed or taken to discharge the Inhabitants of the said County of Southampton from contributing towards building a Bridge over the said River Blackwater at a place called Proctors Ferry but that the same shall be erected built and maintained at the Expence of the said Counties of Isle of Wight and Southampton respectively in proportion to the Number of Tithable Persons in each of the said Counties AND Be it further Enacted by the Authority aforesaid that from and after the aforesaid twentieth day of May the Court for the County of Isle of Wight shall be constantly held on the first Thursday in every Month any Law Custom or Usage to the Contrary in anywise nothwithstanding.

April 18. 1749 Read the third Time & passed the House of Burgesses.

        Peter Randolph C. H. B.
        William Gooch
        John Robinson Speaker

April 20. 1749 Read the third Time & agreed to by the Council.

        N. Walthoe C. G. A.
   Copy William Randolph C. H. B.

[Endorsed:]

Virginia. At a General Assembly begun and held at the College in Williamsburg on Thursday the Twenty seventh day of October in the Twenty second year of the Reign of our Sovereign Lord George the Second by the Grace of God of Great Britain France and Ireland King Defender of the Faith &c. And in the year of our Lord 1748. Num^r 15.

An Act for dividing the County of Isle of Wight into two distinct Counties and for other purposes therein mentioned.

Passed ye 11th of May 1749.
Rec^d with Col^o Lee's Letter dated ye 6th Novr 1749.
Rec^d March ye 19th 1749/50.
Sent to Mr Lamb May ye 21st 1750.
Rec^d back Feb^{ry} ye 8th 1750/1.

           No Objection
           Great Seal of Virg^a
           taken off pr. S. G.

Ex^d 15.

---

* C. O. Class 5. Vol. 1395.

CHAP. XI.

An Act for dividing the County of Henrico into two distinct counties.*

[Passed May 1, 1749.]

FOR the Ease and convenience of the Inhabitants of the County of Henrico in attending Courts and other public Meetings Be it Enacted by the Lieutenant Governor Council and Burgesses of this present General Assembly and it is hereby enacted by the Authority of the same That from and immediately after the twenty fifth day of May next ensuing the said County of Henrico be divided into two Counties that is to say all that Part of the said County of Henrico lying on the south side of James River shall be one distinct County and called by the Name of Chesterfield County and all that other part of the said County of Henrico on the north side of James River aforesaid shall be one other distinct County and retain the Name of Henrico AND that for the due Administration of Justice after the said twenty-fifth day of May a Court for the said County of Chesterfield be constantly held by the Justices thereof upon the first Friday and a Court for the said County of Henrico be constantly held by the Justices thereof upon the first Monday in every Month in such Manner as by the Laws of this Colony is provided and shall be by their Commissions directed PROVIDED alway that nothing herein contained shall be construed to hinder the Sherif or Collector of the said County of Henrico as the same now stands intire and undivided to make Distress for any Levies Fees or Dues which shall be due from the said County of Chesterfield after the said twenty fifth day of May in such Manner and not otherwise as by Law he might have done if this Act had never been made any Law Custom or Usage to the Contrary thereof notwithstanding.

April 27. 1749 Read the third time & passed the House of Burgesses.

William Randolph C. H. B.
William Gooch
John Robinson Speaker

May 1. 1749. Read the third time & agreed to by the Council.

A Copy Test   N. Walthoe C. G. A.

William Randolph C. H. B.

[Endorsed:]

Virginia. At a General Assembly begun and held at the College in Williamsburg on Thursday the Twenty seventh day of October in the Twenty second year of the Reign of our Sovereign Lord George the Second by the Grace of God of Great Britain France and Ireland King Defender of the Faith &c. and in the year of our Lord 1748. Numr 27.

An Act for dividing the County of Henrico into two distinct Counties.
Passed ye 11th of May 1749.
Recd with Colo Lee's Letter dated ye 6th Novr 1749.
Recd March ye 19th 1749/50.
Sent to Mr Lamb May ye 21st 1750.
Recd back Febry ye 8th 1750/1.

Exd 27.

No Objection
Great Seal of Virga
taken off pr. S. G.

---

* C. O. Class 5. Vol. 1395.

PART VII.

BIBLIOGRAPHY

This bibliography in a way follows the plan of the preface as a whole, in that there is a "general" group, which contains the various official Virginia collections of information touching all the counties in a greater or less degree, while there are grouped under the name of each of the counties such additional titles as the Library contains (as of October 1, 1915) which relate to that particular county,—these county-groups being based directly upon Assistant State Librarian Earl G. Swem's "Bibliography of Virginia, Part I" (Virginia State Library Bulletin, vol. 8, Nos. 2, 3, 4— April, July, October, 1915), to which acknowledgment is hereby gratefully made, and to which the student is referred for fuller and more detailed data than are here given. As the Library does not contain separate histories of all the counties resulting from Virginia legislation, which are now in other jurisdictions, there have been utilized in those cases such available histories of Kentucky and West Virginia as seem to contain the desired information, although bearing the titles of state histories; and in the case of Yohogania County recourse has been had to a history of Westmoreland County in western Pennsylvania.

In the titles given under the various counties it has been thought proper to include printed speeches and addresses delivered before audiences in those counties—if in any case such information is conveyed on the title page— books, pamphlets, etc., whose title pages connect their authors with these counties in any way, and in some cases the biographies of natives of the counties. The effort has not been made, however, to collect in the case of any county a full list of the biographies in which information in reference to that county may be found. Such biographies, it is hardly necessary to say, frequently contain a large amount of valuable information for the worker in local history.

One cannot but be struck by the fact that there are at least fourteen counties[*] in the present State of Virginia for which not a single separate title is now available in the Library; and it is hoped that this presentation of the paucity of such material will stimulate others to add to this all-too-meagre collection.

The bibliography follows:

GENERAL:

    Acts of the General Assembly of Virginia, 1776 to 1879-'80.
    Hening's Statutes at Large, vols. 1 to xiii.
    Howe's Historical Collections of Virginia—several editions, the first of which was printed in 1845.

---

[*] Bland, Buchanan, Carroll, Craig, Dickenson, Floyd, Giles, Greene, Lee, Nelson, Patrick, Pulaski, Rappahannock (1833) and Russell.

Journals of the House of Burgesses, 1619 to 1776 (Virginia State Library: 1905-1915).
Journals of the House of Delegates, 1776 to 1879-'80.
Journals of the Senate, 1776 to 1879-'80.
Shepherd's Statutes at Large (continuation of Hening), vols. i to iii.
Williams's Index to Enrolled Bills of the General Assembly of Virginia, 1776 to 1910 (Richmond: 1911).

• ACCOMACK :*

Brent, Frank Pierce. Some unpublished facts, relating to Bacon's rebellion on the Eastern Shore of Virginia, gleaned from the court records of Accomac County. A paper read before the Virginia historical society, Tuesday, December 22, 1891, by Professor Frank P. Brent . . .
    (In Virginia historical society. Collections. Richmond, 1892. new series, v. 11)

Eckenrode, Hamilton James. . . . A calendar of legislative petitions, arranged by counties: Accomac-Bedford. Special report of the Department of archives and history, H. J. Eckenrode, archivist. Richmond, D. Bottom, supt. of public printing, 1908.
    (In Virginia state library. 5th report, 1908)

Joynes, Levin Smith. . . . A sketch of the life of Thomas R. Joynes, of Accomack, Virginia; with a brief notice of his father, Col. Levin Joynes. By Levin S. Joynes, M. D. [n. p.] 1876.
    38 p.

McMaster, John Stephenson. Makemieland. An address delivered May 14, 1908, at the unveiling, etc., of the monument at Holden's Creek, Accomack County, Virginia to the Rev. Francis Makemie, founder of the organized Presbyterian church in America. By John Stevenson McMaster. [1908]
    16 p. plate (port.)

[Scarburgh, George P.] An address to the people of the county of Accomac, [upon the subject of the division of the Methodist Episcopal church]
    29 p.
    Signed by George P. Scarburgh and 15 others.

Segar, Joseph E. To the voters of Accomac and Northampton. n. p. [1863]
    3 p.

Virginia historical society. Collections of the Virginia historical society. New series. v. 11.

Virginia magazine of history and biography. v. 5, 19.

William and Mary college quarterly historical magazine. v. 7, 18.

* Covers both old (1634 to 1642/3) and new (1663) Accomack.

Williamson, Robert. . . . A brief history of the origin and progress of the Baptists on the Eastern Shore of Virginia, embracing an account of the Accomack association and sketches of the churches. By Rev. Robert Williamson. Baltimore, J. F. Weishampel, jr., 1878.
91 [4] p.

Wise, Barton Haxall. Memoir of General John Cropper of Accomack County, Virginia. Reprinted from Virginia historical collections, v. 11. 1892.
43 p.

Wise, Jennings Cropper. Ye kingdome of Accawmacke; or The eastern shore of Virginia in the seventeenth century, by Jennings Cropper Wise . . . Richmond, Va., The Bell book and stationery co., 1911.
x, 406 p.

ALBEMARLE:
Bloomfield academy, Albemarle county, Va. Catalog.
Library has 1859.

Bushnell, David I., jr. "The Indian grave" a Monacan site in Albemarle County, Virginia . . . Reprinted from William & Mary college quarterly historical magazine, vol. 23, no. 2. Oct., 1914. Williamsburg, Va., 1914. Richmond, Va., Whittet & Shepperson, printers, [1914?]
7 p.

Davidson brothers. In the Supreme court of appeals. County of Albemarle & board of education versus the Davidson bros.; S. Miller's ex'or & others. Appeal from decrees of Circuit court of Richmond. Views of counsel for the Davidsons. [no place. no date]
92, 34 p.

Eckenrode, Hamilton James. . . . A calendar of legislative petitions arranged by counties: Accomac-Bedford. Special report of the Department of archives and history, H. J. Eckenrode, archivist. Richmond, D. Bottom, supt. of public printing, 1908.
302 p.
(in Virginia state library. 5th report, 1908)

Holcombe, James Philemon. The election of a Black Republican president an overt act of aggression on the right of property in slaves: the South urged to adopt concerted action for future safety. A speech before the people of Albemarle, on the 2d day of January, 1860. By James P. Holcombe . . . Richmond, C. H. Wynne, printer, 1860.
16 p.

In memory of Col. James Monroe, died September 7, 1870, aged 71 . . . n. p. n. d.
43 p.
Col. Monroe was born in Albemarle county, Va., Sept. 10, 1799.

Nicholas, Wilson Cary. To the electors of the congressional district, composed of the counties of Amherst, Albemarle and Fluvanna. [no date]
20 p.

Rives, Alexander. Speech of Alexander Rives of Albemarle, on the finances and public works of the state of Virginia, delivered 30th April, 1852, in the House of delegates, in committee of the whole on the license bill. Richmond, Va., Elliott & Nye, printers, [1852]
17 p.

Seamon, W. H. Albemarle county, Virginia. A handbook giving a description of its topography, climate, geology, minerals, fruits, plants, history, educational, agricultural and manufacturing advantages, and inducements the county offers the industrious and intelligent farmer and manufacturer. Edited by W. H. Seamon, Crozet, Va., Professor of analytical chemistry, School of mines, University of Missouri; late Instructor in chemistry and natural history, Miller manual labor school. Published by Wm. H. Prout, Charlottesville. Charlottesville, Va., Jeffersonian book and job printing house, 1888.
110 p. illus.

Washburne, E. B. Sketch of Edward Coles, second governor of Illinois, and of the slavery struggle of 1823-4. Prepared for the Chicago historical society, by E. B. Washburne. Chicago, Jansen, McClurg & co., 1882.
253 p. front.
Gov. Coles was born in Albemarle Co., Va., Dec. 15, 1786.

William and Mary college quarterly historical magazine. v. 9.

Woods, Edgar. Albemarle County in Virginia: giving some account of what it was by nature, of what it was made by man, and of some of the men who made it . . . [Charlottesville, Va., The Michie co., 1901]
iv, 412 p.

Woolfolk, C. W. Directory of the counties of Orange, Louisa, Albemarle, Culpeper and Spotsylvania. Comp. and for sale by C. W. Woolfolk, Orange, Va., W. J. Daniel, Bibb's, Va. 1895. [Richmond, Va., Ware & Duke, general printers, 1895]
1, 267 p.

ALEXANDRIA:

Alexandria Co., Va. Board of supervisors. A brief history of Alexandria County, Virginia; its wealth and resources, great and growing industries, educational and social advantages . . . Pub. under authority of the county Board of supervisors by C. G. Boteler, Crandal Mackey, M. E. Church, W. S. Hoge, jr., C. B. Haller, committee. Falls Church, Va., The Newell printing co. [1907]
2 p. l., [9]-56 p. illus., fold. map.

Eckenrode, Hamilton James. . . . A calendar of legislative petitions, arranged by counties: Accomac-Bedford. Special report of the Department of archives and history, H. J. Eckenrode, archivist. Richmond, D. Bottom, supt. of public printing, 1908.
>302 p.
>(In Virginia state library. 5th report, 1908)

Parsons, Arthur J. Books, pamphlets, periodicals, maps, and original plans of the "Centennial exhibition" in the division of prints, Library of Congress, Washington.
>(In Cox, William V. Celebration of the one hundredth anniversary of the establishment of the seat of government in the District of Columbia. p. 329-340).
>Includes some titles relating to Alexandria County, formerly a part of the District of Columbia.

ALLEGHANY:

Covington, Va. Chamber of commerce. Allegheny County, Va., its resources and industries. 1907.
>32 p. illus.

Eckenrode, Hamilton James. . . . A calendar of legislative petitions, arranged by counties: Accomac-Bedford. Special report of the Department of archives and history, H. J. Eckenrode, archivist. Richmond, D. Bottom, supt. of public printing, 1908.
>302 p.
>(In Virginia state library. 5th report, 1908)

Virginia magazine of history and biography. v. 10.

AMELIA:

Bernard, R. S. Directory of the counties of Hanover, Chesterfield, Amelia, Dinwiddie, Greensville and Brunswick. Comp. . . . by R. S. Bernard, Madison Run, Orange County, Va., 1896. Richmond, Ware & Duke, printers, 1896.
>287 p.

Eckenrode, Hamilton James. . . . A calendar of legislative petitions arranged by counties: Accomac-Bedford. Special report of the Department of archives and history, H. J. Eckenrode, archivist. Richmond, D. Bottom, supt. of public printing, 1908.
>302 p.
>(In Virginia state library. 5th report, 1908)

William and Mary college quarterly historical magazine. v. 15, 16, 17, 19.

AMHERST:

Cartwright, Peter. Autobiography of Peter Cartwright, the backwoods preacher. Edited by W. P. Strickland. New York, Carlton & Porter, 1857.
>525 p.
>Peter Cartwright was born in Amherst County, Va., in 1785.

Eckenrode, Hamilton James. . . . A calendar of legislative petitions arranged by counties: Accomac-Bedford. Special report of the Department of archives and history, H. J. Eckenrode, archivist. Richmond, D. Bottom, supt. of public printing, 1908.
302 p.
(In Virginia state library. 5th report, 1908)

Facts of interest about Amherst County, Virginia, especially suited to homeseekers and investors. Published by order of the Board of Supervisors, April, 1907.
15 p.

Nicholas, Wilson Cary. To the electors of the congressional district, composed of the counties of Amherst, Albemarle and Fluvanna. [no date]
20 p.

Ware, James. The pocket farrier; or Gentleman's guide in the management of horses under various diseases. With an explanation of the symptoms attending the different disorders, and the shortest, plainest, and most humane methods of curing them. Directions for judging of the horse's age, and useful observations on the breeding, raising, and training of colts. Hints to purchasers, and general directions for using a horse on a journey, with useful rules for riding with safety, gracefulness, &c. and directions to perform the necessary surgical operations. Receipt for gelding, on a new and improved plan: And for securing horses from the dangers arising from bots, truncheons, &c. To which is added, the horse's skeleton, taken from that of the academy of sciences at Paris. By James Ware, Amherst County, Virginia. T. W. White, printer, 1828.
[9]-xvi, [17]-192 p.

APPOMATTOX:

Caine, Thomas A. Soil survey of Appomattox county, Virginia, by Thomas A. Caine and Hugh H. Bennett.
(In U. S. Bureau of soils. Report, 1904.)

Eckenrode, Hamilton James. . . . A calendar of legislative petitions arranged by counties: Accomac-Bedford. Special report of the Department of archives and history, H. J. Eckenrode, archivist. Richmond, D. Bottom, supt. of public printing, 1908.
302 p.
(In Virginia state library. 5th report, 1908)

AUGUSTA:

Eckenrode, Hamilton James. . . . A calendar of legislative petitions, arranged by counties: Accomac-Bedford. Special report of the Department of archives and history, H. J. Eckenrode, archivist. Richmond, D. Bottom, supt. of public printing, 1908.
302 p.
(In Virginia state library. 5th report, 1908)

Fielding, G. H. John Lewis, the pioneer of Augusta county. By G. H. Fielding.
    (In The John P. Branch historical papers, of Randolph-Macon college. [v. 1] no. 3. June, 1903)

Fullerton, Hugh Stuart. Gov. Allen Trimble, of Ohio. Prepared by Dr. Hugh Stuart Fullerton, of Hillsboro, O., and read by Mr. Clifton M. Nichols
    (In The Scotch-Irish society of America. Fifth congress)
    Gov. Trimble was born in Augusta Co., Va., Nov. 24, 1784.

Geological and analytical report of the Kaolin mines, near Staunton, Augusta County, Virginia. New York, Wm. C. Bryant & co., printers, 1866.
    12 p.

John Howe Peyton. Ceremonies attending the presentation of his portrait to the County of Augusta . . . Printed for private circulation. Staunton, Va., A. B. Blackburn & co., 1894.
    32 p.

Nelson, Thomas Forsythe. Report on the Chalkley manuscripts, 21st congress, the National society, Daughters of the American revolution. [Washington, The McQueen press, 1912]
    24 p.
    Signed: Thomas Forsythe Nelson.
    Report on Judge Chalkley's copy of the Augusta County records at Staunton.

Peyton, John Lewis. History of Augusta county, Virginia . . . Staunton, Va., S. M. Yost & son, 1882.
    vii, 387, [7] p.

Rogers, Mrs. Margaret Fleming. General Benjamin Logan. By Mrs. Margaret Fleming Rogers.
    (In The Scotch-Irish society of America. Seventh congress. 1895)
    General Logan was born in Augusta Co., Va.

Stuart, Alexander Hugh Holmes. Substance of the remarks of Mr. Stuart of Augusta, on the motion of Mr. Segar of Northampton, to postpone indefinitely the consideration of the report of the committee of roads and internal navigation, recommending a general system of improvement. Delivered in the House of delegates on Thursday, the eighth day of Feb., eighteen hundred and thirty-eight. Richmond, Shepherd & Colin, printers, 1838.
    23 p.

The Virginia historical register and literary note book. Ed. by William Maxwell. v. 3 (1850), nos. 1, 2.

Virginia magazine of history and biography. v. 2, 7, 8, 21.

Waddell, Joseph Addison. Annals of Augusta county, Virginia. By Joseph A. Waddell. [no date. no place]
    55 p. plates.

——Annals of Augusta County, Virginia, with reminiscences illustrative of the vicissitudes of its pioneer settlers; biographical sketches of citizens locally prominent, and of those who have founded families in the Southern and Western states; a diary of the war, 1861-'5, and a chapter on reconstruction. By Jos. A. Waddell . . . Richmond, Wm. Ellis Jones, printer, 1886.
vii, 374 p. maps.

——Annals of Augusta County, Virginia, with reminiscences illustrative of the vicissitudes of its pioneer settlers; biographical sketches of the citizens locally prominent, and of those who have founded families in the Southern and Western states; a diary of the war of 1861-'5, and a chapter on reconstruction, with a supplement. By Jos. A. Waddell. Richmond, J. W. Randolph & English, 1888.
vii, 460 p. maps.

——Annals of Augusta County, Virginia. By Jos. A. Waddell. Supplement. Richmond, Va. J. W. Randolph & English, 1888.
1 p. l., ii [381]-492 p.

——Annals of Augusta County, Virginia, from 1726 to 1871, by Jos. A. Waddell . . . 2d ed., rev. and enl. Staunton, Va. C. R. Caldwell, 1902.
x, 545 p. fold. map.

▼ BARBOUR:

Callahan, James Morton. Semi-centennial history of West Virginia, by James Morton Callahan . . . with special articles on development and resources . . . [Charleston, W. Va.] Semi-centennial commission of West Virginia, 1913.
ix, 594 p. 1 illus., plates, maps (part fold.) tables.

Eckenrode, Hamilton James. . . . A calendar of legislative petitions, arranged by counties: Accomac-Bedford. Special report of the Department of archives and history, H. J. Eckenrode, archivist. Richmond, D. Bottom, supt. of public printing, 1908.
302 p.
(In Virginia state library. 5th report, 1908)

Lewis, Virgil Anson. History of West Virginia. In two parts . . . Philadelphia, Hubbard bros., 1889.
744 p. pl.

BATH:

An account of the Hot Springs, Bath County, Va., and an analysis of the waters, with a brief notice by Prof. J. L. Cabell, M. D., of the University of Virginia, resident physician, of the effects of thermal baths in cases of gout, rheumatism, diseases of the liver, etc., . . . Richmond, Clemitt & Jones, steam book and job printers, 1875.
109 p.

Eckenrode, Hamilton James. . . . A calendar of legislative petitions, arranged by counties: Accomac-Bedford. Special report of the Department of archives and history, H. J. Eckenrode, archivist. Richmond, D. Bottom, supt. of public printing, 1908.
    302 p.
    (In Virginia state library. 5th report, 1908)

McAllister, Joseph Thompson. Historical sketches of Virginia Hot Springs, Warm Sulphur Springs and Bath County, Virginia, by J. T. McAllister . . . [Salem, Va., Salem printing and publishing company, 1908]
    51 p.

Virginia magazine of history and biography. v. 2.

BEDFORD:

Bellevue high school, Bedford County, Va. Announcements.
    Library has 1900.

——Bellevue high school nondescript.
    Library has May-June, 1899.

——Catalog.
    Library has 1878, 1883, 1884, 1887-1892, 1895.

Caffey, Francis Gordon. George Washington Stone. 1811-1894.
    (In Lewis, W. D. Great American lawyers, v. 6)
    G. W. Stone was born in Bedford Co., Va., Oct. 24, 1811.

Eckenrode, Hamilton James. . . . A calendar of legislative petitions, arranged by counties: Accomac-Bedford. Special report of the Department of archives and history, H. J. Eckenrode, archivist. Richmond, D. Bottom, supt. of public printing, 1908.
    302 p.
    (In Virginia state library. 5th report, 1908)

Green, William Mercer. Memoir of Rt. Rev. James Hervey Otey, D. D., LL. D., the first bishop of Tennessee. By Rt. Rev. William Mercer Green, D. D., bishop of Mississippi. New York, James Pott and company, 1885.
    3 p. l., 359 p.
    Bishop Otey was born in Bedford County, Virginia, Jan. 27, 1800.

Historical sketch of Bedford County, Virginia. 1753. 1907. [Lynchburg, Va., J. P. Bell co., inc., printers, 1907]
    121 p. (fold. map) illus.

Moseley, George Carrington. Genealogy of Moseley family of Bedford County, Va. By George Carrington Moseley, M. A. [Richmond, 1912?]
    9 p.

William and Mary college quarterly historical magazine. vol. 11.

BERKELEY:

Aler, F. Vernon. Aler's history of Martinsburg and Berkeley county, West Virginia . . . Hagerstown, Md., Printed for the author by the Mail pub. co. [1888]
433 p.

Callahan, James Morton. Semi-centennial history of West Virginia, by James Morton Callahan . . . with special articles on development and resources . . . [Charleston, W. Va.] Semi-centennial commission of West Virginia, 1913.
ix, 594 p. 1 illus., plates, maps (part fold.) tables.

Cartmell, Thomas Kemp. Shenandoah Valley pioneers and their descendants. A history of Frederick County, Virginia (illustrated), from its formation in 1738 to 1908. Comp. mainly from original records of old Frederick County, now Hampshire, Berkeley, Shenandoah, Jefferson, Hardy, Clarke, Warren, Morgan and Frederick . . . [Winchester, Va., Printed by the Eddy press corporation, 1909]
vii, 587 p. plates.

Lewis, Virgil Anson. History of West Virginia. In two parts . . . Philadelphia, Hubbard bros., 1889.
744 p., pl.

Norris, J. E. History of the lower Shenandoah valley counties of Frederick, Berkeley, Jefferson and Clarke, their early settlement and progress to the present time; geological features; a description of their historic . . . localities; cities, towns and villages; portraits of some of the prominent men, and biographies of many of the representative citizens . . . Chicago, A. Warner & co., 1890.
viii, 9-812 p. illus., port.

Rumsey, James. A short treatise on the application of steam, whereby is clearly shown from actual experiments, that steam may be applied to propel boats or vessels of any burthen against rapid currents with great velocity. The same principles are introduced with effect, by a machine of a simple and cheap construction, for the purpose of raising water sufficient for the working of grist mills, saw mills, &c. and for watering meadows and other purposes of agriculture. By James Rumsey, of Berkeley county, Virginia. Philadelphia, Printed by Joseph James: Chestnut street. 1788. [Reprint]
(In O'Callaghan, E. B. The documentary history of the state of New York. v. 2).

William and Mary college quarterly historical magazine. v. 13.

BLAND:

No separate history of this county is now in the Library.

BOONE:

Callahan, James Morton. Semi-centennial history of West Virginia, by James Morton Callahan . . . with special articles on development and resources . . . [Charleston, W. Va.] Semi-centennial commission of West Virginia, 1913.
ix, 594 p. 1 illus., plates, maps (part fold.) tables.

Lewis, Virgil Anson. History of West Virginia. In two parts . . . Philadelphia, Hubbard bros., 1889.
744 p. pl.

BOTETOURT:

Johnston, Charles. A narrative of the incidents attending the capture, detention, and ransom of Charles Johnston, of Botetourt county, Virginia, who was made prisoner by the Indians, on the river Ohio, in the year 1790; together with an interesting account of the fate of his companions, five in number, one of whom suffered at the stake. To which are added, sketches of Indian character and manners, with illustrative anecdotes. New York, Printed by J. & J. Harper, 1827.
vi, [7]-264 p.

Schenck, Ralph. The family physician, treating of the diseases which assail the human system at different periods of life . . . to which are prefixed A treatise on chemistry . . . A brief anatomy and physiology . . . and A materia medica. By Ralph Schenck, physician of Botetourt County, Virginia, formerly of New Jersey. Fincastle, Va.; Printed by Oliver Callahan and Wm. E. M. Word, 1842.
481 p.

BOURBON:

Collins, Lewis. Collins' historical sketches of Kentucky. History of Kentucky . . . revised, enlarged . . . and brought down to . . . 1874, by . . . R. H. Collins . . . Embracing pre-historic, annals for 331 years . . . statistics, antiquities and natural curiosities, geographical and geological descriptions . . . and . . . biographical sketches . . . Covington, Ky., Collins & Co., 1878.
2 v. pl., fold. map.

BRAXTON:

Callahan, James Morton. Semi-centennial history of West Virginia, by James Morton Callahan . . . with special articles on development and resources . . . [Charleston, W. Va.] Semi-centennial commission of West Virginia, 1913.
ix, 594 p. 1 illus., plates, maps (part fold.) tables.

Lewis, Virgil Anson. History of West Virginia. In two parts . . . Philadelphia, Hubbard bros., 1889.
744 p. pl.

w BROOKE:

    Callahan, James Morton. Semi-centennial history of West Virginia, by James Morton Callahan . . . with special articles on development and resources . . . [Charleston, W. Va.] Semi-centennial commission of West Virginia, 1913.
        ix, 594 p. 1 illus., maps (part fold.) tables.

    Lewis, Virgil Anson. History of West Virginia. In two parts . . . Philadelphia, Hubbard bros., 1889.
        744 p. pl.

    Newton, J. H. History of the Pan-handle; being historical collections of the counties of Ohio, Brooke, Marshall and Hancock, West Virginia . . . Comp. and written by J. H. Newton, G. G. Nichols, and A. G. Sprankle. Ed. by J. H. Newton. Wheeling, W. Va., J. A. Caldwell, 1879.
        450 p., 1 l., xxx, [1] p. pl., 2 maps.

BRUNSWICK:

    Bernard, R. S. Directory of the counties of Hanover, Chesterfield, Amelia, Dinwiddie, Greensville and Brunswick. Comp. . . . by R. S. Bernard, Madison Run, Orange County, Va. 1896. Richmond, Ware & Duke, printers, 1896.
        287 p.

    Brown, Aaron Venable. Speeches, congressional and political, and other writings of ex-Governor Aaron V. Brown, of Tennessee. Collected and arranged by the editors of the Union and American. Nashville, Tenn., J. L. Marling and company, 1854-[55]
        v. p., 1 l., 706 p.
        Aaron V. Brown was born in Brunswick Co., Va., Aug. 15, 1795.

    Putnam, A. W. History of middle Tennessee; or, Life and times of Gen. James Robertson . . . Nashville, Tenn., Printed for the author, 1859.
        xvi, [17]-668 p. plates. 3 fold. maps.
        Gen. Robertson was born in Brunswick Co., Va., June 28, 1742.

    Smithey, Marvin. Brunswick county, Virginia. Information for the homeseeker and investor. Prepared under the supervision of the Hon. I. E. Spatig as authorized by the Board of Supervisors of Brunswick County, Virginia, July 23, 1906. Compiled by Marvin Smithey of . . . Lawrenceville, Va. Richmond, Va., Williams printing co., 1907.
        48 p. illus.

Virginia magazine of history and biography. v. 22.

William and Mary college quarterly historical magazine. v. 7, 9, 20.

BUCHANAN:

No separate history of this county is now in the Library.

BUCKINGHAM:

    Harrison, Randolph. Circular to the people of Cumberland, Buckingham and Campbell. [no date]
        8 p.

    Randolph, John. To the freeholders of Charlotte, Buckingham, Prince Edward and Cumberland [containing a speech on the intended declaration of war against Great Britain, May 30, 1812] [n. p., 1812]
        14 p.

    Seven Islands school, Buckingham county, Va. Catalog.
        Library has 1894, 1900.

w CABELL:

    Callahan, James Morton. Semi-centennial history of West Virginia, by James Morton Callahan . . . with special articles on development and resources . . . [Charleston, W. Va.] Semi-centennial commission of West Virginia, 1913.
        ix, 594 p. 1 illus., plates, maps (part fold.) tables.

    Lewis, Virgil Anson. History of West Virginia. In two parts . . . Philadelphia, Hubbard bros., 1889.
        744 p. pl.

w CALHOUN:

    Callahan, James Morton. Semi-centennial history of West Virginia, by James Morton Callahan . . . with special articles on development and resources . . . [Charleston, W. Va.] Semi-centennial commission of West Virginia, 1913.
        ix, 594 p. 1 illus., plates, maps (part fold.) tables.

    Lewis, Virgil Anson. History of West Virginia. In two parts . . . Philadelphia, Hubbard bros., 1889.
        744 p. pl.

CAMPBELL:

    Bell, James Pinkney. Our Quaker friends of ye olden time, being in part a transcript of the minute books of Cedar Creek meeting, Hanover county, and the South River meeting, Campbell county, Va. J. P. Bell company, publishers, Lynchburg, Va., 1905.
        v, 287 p. plates.

    Harrison, Randolph. Circular to the people of Cumberland, Buckingham and Campbell. [no date]
        8 p.

    Winston, R. A. Soil survey of Campbell county, Virginia, by R. A. Winston.
        (In U. S. Bureau of soils. Report. 1909.)

Brown, John Thompson. Catalogue of a valuable collection of old American law books, the property of John Thompson Brown, esq., of Evington, Campbell County, Virginia; including rare early Virginia session laws. Journals of the House of Burgesses, Proceedings of the Convention of Virginia delegates, 1776 (the original edition), and other items of great rarity. To be sold at auction, Dec. 2nd, 1913, by Merwin Sales Co., New York. [n. d.]
30 p.

CAROLINE:

Boucher, Jonathan. A view of the causes and consequences of the American revolution; in thirteen discourses preached in North America between the years 1763 and 1775: with an historical preface. By Jonathan Boucher, Vicar of Epsom in the County of Surrey. London, Printed for G. G. and J. Robinson, 1797.
4 p. l., xciv p., 1 l., 596 p.

> "The Vestry of the Parish of Hanover in the County of King George, in that part of Virginia which is called the Northern Neck, did me the honour to nominate me to the Rectory of their Parish, in 1761, before I was in orders . . . I afterwards held the Parish of St. Mary's in Caroline County, Virginia", p. xc.

Caroline Co., Va. Board of supervisors. A hand-book of Caroline County, Virginia. Pub. by authority of the Board of supervisors of the county. 1907 . . . Bowling Green, Va., 1907.
13 p. fold. map.

William and Mary college quarterly historical magazine. v. 6, 8.

CARROLL:

No separate history of this county is now in the Library.

CHARLES CITY:

The Chesapeake & Ohio railway directory, containing an illustrated history and description of the road, together with improvements and connections already completed and those in contemplation; also, the names of the merchants, manufacturers, professional men, and farmers, with postoffice addresses in the counties of Elizabeth City, Warwick, York, James City, New Kent, Charles City, King William, Henrico . . . together with a description of the surface, soil, average value of lands, county and city officers, and other useful and valuable information. Compiled by J. H. Chataigne. 1881. c 1881 by J. H. Chataigne.
379 p.

Christian, George Llewellyn. John Tyler, address delivered before the Colonial dames of America in the state of Virginia, at Greenway, Charles City county, Va., on Monday, Oct. 27, 1913, at the unveiling of a memorial to mark the birthplace of president Tyler, by George L. Christian, of Richmond, Va. Richmond, Va. Whittet & Shepperson, printers, 1913.

21 p.

——. Lecture; Charles City: some of its noted places and people and personal recollections of some of these. Delivered at Charles City courthouse, June 24, 1910. By Hon. George L. Christian . . . To aid Bethany Presbyterian church, and published at the request and for the benefit of that church . . . [1910]

33 p.

Douthat, Robert. Argument before the committee of privileges and elections, in the case of Robert Douthat, returned delegate from the county of Charles City. Richmond, Printed by Shepherd & Pollard, 1826.

26 p.

History of Elam Baptist church, Charles City co., Va. Published on its one hundredth anniversary. Richmond, Va. Reformer electric print, 1910.

35 p.

Slaughter, Philip. A brief sketch of the life of William Green, LL. D., jurist and scholar, with some personal reminiscences of him. By Philip Slaughter, D. D., historiographer of the P. E. church diocese of Virginia. Also, a historical tract by Judge Green, and some curious letters upon the origin of the proverb "*Vox populi, vox dei.*" Richmond, Wm. Ellis Jones, book and job printer, 1883.

131 p.
Contains: The Genesis of certain counties in Virginia, from cities or towns of the same name.

The vain prodigal life, and tragical penitent death of Thomas Hellier born at Whitchurch near Lyme in Dorset-shire: who for murdering his master, mistress and a maid, was executed according to law at Westover in Charles City, in the country of Virginia, neer the plantation called Hard Labour, where he perpetrated the said murders. He suffered on Munday the 5th of August, 1678. . And was after hanged up in chains at Windmill-Point on James River . . . London, Printed for Sam. Crouch, 1680.

1 p. l., 40 p.

William and Mary college quarterly historical magazine. v. 4, 8, 9, 10, 14.

• CHARLES RIVER:

The county existed only from 1634 to 1642/3. No separate history of this county is now in the Library.

CHARLOTTE:

 Carrington, John Cullen. Charlotte County, Virginia: historical, statistical and present attractions; comp. by J. Cullen Carrington. . . . Richmond, Va., The Hermitage press, inc., 1907.
  5 p. l., 7-142 p. illus. plates. pl.

 Gaines, Richard V. Hand-book of Charlotte County, Virginia. Its history, physical characteristics, climatic conditions, social, moral and religious advantages, statistical and other information, with letters from prominent citizens showing its desirability as a home, and the inducements which it offers to the industrious and intelligent farmer and mechanic. Richmond, Va., Everett Waddey, 1889.
  68 p. illus., map.

 Randolph, John. To the freeholders of Charlotte, Buckingham, Prince Edward and Cumberland [containing a speech on the intended declaration of war against Great Britain, May 30, 1812] [n. p., 1812]
  14 p.

 Vaughan, C. R. Memorial sketch of the late William B. Morton, ruling elder in the church of Roanoke, in the county of Charlotte, Va. Written to aid ruling elders. By Rev. C. R. Vaughan, D. D. Richmond, Va., Presbyterian committee of publication, 1886.
  35 p.

CHESTERFIELD:

 Bennett, Frank. Soil survey of Chesterfield county, Virginia, by Frank Bennett, R. A. Winston, W. J. Geib and C. W. Mann.
  (In U. S. Bureau of soils. Report, 1906.)

 Bernard, R. S. Directory of the counties of Hanover, Chesterfield, Amelia, Dinwiddie, Greensville and Brunswick. Comp. . . . by R. S. Bernard, Madison Run, Orange County, Va. 1896. Richmond, Ware & Duke, printers, 1896.
  287 p.

 Cox, T. B. Chesterfield county, Virginia. Its history and present condition. Prepared under the supervision of the Hon. John B. Watkins, as authorized by the board of supervisors of the county, August, 1906. Compiled by T. B. Cox. Richmond, Va., Williams ptg. co., 1907.
  45 p.

 Haddock's directory of Manchester, Va., and suburbs, for 1893-94, to which is appended a business directory of Chesterfield county. T. M. Haddock & co., publishers. c 1893.
  206 p.

 Raymond, R. W. The natural coke of Chesterfield County, Virginia.
  3 p.
   Extracts from the Transactions of the American institute of mining engineers. v. 3. 1883.)

Ritchie, Thomas. A full report, embracing all the evidence and arguments in the case of the commonwealth of Virginia vs. Thomas Ritchie, jr., tried at the spring term of the Chesterfield Superior court, 1846. To which is added, an appendix, shewing the action of the court in relation to the other parties, Messrs. J. P. Archer, W. Greenhow, and William Scott, connected with the said case. New York, Burgess, Stringer and company, 1846.
91 p., 1 l., (fold. plan)

Virginia magazine of history and biography. v. 11.

William and Mary college quarterly historical magazine. v. 8.

CLARKE:

Cartmell, Thomas Kemp. Shenandoah Valley pioneers and their descendants. A history of Frederick County, Virginia (illustrated), from its formation in 1738 to 1908. Comp. mainly from original records of old Frederick County, now Hampshire, Berkeley, Shenandoah, Jefferson, Hardy, Clarke, Warren, Morgan and Frederick . . . [Winchester, Va., Printed by the Eddy press corporation, 1909]
vii, 587 p. plates.

Gold, Thomas Daniel. History of Clarke County, Virginia, and its connection with the War between the States, with illustrations of colonial homes and of Confederate officers, by Thomas D. Gold; with sketches by Dr. H. C. Sommerville, Geo. H. Burwell, Geo. B. Harrison, A. Moore, jr. and M. W. Jones. [Berryville, Va., Printed by C. R. Hughes, c 1914]
337, [1] p. plates.

[Hammond, Harriot Milton] The story of a long life. A memoir of Elizabeth S. W. Taylor, "Aunt Bet." Jamaica, Queensborough, New York, 1900.
3 p. l., 177 p. front. (port.)
Elizabeth S. W. Taylor was born in Clarke county, Va., in 1800.

Mabry, W. S. Brief sketch of the career of Captain Catesby ap R. Jones. Compiled by request by W. S. Mabry, Selma, Alabama, January, 1912.
55 p.
Capt. Jones was born at Fairfield, Frederick, now Clarke County, Virginia, on the 15th day of April, 1821.

Norris, J. E. History of the lower Shenandoah valley counties of Frederick, Berkeley, Jefferson and Clarke, their early settlement and progress to the present time; geological features; a description of their historic . . . localities; cities, towns and villages; portraits of some of the prominent men, and biographies of many of the representative citizens . . . Chicago, A Warner & co., 1890.
viii, 9-812 p. illus.

CLAY:

>Callahan, James Morton. Semi-centennial history of West Virginia, by James Morton Callahan . . . with special articles on development and resources . . . [Charleston, W. Va.] Semi-centennial commission of West Virginia, 1913.
>>ix, 594 p. illus., plates, maps (part fold.) tables.

>Lewis, Virgil Anson. History of West Virginia. In two parts . . . Philadelphia, Hubbard bros., 1889.
>>744 p. pl.

CRAIG:

>No separate history of this county is now in the Library.

CULPEPER:

>Culpeper exponent. v. 29, no. 11. Culpeper, Va., June 25, 1909.
>>Special edition.

>Culpeper female institute, Culpeper, Va. Catalog.
>>Library has 1875, 1877.

>Culpeper female seminary, Culpeper, Va. Catalog.
>>Library has 1894, 1895.

>Culpeper military institute, Culpeper, Va. Catalog.
>>Library has 1858.

>Green, Ralph Travers. Genealogical and historical notes on Culpeper County, Virginia. Embracing a revised and enlarged edition of Dr. Philip Slaughter's History of St. Mark's parish. Comp. . . . by Raleigh Travers Green. Culpeper, Va., R. T. Green, 1900.
>>5 p. l, ii p., 1 l., [vi]-viii, 120 p., 1 l., 160, xxvi p., 1 l.

>Grimsley, Daniel Amon. Battles in Culpeper County, Virginia, 1861-1865, and other articles by Major Daniel A. Grimsley, of the Sixth Virginia cavalry. Comp. and pub. by R. T. Green . . . Culpeper, Va., R. T. Green, 1900.
>>2 p. l., 56 p.

>Pennsylvania. Culpeper, Virginia, monument commission. Report of the Culpeper, Virginia monument commission of Pennsylvania. Harrisburg, Pa., W. S. Ray, state printer, 1914.
>>62 p. plates.

>St. Mark's parish, Culpeper co., Va. The parish leaflet.
>>Library has no. 1, 1913; no. 2-4, 1914; no. 5, 1915.

>Slaughter, Philip. Genealogical and historical notes on Culpeper County, Virginia. Embracing a revised and enlarged edition of Dr. Philip Slaughter's History of St. Mark's parish. Culpeper, Va., by R. T. Green, 1900.
>>5 p. l., viii, 120 p., 1 l., 160, xxvi p., 1 l.

—— A history of St. Mark's parish, Culpeper county, Virginia, with notes of old churches and old families, and illustrations of the manners and customs of the olden time. By Rev. Philip Slaughter, D. D., rector of Emmanuel Church, Culpeper co., Va. . . . [Baltimore, Md., Innes & co.,], 1877.
x, 200 p. map.

Stringfellow, Thornton. Slavery: its origin, nature and history. Its relation to society, to government, and to true religion,—to human happiness and divine glory. Considered in the light of Bible teachings, moral justice, and political wisdom. By Rev. Thornton Stringfellow, D. D., of Culpeper County, Virginia. Alexandria, Printed at the Virginia sentinel office, 1860.
32 p.

—— Slavery: its origin, nature, and history, considered in the light of Bible teachings, moral justice and political wisdom . . . By Rev. Thornton Stringfellow, D. D., of Culpeper County, Virginia. New York, John F. Trow, 1861.
56 p.

Virginia midland academy, near Culpeper, Va. Catalog.
Library has 1887.

Ward, Robert D. An account of General LaFayette's visit to Virginia, in the years 1824-'25, containing full circumstantial reports of his reception in Washington, Alexandria, Mount Vernon, Yorktown, Williamsburg, Norfolk, Richmond, Petersburg, Goochland, Fluvanna, Monticello, Charlottesville, Gordonsville, Orange Court House, Fredericksburg, Leesburg, University of Virginia, Culpeper, Fauquier, and his departure from the United States, with a portrait of General LaFayette, photographed from his bust, by Houdon, in the capitol of Virginia; compiled from newspapers of the period and other sources, by Robert D. Ward, Richmond. West, Johnston & co., Richmond, Va., 1881.
136 p.

Wayland Blue Ridge Baptist association. Minutes of the eleventh annual session of the Wayland Blue Ridge Baptist association, held with Ebenezer Baptist church, Culpeper Co., Va., August 15th, 16th and 17th, 1900. . . . Richmond, Va., Virginia Baptist press, 1901.
[24] p.

Woolfolk, C. W. Directory of the counties of Orange, Louisa, Albemarle, Culpeper and Spotsylvania. Comp. and for sale by C. W. Woolfolk, Orange, Va., W. J. Daniel, Bibb's, Va. 1895. [Richmond, Va., Ware & Duke, general printers, 1895]
1, 267 p.

CUMBERLAND:

Harrison, Randolph. Circular to the people of Cumberland, Buckingham and Campbell [no date]
8 p.

Randolph, John. To the freeholders of Charlotte, Buckingham, Prince Edward and Cumberland [containing a speech on the intended declaration of war against Great Britain, May 30, 1812] [n. p., 1812]
14 p.

William and Mary college quarterly historical magazine. v. 20.

DICKENSON:

No separate history of this county is now in the Library.

DINWIDDIE:

Bernard, R. S. Directory of the counties of Hanover, Chesterfield, Amelia, Dinwiddie, Greensville and Brunswick. Comp. . . . by R. S. Bernard, Madison Run, Orange County, Va. 1896. Richmond, Ware & Duke, printers, 1896.
287 p.

Epes, William Dandridge. Trial of William Dandridge Epes, for the murder of Francis Adolphua Muir, Dinwiddie County, Virginia . . . Petersburg, Va., J. M. H. Brunet, 1849.
76 p.

Jarratt, Devereux. The life of the Reverend Devereux Jarratt, rector of Bath parish, Dinwiddie County, Virginia. Written by himself, in a series of letters addressed to the Rev. John Coleman, one of the ministers of the Protestant Episcopal church, in Maryland. Baltimore, Printed by Warner & Hanna, 1806.
1 p. L., iv. p., 1 l., [5]-223 p.

——Sermon preached before the convention of the protestant Episcopal church, in Virginia, at Richmond, May 3, 1792. By Devereux Jarratt, rector of Bath Parish, Dinwiddie County. Richmond (Virginia) Printed. New-London, Reprinted by T. Green and son, 1792.
v, [7]-31 p.

——A sermon preached before the convention of the Protestant Episcopal church in Virginia, at Richmond, May 3, 1792. By Devereux Jarratt, rector of Bath parish, Dinwiddie County. 3d ed. New Haven, Sidney's press, 1809.
v, [7]-24 p.

——Thoughts on some important subjects in divinity; in a series of letters to a friend. By the Rev. Devereux Jarratt, rector of Bath parish, in Dinwiddie County, Virginia. Baltimore, Printed by Warner & Hanna, 1806.
84 p.

Petersburg city directory, 1872-'73: containing a complete general and business directory, together with a list of all the prominent business men and farmers in Dinwiddie county. Also, the United States,

state, and city government, with a list of all the streets, lanes, alleys, &c. Compiled by Chataigne & Boyd. Petersburg, Va., Jos. Van Holt Nash, publishers, 1872.
    3, 219 p.

Rives, W. C., of Dinwiddie Co., Va. Historic Dinwiddie county, Virginia; or, The last long camp. Published by order of The Jamestown exhibit committee of Dinwiddie Co., Va. [Petersburg, Va., The Franklin press co., printers, 1907]
    12 p. incl. plates. fold. map.

William and Mary college quarterly historical magazine. v. 8.

w DODDRIDGE:

Callahan, James Morton. Semi-centennial history of West Virginia, by James Morton Callahan . . . with special articles on development and resources . . . [Charleston, W. Va.] Semi-centennial commission of West Virginia, 1913.
    ix, 594 p. 1 illus., plates, maps (part fold.) tables.

Lewis, Virgil Anson. History of West Virginia. In two parts . . . Philadelphia, Hubbard bros., 1889.
    744 p. pl.

e DUNMORE:

This county existed only from 1772-1778. No separate history of this county is now in the Library.

ELIZABETH CITY:

The Chesapeake & Ohio railway directory, containing an illustrated history and description of the road, together with improvements and connections already completed and those in contemplation; also, the names of the merchants, manufacturers, professional men, and farmers, with postoffice addresses in the counties of Elizabeth City, Warwick, York, James City, New Kent, Charles City, King William, Henrico . . . together with a description of the surface, soil, average value of lands, county and city officers, and other useful and valuable information. Compiled by J. H. Chataigne. 1881. c 1881 by J. H. Chataigne.
    379 p.

Segar, Joseph E. Remarks of Mr. Joseph Segar, (of Elizabeth City and Warwick,) on the bill to construct the mountain portion of the Louisa railroad, and to tunnel the Blue Ridge Mountain. Richmond, Printed by Shepherd and Colin, 1849.
    8 p.

——Speech of Mr. Segar, of Elizabeth City and Warwick, on the election of state officers, delivered in the House of delegates, Wednes-

day, the 6th and Tuesday, the 13th February, 1850. Richmond, H. K. Ellyson's power press, 1850.
21 p.
Relating to the Democratic proposal to remove Mr. Heath, first auditor of Va. and a Whig, and defending the policy of the national administration in removals from office for partisan reasons.

——Speech of Mr. Segar, of Elizabeth City, on the bill authorizing a loan of state bonds, to the South-side railroad company, delivered in the House of delegates, January 18th and 19th, 1853. Richmond, H. K. Ellyson, printer, 1853.
21 p.

——Speech of Mr. Joseph Segar, (of Elizabeth City and Warwick,) on the Wilmot proviso. Delivered in the House of delegates, Jan. 19, 1849. Richmond, Printed by Shepherd and Colin, 1849.
22 p.

Slaughter, Philip. A brief sketch of the life of William Green, LL. D., jurist and scholar, with some personal reminiscences of him. By Philip Slaughter, D. D., historiographer of the P. E. church diocese of Virginia. Also, a historical tract by Judge Green, and some curious letters upon the origin of the proverb *"Vox populi, vox dei."* Richmond, Wm. Ellis Jones, book and job printer, 1883.
131 p.
Contains: The Genesis of certain counties in Virginia, from cities or towns of the same name.

William and Mary college quarterly historical papers. v. 1, 2.

William and Mary college quarterly historical magazine. v. 5, 9, 14, 20.

ESSEX:

Garnett, Henry Wise. Historical address on the history of Essex county, Virginia, delivered . . . at Occupacia, Essex co., Virginia, on July 4th, 1876. Washington, Judd & Detwiler, 1876.
34 p.

Garnett, James Mercer. Lectures on female education, comprising the first and second series of a course delivered to Mrs. Garnett's pupils, at Elm-wood, Essex County, Virginia. By James M. Garnett. To which is annexed, The gossips manual. 4th ed. with corrections and additions by the author. Richmond, T. W. White, 1825.
389 p.

——Same. 3d ed.

——Seven lectures on female education. Inscribed to Mrs. Garnett's pupils, at Elm-wood, Essex County; by their very sincere friend James M. Garnett. 2d ed., with corrections and additions by the author. Richmond, T. W. White, 1824.
8, lxviii, [69]-261 p.

Garnett, James Mercer. Biographical sketch of Hon. Muscoe Russell Hunter Garnett (1821-1864) of "Elmwood", Essex Co., Va., by James Mercer Garnett . . . [Williamsburg, 1909]
76 p.
Reprint from July and October numbers (1909) of William and Mary college quarterly magazine.

——Genealogy of the Mercer-Garnett family of Essex County, Virginia. Supposed to be descended from the Garnetts of Lancashire, England. Compiled from original records, and from oral and written statements of members of the family. By James Mercer Garnett. Richmond, Va., Whittet & Shepperson, printers, c 1910.
62 p. plates.

Manufacturers' record, Baltimore. Perpetuation of local history in Virginia [with lists of portraits and memorials in Westmoreland, King and Queen, Essex, Lancaster, Mathews, Middlesex, Northumberland, Gloucester and King William counties] a description of the work of Judge T. R. B. Wright.
13 p.
Reprinted from the Manufacturers' record, Baltimore, Md., July 25, 1907.

Quandary, Christopher, pseud. Some serious considerations on the present state of parties, with regard to the presidential election; with the author's case fairly stated, and submitted to all candid and compassionate men. By Christopher Quandary. Richmond, Printed by Thomas W. White, 1827.
24 p.
Signed: Christopher Quandary, Essex County, Nov. 9, 1827.

Virginia magazine of history and biography. v. 10.

William and Mary college quarterly historical magazine. v. 6, 18, 19.

FAIRFAX:

Choate, Columbus D. Historic Fairfax County. First paper. [c 1911]
[11] p.

Machen, Lewis H. George Mason of Virginia; an address by L. H. Machen presenting a portrait to Fairfax county, May 20th, 1901. [Washington, D. C., B. S. Adams, 1901]
35 p.

William and Mary college quarterly historical magazine. v. 12.

FAUQUIER:

Frederick, Francis. Autobiography of Rev. Francis Frederick of Virginia. Baltimore, J. W. Woods, printer, 1870.
43 p.
Francis Frederick was born on his master's plantation in Fauquier County, Virginia, in 1809.

Morton, J. H. Reports on the Stringfellow gold mine, of Fauquier county, Va., made by Prof. J. H. Morton, M. E. New York, Capt. J. G. Riley, M. E. San Francisco, Prof. F. M. Endlich, Smithsonian Inst. Brooklyn, N. Y., J. F. Baker, printer, 1879.
    16 p.

Piggot, A. S. Reports of Professor A. S. Piggot, of Baltimore, and Prof. Benj. Silliman, Jr., of New York, on the Manassas copper-mine, in Fauquier county, Virginia; together with analysis of the same, by Prof. Piggot, Dr. James R. Chilton, and Prof. Silliman. New York, Oliver & brother, steam printers, April, 1853.
    17 p. map.

Scott, John, of Fauquier. During the war and after the war. Warrenton, Va., Caldwell & Frank [1897?]
    1 p. l., 59 p., 1 l., 13 p. 21 p.

——Same. 2d ed. Warrenton, Va., The True index [1909?]
    5 p. l., 97 p.

——The lost principle; or the sectional equilibrium: how it was created—how destroyed—how it may be restored. By "Barbarossa" . . . Richmond, Va., James Woodhouse & co., 1860.
    viii, [9]-266 p.

——Partisan life with Col. John S. Mosby. By Major John Scott, of Fauquier, late C. S. A. . . . with portraits and engravings on wood . . . New York, Harper & brothers, 1867.
    [iv-xvi] p., 1 l., [19-492] p. illus., fold. map.

——The republic as a form of government; or, The evolution of democracy in America. By John Scott, of Fauquier . . . London, Chapman and Hall, ltd.; Baltimore, J. Murphy and co., 1890.
    x p., 1 l., 323 p.

Six weeks in Fauquier. Being the substance of a series of familiar letters illustrating the scenery, localities, medical virtues and general characteristics of the White Sulphur springs . . . Written in 1838, to a gentleman in New England; by a visitor. New York, S. Colman, 1839.
    67 p.

Ward, Robert D. An account of General LaFayette's visit to Virginia, in the years 1824-'25, containing full circumstantial reports of his reception in Washington, Alexandria, Mount Vernon, Yorktown, Williamsburg, Norfolk, Richmond, Petersburg, Goochland, Fluvanna, Monticello, Charlottesville, Gordonsville, Orange Court House, Fredericksburg, Leesburg, University of Virginia, Culpeper, Fauquier, and his departure from the United States, with a portrait of General LaFayette, photographed from his bust, by Houdon, in the capitol of Virginia; compiled from newspapers of the period and other sources, by Robert D. Ward, Richmond. West, Johnston & co., Richmond, Va., 1881.
    136 p.

Whig party. Virginia. Fauquier County. Appendix. First address of the Whig central committee of vigilance of Fauquier County, Virginia. [1840]
11 p.

——Second address of the Central committee of Fauquier, to the people of that county, on the army bill. Washington, Printed at the Madisonian office, 1840.
xii, 34, 11 p.

William and Mary college quarterly historical magazine. v. 19.

Wise, John Sergeant. Beverley of Beverley. Copied by me from papers loaned me by Col. Robert Beverley of the "The Plains", Fauquier County, Virginia. New York, Oct. 1st, 1890. John S. Wise.
chart. 48½x61½ cm.

k FAYETTE (1780):

Collins, Lewis. Collins' historical sketches of Kentucky. History of Kentucky . . . revised, enlarged . . . and brought down to . . . 1874, by . . . R. H. Collins . . . Embracing pre-historic, annals for 331 years . . . statistics, antiquities and natural curiosities, geographical and geological descriptions . . . and . . . biographical sketches . . . Covington, Ky., Collins & Co., 1878.
2 v. pl., fold. map.

w FAYETTE (1831):

Callahan, James Morton. Semi-centennial history of West Virginia, by James Morton Callahan . . . with special articles on development and resources . . . [Charleston, W. Va.] Semi-centennial commission of West Virginia, 1913.
ix, 594 p. 1 illus., plates, maps (part fold.) tables.

Lewis, Virgil Anson. History of West Virginia. In two parts . . . Philadelphia, Hubbard bros., 1889.
744 p. pl.

• FINCASTLE:

This county existed only from 1772-1777. No separate history of this county is now in the Library.

FLOYD:

No separate history of this county is now in the Library.

FLUVANNA:

Hatcher, Virginia Snead, Mrs. William E. Hatcher. The Sneads of Fluvanna, by Mrs. William E. Hatcher, (Virginia Snead Hatcher)

. . . All rights reserved. Historical and biographical, illustrated, 1910. Roanoke, Va., the Stone printing & mfg. co. [1910]
[118] p. plates.

Nicholas, Wilson Cary. To the electors of the congressional district, composed of the counties of Amherst, Albemarle and Fluvanna. [no date]
20 p.

Smith, A. B. Memoir of Elder P. P. Smith, late pastor of Fork Union, Fork of Willis, and Columbia Baptist churches, Fluvanna, Va., by Elder A. B. Smith, pastor 4th Baptist church, Richmond. Richmond, H. K. Ellyson, printer, 1847.
141 p.

Ward, Robert D. An account of General LaFayette's visit to Virginia, in the years 1824-'25, containing full circumstantial reports of his reception in Washington, Alexandria, Mount Vernon, Yorktown, Williamsburg, Norfolk, Richmond, Petersburg, Goochland, Fluvanna, Monticello, Charlottesville, Gordonsville, Orange Court House, Fredericksburg, Leesburg, University of Virginia, Culpeper, Fauquier, and his departure from the United States, with a portrait of General LaFayette, photographed from his bust, by Houdon, in the capitol of Virginia; compiled from newspapers of the period and other sources, by Robert D. Ward, Richmond. West, Johnston & co., Richmond, Va., 1881.
136 p.

FRANKLIN:

Claiborne, Nathaniel Herbert. Notes on the war in the South; with biographical sketches of the lives of Montgomery, Jackson, Sevier, the late Gov. Claiborne, and others. By Nathaniel Herbert Claiborne, of Franklin County, Va., a member of the executive of Virginia during the late war. Richmond, Published by William Ramsey, 1819.
112 p.

FREDERICK:

Cartmell, Thomas Kemp. Shenandoah Valley pioneers and their descendants. A history of Frederick County, Virginia (illustrated), from its formation in 1738 to 1908. Comp. mainly from original records of old Frederick County, now Hampshire, Berkeley, Shenandoah, Jefferson, Hardy, Clarke, Warren, Morgan and Frederick . . . [Winchester, Va., Printed by the Eddy press corporation, 1909]
vii, 587 p. plates.

In loving memory of a revered father [William Searight, 1791-1852] and a sainted mother [Rachel Brownfield Searight Stidger, 1805-1893] no place. no date.
66 p.
Rachel Brownfield Searight was born in Frederick Co., Va., in 1805.

Ireland, James. The life of the Rev. James Ireland, who was for many years pastor of the Baptist church at Buck Marsh, Waterlick and Happy Creek in Frederick and Shenandoah counties, Virginia. Winchester, Va., Printed for the publishers by J. Foster, 1819.
232 p.

Mabry, W. S. Brief sketch of the career of Captain Catesby ap R. Jones. Compiled by request by W. S. Mabry, Selma, Alabama, January, 1912.
55 p.
> Capt. Jones was born at Fairfield, Frederick, now Clarke County, Virginia, on the 15th day of April, 1821.

Norris, J. E. History of the lower Shenandoah valley counties of Frederick, Berkeley, Jefferson and Clarke, their early settlement and progress to the present time; geological features; a description of their historic . . . localities; cities, towns and villages; portraits of some of the prominent men, and biographies of many of the representative citizens . . . Chicago, A. Warner & co., 1890.
viii, 9-812 p. illus.

Virginia magazine of history and biography. v. 18.

GILES:

No separate history of this county is now in the Library.

w GILMER:

Callahan, James Morton. Semi-centennial history of West Virginia, by James Morton Callahan . . . with special articles on development and resources . . . [Charleston, W. Va.] Semi-centennial commission of West Virginia, 1913.
ix, 594 p. 1 illus., plates, maps (part fold.) tables.

Lewis, Virgil Anson. History of West Virginia. In two parts . . . Philadelphia, Hubbard bros., 1889.
744 p. pl.

GLOUCESTER:

Manufacturers' record, Baltimore. Perpetuation of local history in Virginia [with lists of portraits and memorials in Westmoreland, King and Queen, Essex, Lancaster, Mathews, Middlesex, Northumberland, Gloucester and King William counties], a description of the work of Judge T. R. B. Wright.
13 p.
> Reprinted from the Manufacturers' record, Baltimore, Md., July 25, 1907.

Robins, Mrs. Sally Nelson. Gloucester. One of the first chapters of the commonwealth of Virginia . . . By Sally Nelson Robins. [Richmond, West, Johnston & co., 1893]
21 p. plates.
> On cover: History of Gloucester County, Virginia, and its families.

Stubbs, William Carter. Descendants of Mordecai Cooke, of "Mordecai's Mount", Gloucester County, Virginia, 1650. By William Carter Stubbs, Audubon Park, New Orleans, La. New Orleans, L. Graham & son, ltd., printers, 1896.
48 p. illus.

Virginia magazine of history and biography. v. 12, 13.

William and Mary college quarterly historical papers. v. 2.

William and Mary college quarterly historical magazine. v. 3, 11, 15.

GOOCHLAND:

Massie, David Meade. Nathaniel Massie, a pioneer of Ohio. A sketch of his life and selections from his correspondence. By David Meade Massie. Cincinnati, The Robert Clarke company, 1896.
ix, 11-285 p. map.
Nathaniel Massie was born in Goochland Co., Va., Dec. 28, 1/63.

Rutherfoord, John C. Speech of John C. Rutherfoord, of Goochland, in the House of Delegates of Virginia, 21 February 1860, in favor of the proposed conference of Southern states. Richmond, W. H. Clemmitt, printer, 1860.
(In Political pamphlets. v. 10.)

——Speech of John C. Rutherford of Goochland on the banking policy of Virginia, delivered in the House of delegates of Virginia, February 9, 1856, upon the bill to extend the charter of the bank of Virginia. Richmond, Chas. H. Wynne, printer, 1856.
34 p.

Virginia magazine of history and biography. v. 7.

Ward, Robert D. An account of General LaFayette's visit to Virginia, in the years 1824-'25, containing full circumstantial reports of his reception in Washington, Alexandria, Mount Vernon, Yorktown, Williamsburg, Norfolk, Richmond, Petersburg, Goochland, Fluvanna, Monticello, Charlottesville, Gordonsville, Orange Court House, Fredericksburg, Leesburg, University of Virginia, Culpeper, Fauquier, and his departure from the United States, with a portrait of General LaFayette, photographed from his bust, by Houdon, in the capitol of Virginia; compiled from newspapers of the period and other sources, by Robert D. Ward, Richmond. West, Johnston & co., Richmond, Va., 1881.
136 p.

William and Mary college quarterly historical magazine. v. 5, 7, 8, 15.

GRAYSON:

Nuckolls, B. F. Pioneer settlers of Grayson Co., Va., by B. F. Nuckolls, Galax, Va. Bristol, Tenn., The King printing Co., 1914.
206 p. plates.

w GREENBRIER:

    Callahan, James Morton. Semi-centennial history of West Virginia, by James Morton Callahan . . . with special articles on development and resources . . . [Charleston, W. Va.] Semi-centennial commission of West Virginia, 1913.
        ix, 594 p. 1 illus., plates, maps (part fold.) tables.

    Lewis, Virgil Anson. History of West Virginia. In two parts . . . Philadelphia, Hubbard bros., 1889.
        744 p. pl.

    Miller, Joseph Lyon. Ancestry and descendants of Lieut. John Henderson, of Greenbrier County, Virginia. 1650-1900. From data collected and arranged by his great-great-grandson, Joseph Lyon Miller, M. D., . . . Richmond, Va., Whittet & Shepperson, printers, 1902.
        37 p.

    Virginia magazine of history and biography. v. 19.

    William and Mary college quarterly historical magazine. v. 22.

GREENE:

    No separate history of this county is now in the Library.

GREENSVILLE:

    Bernard, R. S. Directory of the counties of Hanover, Chesterfield, Amelia, Dinwiddie, Greensville and Brunswick. Comp. . . . by R. S. Bernard, Madison Run, Orange County, Va. 1896. Richmond, Ware & Duke, printers, 1896.
        287 p.

    William and Mary college quarterly historical magazine. v. 22.

HALIFAX:

    Morrison, Alfred James. Halifax County, Virginia: a handbook prepared under the direction of the Board of supervisors, by Alfred J. Morrison. Richmond, Va., Everett Waddey co., 1907.
        93 p. (fold. map) illus.

w HAMPSHIRE:

    Callahan, James Morton. Semi-centennial history of West Virginia, by James Morton Callahan . . . with special articles on development and resources . . . [Charleston, W. Va.] Semi-centennial commission of West Virginia, 1913.
        ix, 594 p. 1 illus., plates, maps (part fold.) tables.

    Cartmell, Thomas Kemp. Shenandoah Valley pioneers and their descendants. A history of Frederick County, Virginia (illustrated),

from its formation in 1738 to 1908. Comp. mainly from original records of old Frederick County, now Hampshire, Berkeley, Shenandoah, Jefferson, Hardy, Clarke, Warren, Morgan and Frederick . . . [Winchester, Va., Printed by the Eddy press corporation, 1909]
vii, 587 p. plates.

Lewis, Virgil Anson. History of West Virginia. In two parts . . . Philadelphia, Hubbard bros., 1889.
744 p. pl.

Maxwell, Hu. History of Hampshire county, West Virginia, from its earliest settlement to the present, by Hu Maxwell and H. L. Swisher . . . Morgantown, W. Va., A. B. Boughner, printer, 1897.
744 p. pl.

HANCOCK:

Callahan, James Morton. Semi-centennial history of West Virginia, by James Morton Callahan . . . with special articles on development and resources . . . [Charleston, W. Va.] Semi-centennial commission of West Virginia, 1913.
ix, 594 p. 1 illus., plates, maps (part fold.) tables.

Lewis, Virgil Anson. History of West Virginia. In two parts . . . Philadelphia, Hubbard bros., 1889.
744 p. pl.

Newton, J. H. History of the Pan-handle; being historical collections of the counties of Ohio, Brooke, Marshall and Hancock, West Virginia . . . Comp. and written by J. H. Newton, G. G. Nichols, and A. G. Sprankle. Ed. by J. H. Newton. Wheeling, W. Va., J. A. Caldwell, 1879.
450 p., 1 l., xxx [1] p. pl., 2 maps.

HANOVER:

Bell, James Pinkney. Our Quaker friends of ye olden time, being in part a transcript of the minute book of Cedar Creek meeting, Hanover county, and the South River meeting, Campbell county, Va. J. P. Bell company, publishers, Lynchburg, Va., 1905.
v, 287 p. plates.

Bennett, Hugh Hammond. Soil survey of Hanover County, Virginia, by Hugh H. Bennett and W. E. McLendon.
(In U. S. Bureau of soils. Report, 1905)

Bernard, R. S. Directory of the counties of Hanover, Chesterfield, Amelia, Dinwiddie, Greensville and Brunswick. Comp. . . . by R. S. Bernard, Madison Run, Orange County, Va. 1896. Richmond, Ware & Duke, printers, 1896.
287 p.

Davies, Samuel. The crisis: or, The uncertain doom of kingdoms at particular times. Considered with reference to Great Britain and her colonies in their present circumstances. A sermon, preached in Hanover, Virginia, October 28, 1756; a day appointed by the synod of New York, to be observed as a general fast on account of the present war with France. By the reverend Mr. Samuel Davies, A. M. With a preface by the reverend Mr. Thomas Gibbons. London, Printed for J. Buckland in Pater-noster Row, J. Ward in Cornhill, and T. Field in Cheapside, 1757.
iii-viii, 36 p.

—— The substance of a letter from Mr. Davies, minister of the gospel in Hanover county, Virginia, to Mr. Bellamy of Bethlem, in New England, concerning the state of religion in Virginia, from 1743 to June, 1751. Printed for John Orr, bookseller.
16 p.
Letter dated: "Hanover, June 28, 1751".

Jay, John. Letters, being the whole of the correspondence between the Honorable John Jay, esq., and Mr. Lewis Littlepage; a young man, whom Mr. Jay, when in Spain, patronized and took into his family. A new and correct edition. To which is added an appendix, not before published. New York, Printed by Eleazer Oswald, 1786.
54 p.
Mr. Littlepage was born in Hanover County, Virginia, Dec. 19, 1762.

The Virginia almanack for the year of our Lord 1805 . . . Adapted to the latitude and meridian of Richmond. Calculated by Benjamin Bates of Hanover county, Virginia. Richmond, printed and sold wholesale and retail by Samuel Pleasants, Jr. [1804]
48 p.
[The Library also has a copy of this almanac for the year 1812.]

William and Mary college quarterly historical magazine. v. 6, 9, 21, 22.

▼ HARDY:

Callahan, James Morton. Semi-centennial history of West Virginia, by James Morton Callahan . . . with special articles on development and resources . . . [Charleston, W. Va.] Semi-centennial commission of West Virginia, 1913.
ix, 594 p. 1 illus., plates, maps (part fold.) tables.

Cartmell, Thomas Kemp. Shenandoah Valley pioneers and their descendants. A history of Frederick County, Virginia (illustrated), from its formation in 1738 to 1908. Comp. mainly from original records of old Frederick County, now Hampshire, Berkeley, Shenandoah, Jefferson, Hardy, Clarke, Warren, Morgan and Frederick . . . [Winchester, Va., Printed by the Eddy press corporation, 1909]
vii, 587 p. plates.

Lewis, Virgil Anson. History of West Virginia. In two parts . . . Philadelphia, Hubbard bros., 1889.
  744 p. pl.

w HARRISON:

Callahan, James Morton. Semi-centennial history of West Virginia, by James Morton Callahan . . . with special articles on development and resources . . . [Charleston, W. Va.] Semi-centennial commission of West Virginia, 1913.
  ix, 594 p. 1 illus., plates, maps (part fold.) tables.

Haymond, Henry. History of Harrison County, West Virginia, by Henry Haymond; from the early days of northwestern Virginia to the present . . . Morgantown, W. Va., Acme publishing company [c 1910]
  4 pl., 451 p. plates.

Lewis, Virgil Anson. History of West Virginia. In two parts . . . Philadelphia, Hubbard bros., 1889.
  744 p. pl.

HENRICO:

Cabell, James Branch. Branch of Abingdon, being a partial account of the ancestry of Christopher Branch of "Arrowhattocks" and "Kingsland", in Henrico County, and the founder of the Branch family in Virginia, by James Branch Cabell . . . Richmond, Va., Printed by Wm. E. Jones' sons, inc. [1911]
  9 p. l., [15]-126 p. plates.

The Chesapeake & Ohio railway directory, containing an illustrated history and description of the road, together with improvements and connections already completed and those in contemplation; also, the names of the merchants, manufacturers, professional men, and farmers, with postoffice addresses in the counties of Elizabeth City, Warwick, York, James City, New Kent, Charles City, King William, Henrico . . . together with a description of the surface, soil, average value of lands, county and city officers, and other useful and valuable information. Compiled by J. H. Chataigne. 1881. c 1881 by J. H. Chataigne.
  379 p.

Hardesty's historical and geographical encyclopedia . . . Special Virginia ed., giving a history of the Virginias, biographical sketches of eminent Virginians, written by R. A. Brock . . . New York, Richmond [etc.] H. H. Hardesty & co., 1885.
  417 p. incl. plates, maps.
    The "History of the Virginias" (p. [305]-334) and the chapter "Eminent Virginians" (p. [335]-392) are mainly identical with the work "Virginia and Virginians," 2 v. Richmond, H. H. Hardesty & company, 1888.
    This was issued in several county editions. The edition in the State Library contains special information in regard to Henrico county and city of Richmond.

Harris family. A chart of some of the descendants of Captain Thomas Harris, of Henrico County, who came to Virginia in 1611, with an appendix of illustrative documents. Richmond, Va., Wm. Ellis Jones, printer, 1893.
    chart, 29 p.

Ruffin, Frank G. The judicial usurpation of Judge Hugh L. Bond, judge of the 4th judicial circuit of the U. S., in the case of A. J. Ford, prop'r of Ford's hotel vs. Wm. Taylor, treasurer, Henrico Co. As exposed by Frank G. Ruffin. Richmond, Va., Johns & co., printers, 1886.
    17 p.

Slaughter, Philip. A brief sketch of the life of William Green, LL. D., jurist and scholar, with some personal reminiscences of him. By Philip Slaughter, D. D., historiographer of the P. E. church diocese of Virginia. Also, a historical tract by Judge Green, and some curious letters upon the origin of the proverb "*Vox populi, vox dei*." Richmond, Wm. Ellis Jones, book and job printer, 1883.
    131 p.
    Contains: The Genesis of certain counties in Virginia, from cities or town of the same name.

Virginia magazine of history and biography. v. 5.

William and Mary college quarterly historical magazine. v. 5, 8.

HENRY:

Virginia magazine of history and biography. v. 1, 9, 10, 11, 17, 21.

HIGHLAND:

Morton, Oren Frederic. A history of Highland County, Virginia, by Oren F. Morton. . . . Monterey, Va., The author [1911]
    419 p. plates, 2 maps.

•ILLINOIS:

This county existed only from 1778-1784.

Alvord, Clarence Walworth. . . . Cahokia records, 1778-1790; ed. with introduction and notes by Clarence Walworth Alvord . . . Springfield, Ill., The Trustees of the Illinois state historical library, 1907.
    clvi, 663 p. 2 pl. fold. map.
    (Collections of the Illinois state historical library, vol. II. Virginia series, vol. 1)

Boyd, Carl Evans. The county of Illinois [in Virginia]
    (In American historical review. v. 4, no. 4. July, 1899)

Cahokia, Ill. . . . Cahokia records, 1778-1790; ed. with introduction and notes by Clarence Walworth Alvord . . . Springfield, Ill., The Trustees of the Illinois state historical library, 1907.
    clvi, 563 p. 2 pl. fold. map.
    (Collections of the Illinois state historical library, v. 2. Virginia series, v. 1)

Carter, Clarence Edwin. Great Britain and the Illinois country (1763-1774) by Clarence Edwin Carter [Washington, The American historical association, 1910].
    ix, 223 p. (Half-title: Prize Essays of the American historical association, 1908)

ISLE OF WIGHT:

Crocker, James Francis. The Woodleys of Isle of Wight County, Va., and other ancestors. By James Francis Crocker. Portsmouth, Virginia, 1915.
    var. pag.

[Morrison, E. M.] Isle of Wight County. 1608-1907. [Norfolk? Va., 1907]
    72 p. illus., plates.

Virginia historical register and literary note book. v. 4, no. 4.

Virginia magazine of history and biography. v. 5, 6, 11.

William and Mary college quarterly historical magazine. v. 4, 5, 6, 7.

▼JACKSON:

Callahan, James Morton. Semi-centennial history of West Virginia, by James Morton Callahan . . . with special articles on development and resources . . . [Charleston, W. Va.] Semi-centennial commission of West Virginia, 1913.
    ix, 594 p. 1 illus., plates, maps (part fold.) tables.

Lewis, Virgil Anson. History of West Virginia. In two parts . . . Philadelphia, Hubbard bros., 1889.
    744 p. pl.

JAMES CITY:

Hall, John Leslie. Ancient epitaphs and inscriptions, in York and James City counties, Virginia. A paper read before the Virginia historical society Monday, December 21, 1891, by Prof. J. L. Hall . . . Richmond, 1892.
    (In Virginia historical society. Collections. Richmond, 1892. new ser., v. 11)

Slaughter, Philip. A brief sketch of the life of William Green, LL. D., jurist and scholar, with some personal reminiscences of him. By Philip Slaughter, D. D., historiographer of the P. E. church

diocese of Virginia. Also, a historical tract by Judge Green, and some curious letters upon the origin of the proverb *"Vox populi, vox dei."* Richmond, Wm. Ellis Jones, book and job printer, 1883.
 131 p.
  Contains: The Genesis of certain counties in Virginia, from cities or towns of the same name.

William and Mary college quarterly historical magazine. v. 2, 5, 6, 9, 10, 11, 12, 14, 20.

JEFFERSON (1780):

 Collins, Lewis. Collins' historical sketches of Kentucky. History of Kentucky . . . revised, enlarged . . . and brought down to . . . 1874, by . . . R. H. Collins . . . Embracing pre-historic, annals for 331 years . . . statistics, antiquities and natural curiosities, geographical and geological descriptions . . . and . . . biographical sketches . . . Covington, Ky., Collins & Co., 1878.
  2 v. pl. fold. map.

JEFFERSON (1801):

 Callahan, James Morton. Semi-centennial history of West Virginia, by James Morton Callahan . . . with special articles on development and resources . . . [Charleston, W. Va.] Semi-centennial commission of West Virginia, 1913.
  ix, 594 p. 1 illus., plates, maps (part fold.) tables.

 Cartmell, Thomas Kemp. Shenandoah Valley pioneers and their descendants. A history of Frederick County, Virginia (illustrated), from its formation in 1738 to 1908. Comp. mainly from original records of old Frederick County, now Hampshire, Berkeley, Shenandoah, Jefferson, Hardy, Clarke, Warren, Morgan and Frederick . . . [Winchester, Va., Printed by the Eddy press corporation, 1909]
  vii, 587 p. plates.

 Lewis, Virgil Anson. History of West Virginia. In two parts . . . Philadelphia, Hubbard bros., 1889.
  744 p. pl.

 Norris, J. E. History of the lower Shenandoah valley counties of Frederick, Berkeley, Jefferson and Clarke, their early settlement and progress to the present time; geological features; a description of their historic . . . localities; cities, towns and villages; portraits of some of the prominent men, and biographies of many of the representative citizens . . . Chicago, A. Warner & co., 1890.
  viii, 9-812 p. illus.

KANAWHA:

 Atkinson, George Wesley. History of Kanawha county [W. Va.] from its organization in 1789 until the present time; embracing accounts of early settlements, and thrilling adventures with the Indians . . .

Also, biographical sketches of a large number of the early setlers of the Great Kanawha valley . . . Charleston, Off. of West Virginia journal, 1876.
1 p. l., viii, 9-338 p. pl., plans.

Callahan, James Morton. Semi-centennial history of West Virginia, by James Morton Callahan . . . with special articles on development and resources . . . [Charleston, W. Va.] Semi-centennial commission of West Virginia, 1913.
ix, 594 p. 1 illus., plates, maps (part fold.) tables.

Hale, John P. Daniel Boone. Some facts and incidents not hitherto published. His ten or twelve years' residence in Kanawha County . . . By Dr. John P. Hale . . . Wheeling, L. Baker & co., printers [188-]
18 p.

Lewis, Virgil Anson. History of West Virginia. In two parts . . . Philadelphia, Hubbard bros., 1889.
744 p. pl.

Summers, L. Memorial of manufacturers of salt, in the county of Kanawha, Virginia, against the repeal of the duty on imported salt, Jan. 21, 1828. Printed by order of the senate of the United States. Washington, Printed by Duff Green, 1828.
21 p. fold. table.
Signed by L. Summers and six others.
(U. S. 20th Congress. 1st sess. Sen. doc. 47)

Virginia magazine of history and biography. v. 8.

• KENTUCKY:

This county existed only from 1777-1780.

Collins, Lewis. Collins' historical sketches of Kentucky. History of Kentucky . . . revised, enlarged . . . and brought down to . . . 1874, by . . . R. H. Collins . . . Embracing pre-historic, annals for 331 years . . . statistics, antiquities and natural curiosities, geographical and geological descriptions . . . and . . . biographical sketches . . . Covington, Ky., Collins & Co., 1878.
2 v. pl. fold. map.

KING AND QUEEN:

Bagby, Alfred. King and Queen County, Virginia, by Rev. Alfred Bagby . . . New York and Washington, The Neale publishing company, 1908.
4 pl., [7]-402 p. plates, maps.

Graham, William A. Life and character of the Hon. Thomas Ruffin, late chief justice of North Carolina. A memorial oration by William A. Graham, delivered before the agricultural society of the state,

by its request, at the annual fair in Raleigh, Oct. 21, 1870. Raleigh, N. C., Nichols & Gorman, 1871.
34 p.
Judge Ruffin was born in King & Queen Co., Va., Nov. 17, 1787.

Manufacturers' record, Baltimore. Perpetuation of local history in Virginia [with lists of portraits and memorials in Westmoreland, King and Queen, Essex, Lancaster, Mathews, Middlesex, Northumberland, Gloucester, and King William counties] a description of the work of Judge T. R. B. Wright.
13 p.
Reprinted from the Manufacturers' record, Baltimore, Md., July 25, 1907.

Pollard, Henry Robinson. Addresses delivered at the unveiling of a monument to the memory of Edward Bagby at Bruington church, King & Queen County, Virginia, August 8, 1912, by Hon. Henry R. Pollard and others. Richmond, Va., Everett Waddey company [1912]
53 p.

Smedes, Susan Dabney. A Southern planter. By Susan Dabney Smedes . . . Fourth edition. New York, James Pott & co., publishers, 1890.
342 p.
Memorials of Thomas Smith Gregory Dabney, who was born in King and Queen County, Virginia, Jan. 4, 1798.

Virginia magazine of history and biography. v. 9, 10.

Walker, B. H. King and Queen county, Virginia. Information for the homeseeker and investor. Prepared under the supervision of W. H. Walker, as authorized by the Board of supervisors of King and Queen county, Va., August, 1906. Compiled by Dr. B. H. Walker, Stevensville, Va. Richmond, Chas. E. Picot ptg. co. [1907]
32 p.

William and Mary college quarterly historical magazine. v. 9, 10, 14.

KING GEORGE:

Boucher, Jonathan. A view of the causes and consequences of the American revolution; in thirteen discourses preached in North America between the years 1763 and 1775: with an historical preface. By Jonathan Boucher, Vicar of Epsom in the County of Surrey. London, Printed for G. G. and J. Robinson, 1797.
4 p. l., xciv p., 1 l., 596 p.
"The Vestry of the Parish of Hanover in the County of King George in that part of Virginia which is called the Northern Neck, did me the honour to nominate me to the Rectory of their Parish, in 1761, before I was in orders . . . I afterwards held the Parish of St. Mary's in Caroline County, Virginia" p. xc.

Virginia magazine of history and biography. v. 8.

KING WILLIAM:

The Chesapeake & Ohio railway directory, containing an illustrated history and description of the road, together with improvements and connections already completed and those in contemplation; also, the names of the merchants, manufacturers, professional men, and farmers, with postoffice addresses in the counties of Elizabeth City, Warwick, York, James City, New Kent, Charles City, King William, Henrico . . . together with a description of the surface, soil, average value of lands, county and city officers, and other useful and valuable information. Compiled by J. H. Chataigne. 1881. c 1881 by J. H. Chataigne.
379 p.

Clarke, Peyton Neale. Old King William homes and families; an account of some of the old homesteads and families of King William county, Virginia, from its earliest settlement . . . Louisville, J. P. Morton, 1897.
4 p. l., 211 p. pl.

Magruder, Allan Bowie. Debate on the punishment of the wicked and the kingdom of God; its character, locality and the time of its establishment; between Allan B. Magruder, of Charlottesville, Va., and Edward E. Orvis, of New London, Penn., held at Acquinton church, King William co., Va., on the 11th, 12th, 13th and 14th of June, 1855. P. Kean, stenographic reporter. Richmond, Elliott & Nye, 1855.
435 p.

Manufacturers' record, Baltimore. Perpetuation of local history in Virginia [with lists of portraits and memorials in Westmoreland, King and Queen, Essex, Lancaster, Mathews, Middlesex, Northumberland, Gloucester and King William counties] a description of the work of Judge T. R. B. Wright.
13 p.
Reprinted from the Manufactueres' record, Baltimore, Md., July 25 ,1907.

Pamunkey Baptist association (Colored). Minutes of the second annual session of the Pamunkey Baptist association, held at the Mt. Olive Baptist church, King William Co., Va., Sept. 3, 4 and 5, 1902 . . . Richmond, Va., Virginia Baptist press, 1903.
[16] p.

——Proceedings and constitution held at the Third Union Baptist church, King William county, Va., September 5, 1900. Richmond, Virginia Baptist press, 1901.
8 p.

West Point, Virginia, and King William county. 1888. Richmond, Everett Waddey, 1888.
53 p.

William and Mary college quarterly historical magazine. v. 20.

LANCASTER:

Gordon, Armistead Churchill. Colonel James Gordon of Lancaster (1714-1768). Read at the presentation by his descendants to the county of Lancaster, Virginia, of a portrait of Col. James Gordon, July 21, 1913, by Armistead C. Gordon. [Staunton, Va., 1913]
11, [2] p.

Jeter, Jeremiah Bell. A memoir of Mrs. Henrietta Shuck, the first American female missionary to China. By J. B. Jeter, pastor of the First Baptist Church, Richmond, Va. Boston, Gould, Kendall and Lincoln, 1846.
xii, [13]-251 p.
Henrietta Hall (later Mrs. Shuck) was born in Lancaster County, Virginia, Oct. 28, 1817.

Manufacturers' record, Baltimore. Perpetuation of local history in Virginia [with lists of portraits and memorials in Westmoreland, King and Queen, Essex, Lancaster, Mathews, Middlesex, Northumberland, Gloucester and King William counties] a description of the work of Judge T. R. B. Wright.
13 p.
Reprinted from the Manufacturers' record, Baltimore, Md., July 25, 1907.

Miller, Joseph Lyon. . . . The descendants of Capt. Thomas Carter of "Barford", Lancaster County, Virginia, with genealogical notes of many of the allied families, by Joseph Lyon Miller . . . Thomas, W. Va., 1912.
7 p. l., xxvii, 388 p. plates.

Montague, George William. History and genealogy of Peter Montague, of Nansemond and Lancaster counties, Virginia, and his descendants, 1621-1894. Comp. and pub. by George William Montague . . . Amherst, Mass., Press of Carpenter & Morehouse, 1894.
1 p. l., 494 p.

——History and genealogy of the Montague family of America, descended from Richard Montague of Hadley, Mass., and Peter Montague of Lancaster Co., Va., with genealogical notes of other families by name of Montague. Comp. by George Wm. Montague. Rev. and ed. by William L. Montague . . . Amherst, Mass., Press of J. E. Williams, 1886.
vii, [8]-785 p. plates.

Richmond, Westmoreland, Lancaster & Northumberland counties, Va. Board of immigration. The Northern Neck of Virginia as a home for immigrants, by the board of immigration for the counties of Richmond, Westmoreland, Lancaster & Northumberland, Virginia. New York, Schmidt & Curtius, stationers, 1872.
16 p. map.

Virginia magazine of history and biography. v. 5, 7, 12.

William and Mary college quarterly historical papers. v. 1.

William and Mary college quarterly historical magazine. v. 4, 5, 6, 11, 12, 17, 20, 21.—

LEE:

No separate history of this county is now in the Library.

w LEWIS:

Callahan, James Morton. Semi-centennial history of West Virginia, by James Morton Callahan . . . with special articles on development and resources . . . [Charleston, W. Va.] Semi-centennial commission of West Virginia, 1913.
    ix, 594 p. 1 illus., maps (part fold.) tables.

Lewis, Virgil Anson. History of West Virginia. In two parts . . . Philadelphia, Hubbard bros., 1889.
    744 p. pl.

⋆ LINCOLN:

Collins, Lewis. Collins' historical sketches of Kentucky. History of Kentucky . . . revised, enlarged . . . and brought down to . . . 1874, by . . . R. H. Collins . . . Embracing pre-historic, annals for 331 years . . . statistics, antiquities and natural curiosities, geographical and geological descriptions . . . and . . . biographical sketches . . . Covington, Ky., Collins & Co., 1878.
    2 v. fold. map.

w LOGAN:

Callahan, James Morton. Semi-centennial history of West Virginia, by James Morton Callahan . . . with special articles on development and resources . . . [Charleston, W. Va.] Semi-centennial commission of West Virginia, 1913.
    ix, 594 p. 1 illus., plates, maps (part fold.) tables.

Lewis, Virgil Anson. History of West Virginia. In two parts . . . Philadelphia, Hubbard bros., 1889.
    744 p. pl.

LOUDOUN:

Broun, William Le Roy. Dr. William Le Roy Broun, comp. by Thomas L. Broun, assisted by Bessie Lee Broun and Sally F. Ordway. New York, The Neale publishing company, 1912.
    4 p. l., 247 p.
    Dr. Brown was born in Loudoun Co., Va., in 1827. He was graduated at the University of Virginia in 1850.

Confederate States of America. Congress. Proceedings and speeches on the announcement of the death of Hon. R. L. Y. Peyton of Missouri, in the House of Representatives of the Confederate States, Dec. 19, 1863. Richmond, Sentinel job office, print., 1864.
8 p.
R. L. Y. Peyton was born in Loudoun Co., Va., Dec. 1824.

Garnett, James Mercer. Biographical sketch of Hon. Charles Fenton Mercer, 1778-1858, M. C., 1817-1840, of Aldie, Loudoun County, Virginia, son of Hon. James Mercer, Judge of Court of appeals of Virginia. . . . Richmond, Va., Privately printed by Whittet & Shepperson, 1911.
95 p. plates.

Head, James William. History and comprehensive description of Loudoun County, Virginia, by James W. Head. [Washington, D. C.] Park view press [c 1909]
186 p.

Janney, Samuel McPherson. Memoirs of Samuel M. Janney, late of Lincoln, Loudoun County, Va., a minister in the religious society of Friends (written by himself) . . . Philadelphia, Friends' book association, 1881.
x, 309 p.

Preston, William P. Speech of William P. Preston, esq., of Maryland, delivered October 25, 1856, at the farm of Robert J. T. White, esq., near Hillsborough, Loudoun County, Va. Reported expressly for the National. [1856]
12 p.

William and Mary college quarterly historical magazine. v. 12.

LOUISA:

Bennett, Hugh Hammond. Soil survey of Louisa County, Virginia, by Hugh H. Bennett and W. E. McLendon.
(In U. S. Bureau of soils. Report, 1905. map)

Cottom's Virginia and North Carolina almanack for the year of our Lord 1836 . . . Calculated for the meridian of Richmond, latitude 37° 32' 25'', longitude 77° 21' 24''. By David Richardson of Louisa county, Va. Richmond. Printed and published annually by Peter Cottom and sold by him, C. Hall . . . [1835]
36 p.
[The Library has also copies of this almanac for the years 1838, 1840, 1842, 1844 and 1846.]

Leake, Andrew King. The bench, the bar and citizens of Louisa. An address delivered by Judge A. K. Leake, by request of the Board of Supervisors of Louisa, at the dedication of their new court-house, on Aug. 17, 1905. Richmond, Va., Whittet and Shepperson, printers, 1906.
19 p.

Poindexter, George. Speech on the Seminole war, in the House of representatives, Feb. 1, 1819.
: (In Williston, E. B. Eloquence of the U. S. v. 3)
: George Poindexter was born in Louisa Co., Va., in 1779.

Richardson's Virginia and North Carolina almanac for the year of our Lord 1845 . . . Calculated by David Richardson of Louisa county, Virginia . . . Richmond, Va., published by Drinker & Morris [1844]
: 34 p.
: [The Library has also copies of this almanac for the years 1846, 1847, 1848, 1853, 1854, 1855, 1856, 1861, 1862, 1863, 1864, 1866, 1867 and 1871.]

Richardson's almanac, 1857 . . . Calculated by David Richardson of Louisa county, Va. (Cottom's edition). Richmond, Va., published and for sale by J. W. Randolph [1856]
: 36 p.
: [The Library has also copies of this almanac for the years 1858, 1859 and 1861.]

The Virginia almanac for the year of our Lord 1815 . . . Adapted to the latitude and meridian of Richmond. Calculated by D. B. Bullock of Louisa county, Va. Alexandria, printed and published by J. A. Stewart and sold wholesale and retail at his book-stores on King and Royal streets, Alexandria [1814]
: 36 p.

The Virginia and North Carolina pocket almanack and farmers' companion for the year of our Lord 1820 . . . By David Richardson of Louisa county, Virginia . . . Richmond, printed by John Warrock, street leading to Mayo's Bridge [1819]
: 34 p.
: [The Library has also copies of this almanac for the years 1822, 1823, 1825, 1826, 1827, 1828, 1829, 1830, 1831, 1832, 1833, 1834 and 1835.]

Woolfolk, C. W. Directory of the counties of Orange, Louisa, Albemarle, Culpeper and Spotsylvania. Comp. and for sale by C. W. Woolfolk, Orange, Va., W. J. Daniel, Bibb's, Va. 1895. [Richmond, Va., Ware & Duke, general printers, 1895]
: 1, 267 p.

• LOWER NORFOLK:

This county existed only from 1637-1691.

McIntosh, Charles Fleming. Brief abstract of Lower Norfolk County and Norfolk County wills, 1637-1710, by Charles Fleming McIntosh . . . [Richmond] The Colonial dames of America in the state of Virginia, 1914.
: 2 p. l., [3]-223 p. 24cm.
: In 1691 Lower Norfolk County was divided into Princess Anne County and Norfolk County. cf. Pref.

The lower Norfolk County, Virginia, antiquary. Edited by Edward W James. v. 1-5. 1897-1906.
: 5 v.

Virginia magazine of history and biography. v. 5, 6.

William and Mary college quarterly historical papers. v. 2.

LUNENBURG:

Barry, William Taylor. Letters of William T. Barry, 1806-1810, 1829-1831.
   (In American historical review. v. 16, no. 2.)
   W. T. Barry was born in Lunenburg County, Va., in 1785, graduated from the College of William and Mary in 1807. He represented Kentucky in the House of Representatives 1810-11, and in the Senate, 1815-16. Postmaster General, 1829.

Owen, Thomas McAdory. Bryant Lester of Lunenburg Co., Va., and his descendants.
   (In Southern history association publications. v. 1. 1897)
   Virginia historical register and literary companion. v. 5, no. 2.
   William and Mary college quarterly historical magazine. v. 9.

w McDOWELL:

Callahan, James Morton. Semi-centennial history of West Virginia, by James Morton Callahan . . . with special articles on development and resources . . . [Charleston, W. Va.] Semi-centennial commission of West Virginia, 1913.
   ix, 594 p. 1 illus., plates, maps (part fold.) tables.

Lewis, Virgil Anson. History of West Virginia. In two parts . . . Philadelphia, Hubbard bros., 1889.
   744 p. pl.

k MADISON (1786):

Collins, Lewis. Collins' historical sketches of Kentucky. History of Kentucky . . . revised, enlarged . . . and brought down to . . . 1874, by . . . R. H. Collins . . . Embracing pre-historic, annals for 331 years . . . statistics, antiquities and natural curiosities, geographical and geological descriptions . . . and . . . biographical sketches . . . Covington, Ky., Collins & Co., 1878.
   2 v. fold. map.

MADISON (1793):

Early, Samuel Stockwell. A history of the family of Early in America: being the ancestors and descendants of Jeremiah Early, who came from the county of Donegal, Ireland, and settled in what is now Madison County, Virginia, early in the eighteenth century, by Samuel Stockwell Early. Arranged for publication by Robert Stockwell Hatcher . . . Albany, N. Y., J. Munsell's sons, 1896.
   53 p.

Huddle, William Peter. History of the Hebron Lutheran Church, Madison County, Virginia, from 1717 to 1907. By Rev. W. P. Huddle, pastor. New Market, Va., Henkel & company, 1908.
   xi, 115, [1] p. plates.

Virginia magazine of history and biography. v. 14.

Wayland Blue Ridge Baptist association. Minutes of the twelfth annual session held with Mount Zion Baptist church, Madison Co., Virginia, August 14, 15 & 16, 1902 . . . Richmond, Va., Virginia Baptist press, 1902.
 20 p.

w MARION:

Callahan, James Morton. Semi-centennial history of West Virginia, by James Morton Callahan . . . with special articles on development and resources . . . [Charleston, W. Va.] Semi-centennial commission of West Virginia, 1913.
 ix, 594 p. 1 illus., plates, maps (part fold.) tables.

Lewis, Virgil Anson. History of West Virginia. In two parts . . . Philadelphia, Hubbard bros., 1889.
 744 p. pl.

w MARSHALL:

Callahan, James Morton. Semi-centennial history of West Virginia, by James Morton Callahan . . . with special articles on development and resources . . . [Charleston, W. Va.] Semi-centennial commission of West Virginia, 1913.
 ix, 594 p. 1 illus., plates, maps (part fold.) tables.

Lewis, Virgil Anson. History of West Virginia. In two parts . . . Philadelphia, Hubbard bros., 1889.
 744 p. pl.

Newton, J. H. History of the Pan-handle; being historical collections of the counties of Ohio, Brooke, Marshall and Hancock, West Virginia . . . Comp. and written by J. H. Newton, G. G. Nichols, and A. G. Sprankle. Ed. by J H. Newton. Wheeling, W. Va., J. A. Caldwell, 1879.
 450 p., 1 l., xxx, [1] p. pl., 2 maps.

k MASON (1789):

Collins, Lewis. Collins' historical sketches of Kentucky. History of Kentucky . . . revised, enlarged . . . and brought down to . . . 1874, by R. H. Collins . . . Embracing pre-historic, annals for 331 years . . . statistics, antiquities and natural curiosities, geographical and geological descriptions . . . and . . . biographical sketches . . . Covington, Ky., Collins & Co., 1878.
 2 v. fold. map.

w MASON (1804):

Callahan, James Morton. Semi-centennial history of West Virginia, by James Morton Callahan . . . with special articles on development

and resources . . . [Charleston, W. Va.] Semi-centennial commission of West Virginia, 1913.
ix, 594 p. 1 illus., plates, maps (part fold.) tables.

Lewis, Virgil Anson. History of West Virginia. In two parts . . . Philadelphia, Hubbard bros., 1889.
744 p. pl.

MATHEWS:

William and Mary college quarterly historical magazine. v. 3.

MECKLENBURG:

Alexander, Charles. Mecklenburg county, Virginia; its history, resources and advantages. The place for homes, health, happiness, and inviting business prospects. Come and see! Published for free distribution. 1907. [This publication prepared by Charles Alexander, H. F. Hutcheson, and Thos. D. Jeffress, of Mecklenburg County, Va.]
16 p.

Buffalo lithia springs, Mecklenburg County, Va. Thomas F. Goode, proprietor. [n. p. 1879?]
80 p.

Daves, Graham. A sketch of the military career of Captain John Daves of the North Carolina continental line of the army of the revolution; together with some facts of local and family history; by his grandson, Major Graham Daves . . . Baltimore, Press of the Friedenwald co., 1892.
16 p.
John Daves was born in Mecklenburg County, Virginia, in 1748.

Lee, A. Sharpe. Case of A. S. Lee and trial in the county court of Mecklenburg, Va. [n. p. n. d.]
32 p.

Munford, Robert. A collection of plays and poems, by the late Col. Robert Munford, of Mecklenburg County, in the state of Virginia. Now first published together. Petersburg, Printed by William Prentis, 1798.
xii, [13]-206 (i. e. 188) p.

Munford, William. Poems, and compositions in prose on several occasions. By William Munford, of the county of Mecklenburg, and state of Virginia. Richmond, Printed by Samuel Pleasants, jun., 1798.
1 l., 189 p.

Ravenscroft, John S. A sermon preached in St. Paul's church, Alexandria, at the opening of the Virginia convention, May 11, 1820. By the Rev. James S. Ravenscroft, of St. James parish, Mecklenburg. Published by desire of the members of the convention. Philadelphia, Printed by William Fry, 1820.
31 p.

MERCER (1786):

Collins, Lewis. Collins' historical sketches of Kentucky. History of Kentucky . . . revised, enlarged . . . and brought down to . . . 1874, by . . . R. H. Collins . . . Embracing pre-historic, annals for 331 years . . . statistics, antiquities and natural curiosities, geographical and geological descriptions . . . and . . . biographical sketches . . . Covington, Ky., Collins & Co., 1878.
    2 v. fold. map.

MERCER (1837):

Callahan, James Morton. Semi-centennial history of West Virginia, by James Morton Callahan . . . with special articles on development and resources . . . [Charleston, W. Va.] Semi-centennial commission of West Virginia, 1913.
    ix, 594 p. 1 illus., plates, maps (part fold.) tables.

Lewis, Virgil Anson. History of West Virginia. In two parts . . . Philadelphia, Hubbard bros., 1889.
    744 p. pl.

MIDDLESEX:

Christ church, Middlesex co., Va. The parish register of Christ church, Middlesex county, Va., from 1653 to 1812 . . . Richmond, W. E. Jones, 1897.
    341 p.
    Published by the National society of the colonial dames of America, Virginia.

Manufacturers' record, Baltimore. Perpetuation of local history in Virginia [with lists of portraits and memorials in Westmoreland, King and Queen, Essex, Lancaster, Mathews, Middlesex, Northumberland, Gloucester and King William counties] a description of the work of Judge T. R. B. Wright.
    13 p.
    Reprinted from the Manufacturers' record, Baltimore, Md., July 25, 1907.

Virginia magazine of history and biography. v. 2, 12, 15.

William and Mary college quarterly historical magazine. v. 4, 7, 12, 18.

MONONGALIA:

Callahan, James Morton. Semi-centennial history of West Virginia, by James Morton Callahan . . . with special articles on development and resources . . . [Charleston, W. Va.] Semi-centennial commission of West Virginia, 1913.
    ix, 594 p. 1 illus., plates, maps (part fold.) tables.

Lewis, Virgil Anson. History of West Virginia. In two parts . . . Philadelphia, Hubbard bros., 1889.
    744 p. pl.

Willey, Waitman Thomas. Speech delivered by Waitman T. Willey, of Monongalia, on Mr. Moore's resolutions on federal relations in the Virginia convention, March 4th, 1861. Richmond, Chas. H. Wynne, 1861.
    (In Political pamphlets. v. 31.)

Willey, Waitman Thomas. Speeches of Waitman T. Willey, of Monongalia county, before the state convention of Virginia on the basis of representation; on county courts & county organization, and on the election of judges by the people. Richmond, William Culley [1851]
    42 p.

MONROE:

Callahan, James Morton. Semi-centennial history of West Virginia, by James Morton Callahan . . . with special articles on development and resources . . . [Charleston, W. Va.] Semi-centennial commission of West Virginia, 1913.
    ix, 594 p. 1 illus., plates, maps (part fold.) tables.

Lewis, Virgil Anson. History of West Virginia. In two parts . . . Philadelphia, Hubbard bros., 1889.
    744 p. pl.

MONTGOMERY:

Winston, R. A. Soil survey of Montgomery county, Virginia, by R. A. Winston and Ora Lee Jr.
    (In U. S. bureau of soils. Report, 1907.)

MORGAN:

Callahan, James Morton. Semi-centennial history of West Virginia, by James Morton Callahan . . . with special articles on development and resources . . . [Charleston, W. Va.] Semi-centennial commission of West Virginia, 1913.
    ix, 594 p. 1 illus., plates, maps (part fold.) tables.

Cartmell, Thomas Kemp. Shenandoah Valley pioneers and their descendants. A history of Frederick County, Virginia (illustrated), from its formation in 1738 to 1908. Comp. mainly from original records of old Frederick County, now Hampshire, Berkeley, Shenandoah, Jefferson, Hardy, Clarke, Warren, Morgan and Frederick . . . [Winchester, Va., Printed by the Eddy press corporation, 1909]
    vii, 587 p. plates.

Lewis, Virgil Anson. History of West Virginia. In two parts . . . Philadelphia, Hubbard bros., 1889.
    744 p. pl.

NANSEMOND:

> Dunn, Joseph Bragg. The history of Nansemond County, Virginia, by Jos. B. Dunn. [n. p., 1907]
> 71 p. incl. illus., front. (map)
>
> Montague, George William. History and genealogy of Peter Montague, of Nansemond and Lancaster counties, Virginia, and his descendants, 1621-1894. Comp. and pub. by George William Montague . . . Amherst, Mass., Press of Carpenter & Morehouse, 1894.
> 1 p. l., 494 p.
>
> Virginia magazine of history and biography. v. 5, 7.
>
> William and Mary college quarterly historical magazine. v. 4.

k NELSON (1785):

> Collins, Lewis. Collins' historical sketches of Kentucky. History of Kentucky . . . revised, enlarged . . . and brought down to . . . 1874, by R. H. Collins . . . Embracing pre-historic, annals for 331 years . . . statistics, antiquities and natural curiosities, geographical and geological descriptions . . . and . . . biographical sketches . . . Covington, Ky., Collins & Co., 1878.
> 2 v. fold. map.

NELSON (1808):

No separate history of this county is now in the Library.

NEW KENT:

> The Chesapeake & Ohio railway directory, containing an illustrated history and description of the road, together with improvements and connections already completed and those in contemplation; also, the names of the merchants, manufacturers, professional men, and farmers, with postoffice addresses in the counties of Elizabeth City, Warwick, York, James City, New Kent, Charles City, King William, Henrico . . . together with a description of the surface, soil, average value of lands, county and city officers, and other useful and valuable information. Compiled by J. H. Chataigne. 1881. c 1881 by J. H. Chataigne.
> 379 p.
>
> Davies, Samuel. The vessels of mercy, and the vessels of wrath, delineated, in a new, uncontroverted, and practical light. A sermon first preached in New Kent, Virginia, August 22, 1756. By Samuel Davies, A. M. London, Printed for J. Buckland, 1758.
> vi, 7-35 p.
>
> Page, John. A deed of gift to my dear son, Captain Matt. Page, one of his majesty's justices for New Kent county, in Virginia. 1687. Philadelphia, Henry B. Ashmead, 1856.
> ix, [11]-276 p.
> Preface by Bishop Meade of Virginia.

Saint Peter's parish, New Kent County, Va. The parish register of
Saint Peter's, New Kent County, Va., from 1680 to 1787, published
by The National society of the colonial dames of America in the
state of Virginia. Richmond, Wm. Ellis Jones, book and job printer,
1904.
2 p. l., 206 p.
(Parish record series. no. 2)

—— The vestry book of Saint Peter's, New Kent County, Va., from 1682-
1758. Pub. by the National society of the colonial dames of America
in the state of Virginia . . . Richmond, W. E. Jones, book and
job printer, 1905.
242 p.
(Parish record series, no. 3)

Webb, George. The office and authority of a justice of the peace.
And also the duty of sheriffs, coroners, churchwardens, surveiors
of highways, constables, and officers of militia. Together with precedents of warrants, judgments, executions, and other legal process,
issuable by magistrates within their respective jurisdictions, in cases
civil or criminal. And the method of judicial proceedings, before
justices of peace, in matters within their cognisance out of session.
Collected from the common and statute laws of England, and acts
of assembly, now in force; and adapted to the constitution and
practice of Virginia. By George Webb, gent. One of His Majesty's
justices of peace of the county of New-Kent. Williamsburg, Printed
by William Parks, 1736.
x, 364 p., 2 l.

William and Mary college quarterly historical magazine. v. 4, 5, 8.

• NEW NORFOLK:

This county existed only from 1636 to 1637. No separate history of
this county is now in the Library.

w NICHOLAS:

Callahan, James Morton. Semi-centennial history of West Virginia, by
James Morton Callahan . . . with special articles on development
and resources . . . [Charleston, W. Va.] Semi-centennial commission of West Virginia, 1913.
ix, 594 p. 1 illus., plates, maps (part fold.) tables.

Lewis, Virgil Anson. History of West Virginia. In two parts . . .
Philadelphia, Hubbard bros., 1889.
744 p. pl.

NORFOLK:

Democratic party. Virginia. Norfolk county. A political cancer; being
an abridged history of the Norfolk county conspiracy, and an inci-

dental personal controversy. Published by the Democratic executive committee of Norfolk county, Virginia. January, 1904.
16 p.

The lower Norfolk County, Virginia, antiquary. Edited by Edward W. James. v. 1-5. 1897-1906.
5 v.

Porter, John W. H. A record of events in Norfolk County, Virginia, from April 19, 1861, to May 10, 1862, with a history of the soldiers and sailors of Norfolk County, Norfolk City and Portsmouth, who served in the Confederate States army or navy. By John W. H. Porter, a comrade of Stonewall camp, Confederate veterans, of Portsmouth, Va. Portsmouth, Va., W. A. Fiske, printer, 1892.
366 p.

Stewart, William Henry. History of Norfolk County, Virginia, and representative citizens, edited and compiled by Col. William H. Stewart . . . 1637-1900. Published by Biographical publishing company, . . . Chicago, Ill., 1902.
1042 p. plates, map.

Virginia magazine of history and biography. v. 2, 7.

William and Mary college quarterly historical papers. v. 1.

NORTHAMPTON:

Segar, Joseph E. To the voters of Accomac and Northampton. n. p. [1863]
3 p.

The Virginia historical register and literary advertiser. v. 1, no. 4.

Virginia magazine of history and biography. v. 2, 4, 5, 10, 13.

William and Mary college quarterly historical papers. v. 1.

William and Mary college quarterly historical magazine. v. 5, 18.

NORTHUMBERLAND:

Manufacturers' record, Baltimore. Perpetuation of local history in Virginia [with lists of portraits and memorials in Westmoreland, King and Queen, Essex, Lancaster, Mathews, Middlesex, Northumberland, Gloucester and King William counties] a description of the work of Judge T. R. B. Wright.
13 p.
Reprinted from the Manufacturers' record, Baltimore, Md., July 25, 1907.

Richmond, Westmoreland, Lancaster, & Northumberland counties, Va. Board of immigration. The Northern Neck of Virginia as a home

for immigrants, by the board of immigration for the counties of Richmond, Westmoreland, Lancaster, & Northumberland, Virginia. New York, Schmidt & Curtius, stationers, 1872.
16 p. map.

William and Mary college quarterly historical magazine. v. 4, 8, 9, 11, 13, 17, 18, 20, 21, 22.

NOTTOWAY:

Irby, Richard. Historical sketch of the Nottoway Grays, afterwards Company G, Eighteenth Virginia regiment, Army of Northern Virginia; prepared at the request of the surviving members of the company at their first reunion at Bellefont church, July 21, 1877. By Richard Irby . . . Richmond, J. W. Fergusson & son, 1878.
48 p., 1 l.

w OHIO:

Callahan, James Morton. Semi-centennial history of West Virginia, by James Morton Callahan . . . with special articles on development and resources . . . [Charleston, W. Va.] Semi-centennial commission of West Virginia, 1913.
ix, 594 p. 1 illus., plates, maps (part fold.) tables.

Lewis, Virgil Anson. History of West Virginia. In two parts . . . Philadelphia, Hubbard bros., 1889.
744 p.

Newton, J. H. History of the Pan-handle; being historical collections of the counties of Ohio, Brooke, Marshall and Hancock, West Virginia . . . Comp. and written by J. H. Newton, G. G. Nichols, and A. G. Sprankle. Ed. by J. H. Newton. Wheeling, W. Va., J. A. Caldwell, 1879.
450 p., 1 l., xxx, [1] p. pl., 2 maps.

ORANGE:

Cottom's new Virginia almanack for the year of our Lord 1818 . . . Adapted to the latitude and meridian of Richmond. Calculated by Joseph Cave of Orange county, Virginia. Richmond, published annually by Peter Cottom and for sale in his book-stores in Richmond and Lynchburg [1817]
36 p.

Goshen Baptist association. Minutes of the one hundred and eighteenth session of the Goshen Baptist association held with Zion church, Orange Co., Va., September 6-8, 1910 . . . Richmond press, Inc., printers, Richmond, Virginia, 1910.
31 p.

Payne, John. Payne's vindication; addressed to the people of Virginia . . . Printed and published for John Payne, of Orange County, Va., 1838.
36 p.

Scott, William Wallace. A history of Orange County, Virginia, from
its formation in 1734 (o. s.) to the end of reconstruction in 1870;
compiled mainly from original records, with a brief sketch of the
beginnings of Virginia, a summary of local events to 1907, and a
map. By W. W. Scott . . . Richmond, Va., E. Waddey co., 1907.
292 p. 17 pl. double map.

William and Mary college quarterly historical magazine. v. 4, 5, 6.

Woolfolk, C. W. Directory of the counties of Orange, Louisa, Albemarle, Culpeper and Spotsylvania. Comp. and for sale by C. W.
Woolfolk, Orange, Va., W. J. Daniel, Bibb's, Va. 1895. [Richmond,
Va., Ware & Duke, general printers, 1895.]
1, 267 p.

——Orange County directory. Comp. and for sale by C. W. Woolfolk,
Orange, Va. 1894. Lynchburg, Va., J. P. Bell co., book, job and
commercial printers, 1894.
60 p.

PAGE:

Mason, Otis Tufton. Report of a visit to the Luray Cavern, in Page
County, Virginia, under the auspices of the Smithsonian institution, July 13 and 14, 1880.
(In Smithsonian institution. Annual report of the Board of regents.
. . . 1880. Washington, 1881. illus.)

PATRICK:

No separate history of this county is now in the Library.

w PENDLETON:

Callahan, James Morton. Semi-centennial history of West Virginia, by
James Morton Callahan . . . with special articles on development
and resources . . . [Charleston, W. Va.] Semi-centennial commission of West Virginia, 1913.
ix, 594 p. 1 illus., plates, maps (part fold.) tables.

Lewis, Virgil Anson. History of West Virginia. In two parts . . .
Philadelphia, Hubbard bros., 1889.
744 p. pl.

Morton, Oren Frederic. A history of Pendleton County, West Virginia,
by Oren F. Morton . . . Franklin, W. Va., The author, 1910.
viii, 493 p. front. (fold. map) plates.

PITTSYLVANIA:

Virginia magazine of history and biography. v. 16, 17, 20, 22.

William and Mary college quarterly historical magazine. v. 6, 7, 20.

w PLEASANTS:

    Callahan, James Morton. Semi-centennial history of West Virginia, by James Morton Callahan . . . with special articles on development and resources . . . [Charleston, W. Va.] Semi-centennial commission of West Virginia, 1913.
        ix, 594 p. 1 illus., plates, maps (part fold.) tables.

    Lewis, Virgil Anson. History of West Virginia. In two parts . . . Philadelphia, Hubbard bros., 1889.
        744 p. pl.

w POCAHONTAS:

    Callahan, James Morton. Semi-centennial history of West Virginia, by James Morton Callahan . . . with special articles on development and resources . . . [Charleston, W. Va.] Semi-centennial commission of West Virginia, 1913.
        ix, 594 p. 1 illus., plates, maps (part fold.) tables.

    Lewis, Virgil Anson. History of West Virginia. In two parts . . . Philadelphia, Hubbard bros., 1889.
        744 p. pl.

POWHATAN:

    Tyree, Cornelius. The living epistle: or, The moral power of a religious life. By Cornelius Tyree, of Powhatan county, Va. With an introduction by Rev. R. Fuller, D. D. New York, Sheldon & co., Richmond, T. J. Starke, 1859.
        185 p.

    Virginia magazine of history and biography. v. 5.

    Wesson, William H. "Calais-morale"; or, Fifty years' gleanings in the sea of readings. By Wm. H. Wesson, of Calais, Powhatan County, Virginia . . . Richmond, Va., Patrick Keenan, book publisher and printer, 1882.
        1 l., 288 p.

w PRESTON:

    Callahan, James Morton. Semi-centennial history of West Virginia, by James Morton Callahan . . . with special articles on development and resources . . . [Charleston, W. Va.] Semi-centennial commission of West Virginia, 1913.
        ix, 594 p. 1 illus., plates, maps (part fold.) tables.

    Lewis, Virgil Anson. History of West Virginia. In two parts . . . Philadelphia, Hubbard bros., 1889.
        744 p. pl.

Morton, Oren Frederic. A history of Preston County, West Virginia, by Oren F. Morton . . . Kingwood, W. Va., The Journal publishing company, 1914.
>2 v. plates.

Wiley, Samuel T. History of Preston county (West Virginia). By S. T. Wiley, assisted by A. W. Frederick, Kingwood, W. Va., The Journal printing house, 1882.
> xv, 529 p.

PRINCE EDWARD:

Dorsey, Sarah A. Recollections of Henry Watkins Allen, Brigadier-General Confederate States Army, ex-Governor of Louisiana. New York, M. Doolady; New Orleans, James A. Gresham [c 1866]
> 420 p.
>> Gov. Allen was born in Prince Edward County, Virginia, April 29, 1820.

Jeter, Jeremiah Bell. The life of Rev. Daniel Witt, D. D., of Prince Edward County, Virginia. By J. B. Jeter. Richmond, J. T. Ellyson, 1875.
> 267 p.

Randolph, John. To the freeholders of Charlotte, Buckingham, Prince Edward and Cumberland [containing a speech on the intended declaration of war against Great Britain, May 30, 1812] [n. p., 1812]
> 14 p.

William and Mary college quarterly historical magazine. v. 11.

PRINCE GEORGE:

[Bland, Richard]. A letter to the clergy of Virginia, in which the conduct of the General assembly is vindicated against the reflexions contained in a letter to the Lords of trade and plantations, from the Lord-bishop of London. By Richard Bland, esq.; one of the representatives in assembly for the county of Prince-George. . . . Williamsburg, Printed by William Hunter, 1760.
> vi, 3-20 p.

Bland, Theodorick, jr. The Bland papers: being a selection from the manuscripts of Colonel Theodorick Bland, jr., of Prince George county, Virginia. To which are prefixed an introduction and memoir of Colonel Bland . . . Edited by Charles Campbell. Petersburg, Printed by Edmund and Julian C. Ruffin, 1840-1843.
> 2 v.

Cooke, John Esten. Henry St. John, gentleman, of "Flower of Hundreds," in the County of Prince George, Virginia. A tale of 1774-'75 . . . New York, Harper & brothers, 1859.
> [xvi], [17]-503 p.

Haywood, Marshall De Lancey. Lives of the bishops of North Carolina from the establishment of the episcopate in that state down to the division of the diocese . . . Raleigh, N. C., Alfred Williams & company, 1910.
> 270 p. plates.
> Includes the lives of John Stark Ravenscroft, born in Prince George County, Va., May 17, 1772; and Thomas Atkinson, born near Petersburg, Aug. 6, 1807.

Rives, Timothy. Speech of Mr. Timothy Rives, of Prince George and Surry, in the Virginia state convention, on the 29th March, 1861, report of the Committee on federal relations being under consideration in committee of the whole. Richmond, Printed by Chas. H. Wynne [1861]
> (In Political pamphlets. v. 38.)

Spooner, John Jones. Topographical description of the county of Prince George, in Virginia, 1793. By the Rev. John Jones Spooner, rector of Martin's Brandon, in said county.
> (In Massachusetts historical society. Collections. v. 3, 1794)

Virginia magazine of history and biography. v. 4, 6.

William and Mary college quarterly historical magazine. v. 14.

PRINCE WILLIAM:

Hunter, Alexander. The women of the Debatable land, by Alexander Hunter . . Illustrated by Miss Elizabeth C. Harmon. Washington, D. C., Cobden publishing company, 1912.
> viii p., 2 l., 261 p. illus., plates fold. map.
> The region comprises the counties of Fairfax, Prince William, Culpeper and Fauquier, Va.

The Manassas journal, Manassas, Va., May 19, 1911.
> [4], 40 p.
> Contains much historical information concerning Manassas and Prince William County.

Dunlop, William. William Dunlop's library from the appraisal of his estate in Prince William county, Virginia, May 25, 1740, reported by Captain Benjamin Grayson.
> (In William and Mary college quarterly historical magazine. v. 15)

PRINCESS ANNE:

The lower Norfolk County, Virginia, antiquary. Edited by Edward W. James. v. 1-5. 1897-1906.
> 5 v.

Sherwood, Grace. Record of Grace Sherwood's trial for witchcraft, in 1705, in Princess Anne county, Virginia. Presented by . . . [J. P.] Cushing, to the Virginia historical and philosophical society on the 4th of February, 1833.
> (In Virginia historical society. Collections. Richmond, 1833. old series, v. 1)

Virginia historical and philosophical society. Collections. v. 1.

Virginia magazine of history and biography. v. 2, 6, 7.

William and Mary college quarterly historical papers. v. 1, 2.

William and Mary college quarterly historical magazine. v. 3.

PULASKI:

No separate history of this county is now in the Library.

w PUTNAM:

Callahan, James Morton. Semi-centennial history of West Virginia, by James Morton Callahan . . . with special articles on development and resources . . . [Charleston, W. Va.] Semi-centennial commission of West Virginia, 1913.
ix, 594 p. 1 illus., plates, maps (part fold.) tables.

Lewis, Virgil Anson. History of West Virginia. In two parts . . . Philadelphia, Hubbard bros., 1889.
744 p. pl.

w RALEIGH:

Callahan, James Morton. Semi-centennial history of West Virginia, by James Morton Callahan . . . with special articles on development and resources . . . [Charleston, W. Va.] Semi-centennial commission of West Virginia, 1913.
ix, 594 p. 1 illus., plates, maps (part fold.) tables.

Lewis, Virgil Anson. History of West Virginia. In two parts . . . Philadelphia, Hubbard bros., 1889.
744 p. pl.

w RANDOLPH:

Callahan, James Morton. Semi-centennial history of West Virginia, by James Morton Callahan . . . with special articles on development and resources . . . [Charleston, W. Va.] Semi-centennial commission of West Virginia, 1913.
ix, 594 p. 1 illus., plates, maps (part fold.) tables.

Lewis, Virgil Anson. History of West Virginia. In two parts . . . Philadelphia, Hubbard bros., 1889.
744 p. pl.

e RAPPAHANNOCK (1656):

This county existed only from 1656-1692. No separate history of this county is now in the Library.

Virginia magazine of history and biography. v. 5.

RAPPAHANNOCK (1833):

No separate history of this county is now in the Library.

RICHMOND:

Richmond, Westmoreland, Lancaster, & Northumberland counties, Va. Board of immigration. The Northern Neck of Virginia as a home for immigrants, by the board of immigration for the counties of Richmond, Westmoreland, Lancaster & Northumberland, Virginia. New York, Schmidt & Curtius, stationers, 1872.
16 p. map.

Virginia magazine of history and biography. v. 7.

William and Mary college quarterly historical magazine. v. 5, 11, 13, 17.

w RITCHIE:

Callahan, James Morton. Semi-centennial history of West Virginia, by James Morton Callahan . . . with special articles on development and resources . . . [Charleston, W. Va.] Semi-centennial commission of West Virginia, 1913.
ix, 594 p. 1 illus., plates, maps (part fold.) tables.

Lewis, Virgil Anson. History of West Virginia. In two parts . . . Philadelphia, Hubbard bros., 1889.
744 p. pl.

w ROANE:

Callahan, James Morton. Semi-centennial history of West Virginia, by James Morton Callahan . . . with special articles on development and resources . . . [Charleston, W. Va.] Semi-centennial commission of West Virginia, 1913.
ix, 594 p. 1 illus., plates, maps (part fold.) tables.

·Lewis, Virgil Anson.· History of West Virginia. In two parts . . . Philadelphia, Hubbard bros., 1889.
744 p. pl.

ROANOKE:

Stearnes, O. L. Tax segregation and tax reform by O. L. Stearnes, member of the House of Delegates from Roanoke Co. [n. p. 1915?]
31 p.

ROCKBRIDGE:

Claiborne, J. F. H. Life and times of Gen. Sam. Dale, the Mississippi partisan . . . Illustrated by John M'Lenan. New York, Harper & brothers, 1860.
233 p. plates.
Gen. Dale was born in Rockbridge Co., Va.

Paxton, John D. A memoir of J. D. Paxton, D. D., late of Princeton, Indiana. Philadelphia, J. B. Lippincott & co., 1870.
>xi [13]-258 p.
>Dr. Paxton was born in Rockbridge Co., Va., in 1784.

Ridenbaugh, Mary Young. The biography of Ephraim McDowell, M. D., "the father of ovariotomy". By his granddaughter, Mary Young Ridenbaugh. Together with valuable scientific treatises and articles relating to ovariotomy, and eulogistic letters from eminent members of the medical profession in Europe and America. New York, Charles L. Webster and company, 1890.
>xvi, 558 p. pl.
>Dr. McDowell was born in Rockbridge County, Va., Nov. 11, 1771.

Valentine, Edward Pleasants. Report of the exploration of the Hayes' Creek mound, Rockbridge county, Va. Pub. by the Valentine Museum, Richmond, Va., 1901?
>1 l., diagr., 6 pl. 24x32cm.

ROCKINGHAM:

Ruffner, Anne H. Robert Gray, of Rockingham. By Anne H. Ruffner.
>(In The Scotch-Irish society of America. Seventh congress. 1895.)

Virginia magazine of history and biography. v. 7.

[Wayland, John W.] Bibliography [of Rockingham county, Va.]
>(In his A history of Rockingham county, Virginia. 1912.)

Wayland, John Walter. A history of Rockingham County, Virginia, by John W. Wayland . . . Dayton, Va., Ruebush-Elkins company, 1912.
>4 p. l., v-vii, [2], 10-466, [7] p. 1 illus., plates, maps. (part fold.)

——Writers and printers: books and periodicals [of Rockingham county, Va.]
>(In his A history of Rockingham county, Virginia. 1912.)

William and Mary college quarterly historical magazine. v. 13.

RUSSELL:

No separate history of this county is now in the Library.

SCOTT:

[Addington, Robert M.] The old-time school in Scott County . . . East Radford, Va. [1914]
>37 p.
>(The Radford normal bulletin. v. 2, no. 2)

SHENANDOAH:

Cartmell, Thomas Kemp. Shenandoah Valley pioneers and their descendants. A history of Frederick County, Virginia (illustrated),

from its formation in 1738 to 1908. Comp. mainly from original records of old Frederick County, now Hampshire, Berkeley, Shenandoah, Jefferson, Hardy, Clarke, Warren, Morgan and Frederick . . . [Winchester, Va., Printed by the Eddy press corporation, 1909]
vii, 587 p. plates.

Ireland, James. The life of the Rev. James Ireland, who was, for many years, pastor of the Baptist church at Buck Marsh, Waterlick and Happy Creek, in Frederick and Shenandoah counties, Virginia. Winchester, Va., Printed for the publishers by J. Foster, 1819.
232 p.

Pence, Kingsley Adolphus. The history of Judge John Pence and descendants, born in Shenandoah County, Virginia, January 15, 1775. Resided in Champaign County, Ohio, Bartholomew County, Indiana, and Henderson County, Illinois. Comp. and pub. by Kingsley Adolphus Pence, his grandson . . . Denver, Col., 1912.
126 p. plates.

SMYTH:

Sheffey, John P. General resources and advantages of Smyth County, in the most attractive section of Appalachian Virginia; comp. by John P. Sheffey, and printed by order of the Board of supervisors, in the year of the Jamestown exposition, 1907. [Roanoke, Va., The Stone printing & manufacturing co., 1907]
63 p. [1] p. illus.

SOUTHAMPTON:

[Account of the Southampton (Nat Turner's) insurrection; in the biography of Nat Turner]
(In National cyclopedia of American biography, vol. xiii, p. 597)

Asplund, John. The annual register of the Baptist denomination, in North America; to the first of November, 1790. Containing an account of the churches and their constitutions, ministers, members, associations, their plan and sentiments, rule and order, proceedings and correspondence. Also remarks upon practical religion. Humbly offered to the public, by John Asplund. [1791]
iv, 5-70 p.
Preface dated Southampton County, Virginia, July 14, 1791.

Authentic and impartial narrative of the tragical scene which was witnessed in Southampton County (Virginia) on Monday the 22d of August last, when fifty five of its inhabitants (mostly women and children) were inhumanly massacred by the blacks! Communicated by those who were eye witnesses of the bloody scene, and confirmed by the confessions of several of the blacks while under sentence of death. Printed for Warner & West, 1831.
[3]-38 p.

De Jarnette, Eva M. Parable of the untold gold by Eva M. De Jarnette; The Nat Turner insurrection, by William H. Parker; The hidden path to Long Ridge, by William H. Stewart; Progress of the South, [by] William H. Stewart. [no place. no date]
    43 p. 20cm.

Drewry, William Sidney. Southampton insurrection. Washington, The Neale co., 1900.
    201 p. pl., port. maps.

Gray, Thomas R. The confessions of Nat Turner, the leader of the late insurrection in Southampton, Va. As fully and voluntarily made to Thomas R. Gray, in the prison, where he was confined, and acknowledged by him to be such when read before the Court of Southampton; with the certificate under seal of the Court convened at Jerusalem, Nov. 5, 1831, for his trial. Also, an authentic account of the whole insurrection, with lists of the whites who were murdered, and of the negroes brought before the Court of Southampton, and there sentenced, etc. Baltimore, Thomas R. Gray, 1831.
    23 p. 19cm.

Same ——. Richmond. 1832.
    24 p. 19.5cm.

Virginia magazine of history and biography. v. 22.

Wallace, Charles M. The light dragoons.
    (In Southern historical society papers. v. 29, p. 366-371)

SPOTSYLVANIA:

Crozier, William Armstrong. Virginia county records. Spotsylvania county, 1721-1800 . . . New York, Published for the Genealogical ass'n by Fox, Duffield & co., 1905.
    vii, 576 p.
    (Virginia county records. v. 1)

Slaughter, Philip. History of St. George's parish, in the county of Spotsylvania, and diocese of Virginia . . . New York, 1847.
    61 [1] p.

——History of St. George's parish, in the county of Spotsylvania, and diocese of Virginia . . . Edited by R. A. Brock, with a biography by the author, and a continuation, embracing the history of St. George's and Trinity churches to the present time. Richmond, Va., J. W. Randolph & English, 1890.
    xix, 78 p. pl.

Virginia magazine of history and biography. v. 4.

William and Mary college quarterly historical papers. v. 1.

William and Mary college quarterly historical magazine. v. 11, 19.

Woolfolk, C. W. Directory of the counties of Orange, Louisa, Albemarle, Culpeper and Spotsylvania. Comp. and for sale by C. W. Woolfolk, Orange, Va., W. J. Daniel, Bibb's, Va. 1895. [Richmond, Va., Ware & Duke, general printers, 1895]
 1, 267 p.

STAFFORD:

 Boogher, William Fletcher. Virginia. Overwharton parish register, 1720 to 1760. Old Stafford County. Washington, D. C., The Saxton printing co., 1899.
  xiii, [1], 195 p.

 Virginia magazine of history and biography. v. 8.

 William and Mary college quarterly historical magazine. v. 15.

SURRY:

 Jones, Benjamin Washington. Battle roll of Surry County, Virginia, in the war between the states, with historical and personal notes . . . [By] B. W. Jones. Richmond, Everett Waddey company, 1913.
  70 p.

 Mason, Richard. The gentleman's new pocket farrier, comprising a general description of the noble and useful animal, the horse . . . by Richard Mason, M. D., formerly of Surry County, Virginia. 6th ed., with additions. To which is added, a prize essay on mules; and an appendix . . . also, an addenda, containing annals of the turf, American stud book, rules for training, racing, etc. Richmond, Printed by P. Cottom, 1835.
  419 p. plates.

 Rives, Timothy. Speech of Mr. Timothy Rives, of Prince George and Surry, in the Virginia state convention, on the 29th March, 1861, report of the Committee on federal relations being under consideration in committee of the whole. Richmond, Printed by Chas. H. Wynne [1861]
  (In Political pamphlets. v. 38)

 Surry county negro farmers' fair. Catalogue of the first annual exhibition of the Surry County negro farmers' fair, Lebanon Baptist church, Surry County, Va., Wednesday, November 3, 1915. [1915]
  13 [5] p.

 Virginia magazine of history and biography. v. 5.

 William and Mary college quarterly historical magazine. v. 3, 5, 8, 10, 11, 15, 16.

SUSSEX:

 Cocke, William B. Sussex County, Virginia, the home seeker's paradise. A guide to homeseekers and investors . . . Compiled prin-

cipally by Commissioner William B. Cocke, Booker, Va. Richmond, Va., Williams printing co., 1907.
 16 p. illus.

Virginia magazine of history and biography. v. 19, 21.

William and Mary college quarterly historical magazine. v. 11, 12, 14.

w TAYLOR:

Callahan, James Morton. Semi-centennial history of West Virginia, by James Morton Callahan . . . with special articles on development and resources . . . [Charleston, W. Va.] Semi-centennial commission of West Virginia, 1913.
 ix, 594 p. 1 illus., plates, maps (part fold.) tables.

Lewis, Virgil Anson. History of West Virginia. In two parts . . . Philadelphia, Hubbard bros., 1889.
 744 p. pl.

TAZEWELL:

Bickley, George W. L. History of the settlement and Indian wars of of Tazewell county, Virginia. Cincinnati, Morgan & co., 1852.
 267 p. pl. map.

w TUCKER:

Callahan, James Morton. Semi-centennial history of West Virginia, by James Morton Callahan . . . with special articles on development and resources . . . [Charleston, W. Va.] Semi-centennial commission of West Virginia, 1913.
 ix, 594 p. 1 illus., plates, maps (part fold.) tables.

Lewis, Virgil Anson. History of West Virginia. In two parts . . . Philadelphia, Hubbard bros., 1889.
 744 p. pl.

w TYLER:

Callahan, James Morton. Semi-centennial history of West Virginia, by James Morton Callahan . . . with special articles on development and resources . . . [Charleston, W. Va.] Semi-centennial commission of West Virginia, 1913.
 ix, 594 p. 1 illus., plates, maps (part fold.) tables.

Lewis, Virgil Anson. History of West Virginia. In two parts . . . Philadelphia, Hubbard bros., 1889.
 744 p. pl.

e UPPER NORFOLK:

This county existed only from 1637-1645/6. No separate history of this county is now in the Library.

w UPSHUR:

Callahan, James Morton. Semi-centennial history of West Virginia, by James Morton Callahan . . . with special articles on development and resources . . . [Charleston, W. Va.] Semi-centennial commission of West Virginia, 1913.
ix, 594 p. 1 illus., plates, maps (part fold.) tables.

Lewis, Virgil Anson. History of West Virginia. In two parts . . . Philadelphia, Hubbard bros., 1889.
744 p. pl.

WARREN:

Cartmell, Thomas Kemp. Shenandoah Valley pioneers and their descendants. A history of Frederick County, Virginia (illustrated), from its formation in 1738 to 1908. Comp. mainly from original records of old Frederick County, now Hampshire, Berkeley, Shenandoah, Jefferson, Hardy, Clarke, Warren, Morgan and Frederick . . . [Winchester, Va., Printed by the Eddy press corporation, 1909]
vii, 587 p. plates.

Randolph-Macon academy, Front Royal, Va. Randolph-Macon academy at Front Royal the county seat of Warren county in the northern end of the Shenandoah Valley of Virginia. [Lynchburg, Va., J. P. Bell co.]
47 p. illus.

Yerger, Jacob S. Decision of Judge Jacob S. Yerger, on the stay law. Delivered at the December term of the circuit court of Warren County. [n. p.], Printed at the Daily herald book and job office, 1866.
12 p.

° WARROSQUYOAKE:

This county existed only from 1634-1637. No separate history of this county is now in the Library.

WARWICK:

The Chesapeake & Ohio railway directory, containing an illustrated history and description of the road, together with improvements and connections already completed and those in contemplation; also, the names of the merchants, manufacturers, professional men, and farmers, with postoffice addresses in the counties of Elizabeth City, Warwick, York, James City, New Kent, Charles City, King William, Henrico . . . together with a description of the surface, soil, average value of lands, county and city officers, and other useful and valuable information. Compiled by J. H. Chataigne. 1881. c 1881 by J. H. Chataigne.
379 p.

Segar, Joseph E. Remarks of Mr. Joseph Segar, (of Elizabeth City and Warwick,) on the bill to construct the mountain portion of the

Louisa railroad, and to tunnel the Blue Ridge Mountain. Richmond, Printed by Shepherd and Colin, 1849.
8 p.

—— Speech of Mr. Segar, of Elizabeth City and Warwick, on the election of state officers, delivered in the House of delegates, Wednesday, the 6th, and Tuesday, the 13th February, 1850. Richmond, H. K. Ellyson's power press, 1850.
21 p.

—— Speech of Mr. Joseph Segar, (of Elizabeth City and Warwick,) on the Wilmot proviso. Delivered in the House of delegates, Jan. 19, 1849. Richmond, Printed by Shepherd and Colin, 1849.
22 p.

William and Mary college quarterly historical magazine. v. 4, 6, 14.

• WARWICK RIVER:

This county existed only from 1634-1642/3. No separate history of this county is now in the Library.

WASHINGTON:

Draper, Lyman Copeland. King's Mountain and its heroes: history of the battle of King's Mountain, October 7th, 1780, and the events which led to it, by Lyman C. Draper, Secretary of the State historical society of Wisconsin . . . Cincinnati, P. G. Thomson, 1881.
xv, [6]-612 p. pl., map.
Contains many references to frontier Virginians. 400 of the militia of Washington County, Virginia, under Col. Wm. Campbell, took part in the battle.

Harris, Findlay. Virginia, Washington County, its location, climate, resources, attractions and advantages . . . Compiled at the request of The board of supervisors of Washington County, by Findlay Harris, Editor Abingdon Virginian, Abingdon, Va., nineteen hundred and seven. [Bristol, Tenn., The King printing co., 1907]
46 p. illus., map.

Summers, Lewis Preston. History of southwest Virginia, 1746-1786, Washington County, 1777-1870. By Lewis Preston Summers . . . Richmond, Va., J. L. Hill printing company, 1903.
921 p. illus., plates, map.

▼ WAYNE:

Callahan, James Morton. Semi-centennial history of West Virginia, by James Morton Callahan . . . with special articles on development and resources . . . [Charleston, W. Va.] Semi-centennial commission of West Virginia, 1913.
ix, 594 p. 1 illus., plates, maps (part fold.) tables.

Lewis, Virgil Anson. History of West Virginia. In two parts . . . Philadelphia, Hubbard bros., 1889.
744 p. pl.

WEBSTER:

    Callahan, James Morton. Semi-centennial history of West Virginia, by James Morton Callahan . . . with special articles on development and resources . . . [Charleston, W. Va.] Semi-centennial commission of West Virginia, 1913.
        ix, 594 p. 1 illus., plates, maps (part fold.) tables.

    Lewis, Virgil Anson. History of West Virginia. In two parts . . . Philadelphia, Hubbard bros., 1889.
        744 p. pl.

WESTMORELAND:

    Crozier, William Armstrong. . . . Westmoreland County; ed. by the late William Armstrong Crozier . . . and published posthumously by Mrs. Wm. Armstrong Crozier. Hasbrouck Heights, N. J., 1913.
        1 p. l., 102.
        (Virginia county record publications. New series. v. 1)

    Manufacturers' record, Baltimore. Perpetuation of local history in Virginia [with lists of portraits and memorials in Westmoreland, King and Queen, Essex, Lancaster, Mathews, Middlesex, Northumberland, Gloucester and King William counties] a description of the work of Judge T. R. B. Wright.
        13 p.
        Reprinted from the Manufacturers' record, Baltimore, Md., July 25, 1907.

    Mayo, Wat Tyler. A sketch of Yeocomico church (built 1706) in Cople parish, Westmoreland county, Va. With a reference to the bi-centennial celebration on July 15, 1906, and the movement to raise an endowment fund for the preservation of the church. By Wat Tyler Mayo, Walter Randolph Crabbe, S. Downing Cox, committee of the congregation. [1906]
        20 p. plates.

    Richmond, Westmoreland, Lancaster, & Northumberland counties, Va. Board of immigration. The Northern Neck of Virginia as a home for immigrants, by the board of immigration for the counties of Richmond, Westmoreland, Lancaster & Northumberland, Virginia. New York, Schmidt & Curtius, stationer, 1872.
        16 p. map.

    Virginia historical register and literary advertiser. v. 2, no. 1.

    Virginia magazine of history and biography. v. 10.

    William and Mary college quarterly historical magazine. v. 7, 8, 9, 11, 15.

    [Wright, Thomas Roane Barnes] . . . Westmoreland County, Virginia . . . A short chapter and bright day in its history; addresses

delivered by Lawrence Washington, esq., Rev. Randolph Harrison
McKim . . . and Rev. George Wm. Beale . . . at Montross, Va.,
May 3, 1910 . . . Richmond, Va., Whittet & Shepperson, printers,
1912.
153, xi p. plates.

w WETZEL:

Callahan, James Morton. Semi-centennial history of West Virginia, by
James Morton Callahan . . . with special articles on development
and resources . . . [Charleston, W. Va.] Semi-centennial commission of West Virginia, 1913.
ix, 594 p. 1 illus., plates, maps (part fold.) tables.

Lewis, Virgil Anson. History of West Virginia. In two parts . . .
Philadelphia, Hubbard bros., 1889.
744 p. pl.

w WIRT:

Callahan, James Morton. Semi-centennial history of West Virginia, by
James Morton Callahan . . . with special articles on development
and resources . . . [Charleston, W. Va.] Semi-centennial commission of West Virginia, 1913.
ix, 594 p. 1 illus., plates, maps (part fold.) tables.

Lewis, Virgil Anson. History of West Virginia. In two parts . . .
Philadelphia, Hubbard bros., 1889.
744 p. pl.

WISE:

McCreath, Andrew Smith. Geological and chemical report on a portion
of the Virginia and Tennessee coal and iron company's property,
embracing about 15,000 acres along the Clinch Valley division of
the Norfolk and Western R. R., Wise County, Virginia, by Messrs.
A. S. McCreath and E. V. D'Invilliers. [n. p. 1892]
iv, 67 p.

St. Paul, Virginia. Ordinances and by-laws of St. Paul, Wise County,
Virginia. Together with certain general laws relating to the government of towns. [1915]
59 p.

w WOOD:

Callahan, James Morton. Semi-centennial history of West Virginia, by
James Morton Callahan . . . with special articles on development
and resources . . . [Charleston, W. Va.] Semi-centennial commission of West Virginia, 1913.
ix, 594 p. 1 illus., plates, maps (part fold.) tables.

Lewis, Virgil Anson. History of West Virginia. In two parts . . . Philadelphia, Hubbard bros., 1889.
744 p. pl.

k WOODFORD:

Collins, Lewis. Collins' historical sketches of Kentucky. History of Kentucky . . . revised, enlarged . . . and brought down to . . . 1874, by . . . R. H. Collins . . . Embracing pre-historic, annals for 331 years . . . statistics, antiquities and natural curiosities, geographical and geological descriptions . . . and . . . biographical sketches . . . Covington, Ky., Collins & Co., 1878.
2 v. fold. map.

w WYOMING:

Callahan, James Morton. Semi-centennial history of West Virginia, by James Morton Callahan . . . with special articles on development and resources . . . [Charleston, W. Va.] Semi-centennial commission of West Virginia, 1913.
ix, 594 p. 1 illus., plates, maps (part fold.) tables.

Lewis, Virgil Anson. History of West Virginia. In two parts. . . . Philadelphia, Hubbard bros., 1889.
744 p. pl.

WYTHE:

Heuser, H. M. A short historical and physical description of Wythe County, Virginia . . . Published by order of the Board of supervisors for distribution at the Jamestown ter-centennial exposition, 1907. Compiled by H. M. Heuser, Wytheville, Virginia.
35 p. illus.

e YOHOGANIA:

This county existed only from 1776-1786.

Callahan, James Morton. Semi-centennial history of West Virginia, by James Morton Callahan . . . with special articles on development and resources . . . [Charleston, W. Va.] Semi-centennial commission of West Virginia, 1913.
ix, 594 p. 1 illus., plates, maps (part fold.) tables.

Lewis, Virgil Anson. History of West Virginia. In two parts . . . Philadelphia, Hubbard bros., 1889.
744 p.

Hassler, Edgar Wakefield. Old Westmoreland: a history of western Pennsylvania during the revolution. By Edgar W. Hassler. Pittsburg, J. R. Weldin & co., 1900.
4, vi, 5-200 p.

YORK:

The Chesapeake & Ohio railway directory, containing an illustrated history and description of the road, together with improvements and connections already completed and those in contemplation; also, the names of the merchants, manufacturers, professional men, and farmers, with postoffice addresses in the counties of Elizabeth City, Warwick, York, James City, New Kent, Charles City, King William, Henrico . . . together with a description of the surface, soil, average value of lands, county and city officers, and other useful and valuable information. Compiled by J. H. Chataigne. 1881. c 1881 by J. H. Chataigne.
    379 p.

Hall, John Leslie. Ancient epitaphs and inscriptions, in York and James City counties, Virginia. A paper read before the Virginia historical society Monday, December 21, 1891, by Prof. J. L. Hall . . . Richmond, 1892.
    (In Virginia historical society. Collections. Richmond, 1892. new ser., v. 11)

William and Mary college quarterly historical papers. v. 1, 2.

William and Mary college quarterly historical magazine. v. 8, 9, 11, 12, 13, 14, 20, 22.

INDEX

Note.—Only the county formed (the child-county) is indexed, except in the case of the charts,—no notice being taken of the parent-counties; for reference to the name of any county (in Parts I to III) will show all legislation taking territory from that county.

The six references immediately following the name of each county are to the Alphabetical, Chronological, Geographical, and "Genealogical" arrangements (Parts I, II, III, IV), the Origin of County Names (Part V), and the Bibliography (Part VII), respectively; while references to the Texts (Part VI) follow under their several counties. The reference "M" is to the maps inserted opposite p. 124 (in Part III), and the reference "C", followed by a numeral, is to the chart of that number in Part IV.

A.

Abbreviations, used in text....... 21
Accawmack (1634), 42, 90, 125 (M), C. 1, 173, 210
   bounds and population of.... 36
Accomack (1663), 42, 93, 128 (M), C. 1, 173, 210
   proceedings of first court of... 5
   two counties by name of...... 14
Acknowledgments 20
Acts of Assembly, not in Hening, Part VI 6, 18, 197
   unpublished 19
Albemarle, 42, 97, 133 (M), C. 5, 173, 211
   efforts to save records of..14, 73
Alexandria, 42, 119, 138, C. 9, 174, 212
Alleghany, 42, 116, 155, C. 9 a, 174, 213
Alphabetical section (of Preface), 14
   arrangement 41
Amelia 43, 96, 132 (M), C. 2, 174, 213
Amherst, 43, 100, 135, C. 5, 174, 213
Appomattox, 43, 119, 138, C. 5, 174, 214
Appomattox River, Smith explores 25
Argall, arrives and finds conditions poor 29
   charges against 29
Argall's Gift, located (1617)...... 28
   burgesses from, in First Assembly ....30, n.
   location of 31
Archer's Hope, located (1619)..... 30
Augusta, 43, 98, 139 (M), C. 9 & 9 a, 175, 214

B.

Barbour, 44, 119, 157, C. 9 c, 175, 216
Bath,......44, 110, 150, C. 9 a, 175, 216
Bedford,......44, 99, 134, C. 2, 175, 217
Berkeley, 44, 101, 144 (M), C. 9, 175, 218
Berkeley (plantation), located (1619) 30
Bermuda Hundred, located (1612). 28
Bibliography (Section of Preface), 19
   (of Introductory) 39
   (of Bulletin), Part VII...... 209
Bland....45, 121, 159, C. 9 b, 175, 218
Boone,....45, 119, 157, C. 9 b, 175, 219
Botetourt, 45, 101, 140, C. 9 a & 9 b, 175, 219
Bourbon....45, 107, 147, C. 9 d, 175, 219
Brandon (Martin's), located (1617) 28
Braxton, 45, 117, 156, C. 9 c, 175, 219
Brooke, 45, 111, 150, C. 9 a, 176, 220
Brunswick, 46, 95, 131 (M), C. 2, 176, 220
   proceedings of first court of, 5, 75
   Masonic flag saves records of, 6, 76
Buchanan, 46, 121, 159, C. 9 b, 176, 220
Buckingham, 46, 100, 135, C. 5, 176, 221
Burgesses, election of, provided for 29
   origin of name..............30, n.
   in first General Assembly.... 30
   number in Assembly of 1625 35
   number in Assembly of 1632 35
   number in Assembly of 1632/3 35

C.

Cabell, 46, 114, 153, C. 9 b, 176, 221
Calhoun, 46, 121, 159, C. 9 c, 176, 221
Campbell....47, 106, 136, C. 2, 176, 221
Campbell's "History of Virginia", error in, and result of it......24, n.
Caroline, 47, 95, 130 (M), C. 9, 176, 222
   Act of Assembly forming.... 202
Carroll, 47, 118, 138, C. 9 b, 177, 222

Cattle, in colony (1618).......... 29
Census, see "Population".
Chaplin's Choice, located (1619).. 30
Charles City, 47, 90, 125 (M), C. 2,
　　　　　　　　　　　　177, 222
Charles City Hundred, located
　(1612) 28
　　location of 31
　　courts kept at 34
　　bounds and population of.... 36
Charles City Incorporation, located
　(1619) 29
Charles River, 47, 90, 125 (M), C. 3,
　　　　　　　　　　　　177, 223
　　bounds and population of..... 36
Charlotte, 47, 100, 135, C. 2, 177, 224
Charts ("Genealogical"), construc-
　tion of 16
　in Part IV 163
Chesterfield, 47, 99, 134 (M), C. 5,
　　　　　　　　　　　　177, 224
　　Act of Assembly forming.... 208
"Chickacoan" ("Chickawane", "Chick-
　acoun"), ... 9
Chickahominies, Dale makes agree-
　ment with 28
　　refuse to keep their agreement
　　　with Dale 28
　　fight with 28
Chickahominy River, Smith ex-
　plores 25
Chronological section of preface.. 14
　　arrangement (Part II)....... 89
Church, services after landing... 23
　　at Henricopolis (1611)....... 28
　　first Assembly meets in, at
　　　Jamestown 30
Clarke, 47, 117, 143, C. 9, 177, 225
Clay, 48, 121, 159, C. 9 c, 177, 226
Coastal Plain, see "Tidewater".
Colonists, number of, see "Population".
Company, see "London Company".
Counties (or shires), of 1634..... 36
　　use of word "county",......32, n.
　　bounds and population of.... 36
　　change of names of.......... 37
　　number existing (1634), 36,—
　　　(1640), 37, — (1648), 37, —
　　　(1656), 37, — (1673), 37, —
　　　(1700), 37, — (1754), 38, —
　　　(1775), 38, — (1792), 38, —
　　　　(1860), 38,—(1880), 38
Counties having no separate his-
　tories in State Library.......20, n.
County courts, origin of......... 34
County names, origin of, Part V.. 173
Courts, inferior, established (1623/4　34
　　outlying, established (1631/2) 35
Coxendale, part of Henricopolis
　(1611) 28
Craig, 48, 120, 158, C. 9 b, 177, 226

"Create", use of word, in Acts of
　Assembly forming counties..... 9
Culpeper, 48, 98, 133 (M), C. 9, 177, 226
　　Act of Assembly forming..... 204
Cumberland, 48, 98, 133 (M), C. 5,
　　　　　　　　　　　　178, 227
　　Act of Assembly forming..... 205
Curls, located (1612)............. 28

D.

Dale, Sir Thomas, arrives and ex-
　plores 127
　makes agreement with Chicka-
　　hominies 28
　military rule of, not helpful... 28
　tries to suppress tobacco cul-
　　ture 28
　Yeardley, "only Sir Thomas
　　Dale's Man", ... 28
Deaths, see "Mortality", "Population".
Delawarr, Lord, arrives and saves
　colony 27
　dies 29
"Denbigh (Denby), county of",... 9
Dickenson, 48, 121, 159, C. 9 b, 178, 228
Dinwiddie, 48, 99, 134, C. 2, 178, 228
Director of publication of Revolu-
　tionary military records....... 6
Discovery (pinnace), arrives (1607) 23
Doddridge, 48, 119, 157, C. 9 c, 178, 229
Dunmore, 49, 101, 140, C. 9, 178, 229
Dutch Gap 27

E.

East India Sea, efforts to reach.26, n.
Eastern Shore, burgess from..... 35
Elizabeth City, 49, 90, 125 (M),
　　　　　　　　　C. 4, 178, 229
　efforts to save records of..... 14
　courts to be kept at......... 34
　bounds and population of.... 36
　loss of records of........... 79
Essex, 49, 94, 129 (M), C. 9, 179, 230
"Erect", use of word, in Acts of
　Assembly forming counties.... 9
"Establish", use of word in Acts
　of Assembly forming counties.. 9
Extinct counties 8, 9
　definition of ....7, n.

F.

Fairfax, 49, 96, 132 (M), C. 9, 179, 231
Falls of Powhatan (James) River,
　first visit of white men to and
　erroneous date 24
　　Newport explores beyond.... 26
"Family Trees" (of counties), con-
　struction of 16
Fauquier, 49, 100, 134, C. 9, 179, 231

Fayette (1780), 49, 105, 146, C. 9 d, 179, 233
Fayette (1831), 49, 116, 155, C. 9 b, 179, 233
   two counties by name of..... 14
Fincastle, 50, 101, 140, C. 9 b, 179, 233
First Supply arrives............. 25
Flower de Hundred, located (1618) 29
   burgesses from, in first Assembly ....30, n.
   location of 31
   concentration at ....33, n.
Floyd, 50, 116, 137, C. 9 b, 179, 233
Fluvanna, 50, 104, 136, C. 5, 179, 233
"Form", use of word, in Acts of Assembly forming counties..... 9
Fort Charles, built............... 27
Fort Henry, built................ 27
Franklin, 50, 107, 136, C. 2, 179, 234
Frederick, 50, 97, 139 (M), C. 9, 180, 234

G.

Gates, Sir Thomas, military rule of, not helpful 28
   tries to suppress tobacco culture 28
General Assembly, Yeardley issues writs for 29
   first meets in church at Jamestown 30
   plantations represented in first 30
   members of first............. 30
   number of burgesses in, of 1625 35
   number of burgesses in, of 1632 35
   number of burgesses in, of 1632/3 35
General section of preface....... 6
"Genealogical" section of preface 16
   arrangement, Part IV........ 161
Geographical section of preface.. 15
   arrangement, Part III........ 123
Geological divisions of state..... 15
Giles, 51, 113, 152, C. 9 b, 180, 235
Gilmer, 51, 119, 157, C. 9 c, 180, 235
Gloucester, 51, 92, 127 (M), C. 3, 180, 235
Goochland, 52, 95, 131 (M), C. 5, 180, 236
   early exploration of (1608)... 26
   Act of Assembly forming..... 201
"Goodspeed" (ship), arrives (1607) 23
Gosnold, Capt. Bartholomew, of "Goodspeed" in 1607............ 23
"Graft", Argall charged with.... 29
Grayson, 52, 111, 137, C. 9 b, 180, 236
Greenbrier, 52, 104, 145, C. 9 b, 180, 237
Greene, 53, 118, 137, C. 9, 180, 237
Greensville, 53, 106, 130, C. 2, 181, 237

H.

Halifax, 53, 99, 134, C. 2, 181, 237

Hampton, "quarantine station" at (1610) ....27, n.
Hampshire, 53, 99, 144 (M), C. 9 a, 181, 237
Hancock, 53, 120, 157, C. 9 a, 181, 238
Hanover, 53, 95, 129 (M), C. 3, 181, 238
   efforts to save records of...14, 80
   Act of Assembly forming..... 200
Hardy, 53, 107, 147, C. 9 a, 181, 239
Harrison, 54, 106, 147, C. 9 c, 181, 240
Hening, Acts of Assembly not in.6, 18
Henrico, 54, 90, 125 (M), C. 5, 181, 240
   efforts to save records of....14, 80
Henricopolis, Dale builds......... 27
   Coxendale a part of.......... 28
Henricus Incorporation, located (1617) 29
   burgesses from, in first Assembly ....30, n.
   location of 31
   bounds and population of.... 36
Henry, 54, 102, 135, C. 2, 182, 241
Highland, 55, 120, 157, C. 9 a, 182, 241
Hogs, in colony (1618).......... 29
"Humble Petition" 34
Hundreds, status of............28, n.
Hunt, Rev. Robert, prayer offered by, at first landing............ 23

I.

Illinois, 55, 105, 146, C. 9 a, 182, 241
Instructions to colonists.......... 24
Introductory 23
Isle of Wight, 55, 91, 126 (M), C. 7, 182, 242
   Act of Assembly giving bounds of 197, 198
   Smith explores to............ 25

J.

Jackson, 55, 117, 156, C. 9 b, 182, 242
James City, 55, 90, 125 (M), C. 6, 183, 242
James Citty Incorporation, located (1617) 29
   burgesses from, in first Assembly ....30, n.
   location of 31
   bounds and population of.... 36
"James County", evidently transcriber's error for James City County 9
James River, first visit of white men to falls of, and erroneous date 24
Jamestown, first landing at...... 23
   abandoned, but saved by arrival of Delawarr.....27 and n.
   Argall finds poor conditions at 29
   proposal to abandon, rejected 33
   concentration at ....33, n.

280 Index

Jefferson (1780), 55, 105, 146, C. 9 d, 183, 243
Jefferson (1801), 55, 113, 152, C. 9, 183, 243
    two counties by name of..... 14
Jury trials 25
Jordan's Journey, located (1619).. 30
    concentration at ....33, n.

K.

Kanawha, 56, 109, 149, C. 9 b, 183, 243
Kentucky, 56, 103, 145, C. 9 b & 9 d, 183, 244
Kentucky (state), counties now in, 8, 9
Kentucky District................9, 82
Kiccoughtan, Smith explores to... 25
Kiccowtan Incorporation, located (1617) 29
    burgesses from, in first Assembly ....30, n.
    location of 31
    concentration at ....33, n.
    bounds and population of.... 36
King and Queen, 57, 93, 128 (M), C. 9, 183, 244
King Charles, follows father's policy towards colony 35
King George, 57, 94, 129 (M), C. 9, 183, 245
    Act of Assembly forming..... 199
King James, oppressive measures of 33
    demands surrender of charters 34
    good governors sent by...... 35
    dies 35
King's River, name of Powhatan River changed to.............. 24
    Smith explores 25
King William, 57, 94, 129 (M), C. 3, 184, 246
Knights of Horseshoe......37 and n.

L.

"Lady Rebecca", Pocahontas called 28
Lancaster, 57, 92, 127 (M), C. 9, 184, 247
    proceedings of first court of, 5, 83
Lawne's Plantation, located (1619) 30
    burgesses from, in first Assembly ....30, n.
    location of 31
Lee......57, 111, 150, C. 9 b, 184, 248
Lewis, 58, 115, 154, C. 9 c, 184, 248
Lincoln, 58, 105, 146, C. 9 b, 184, 248
Logan, 58, 116, 155, C. 9 b, 184, 248
London Company, accomplishments of 34
    king demands surrender of charters of 34
    dissolution of, not desired by colonists 34
    dissolved 34

Lottery, necessary to keep colony in existence 28
Loudoun, 58, 100, 134, C. 9, 184, 248
Louisa, 59, 96, 132 (M), C. 3, 184, 249
    efforts to save records of, 14, 8.
Lower Norfolk, 59, 91, 126 (M), C. 4, 184, 250
    bounds of 197
Lunenburg, 59, 98, 133 (M), C. 2, 184, 251

M.

McDowell, 59, 121, 159, C. 9 b, 184, 251
Madison (1786), 59, 107, 147, C. 9 d, 185, 251
Madison (1793), 59, 111, 137, C. 9, 185, 251
    two counties by name of..... 14
Map, illustrating geological divisions of State, see frontispiece.
Maps, unpublished 6, 15
Marion, 59, 118, 156, C. 9 c, 185, 252
Marshall, 60, 117, 156, C. 9 a, 185, 252
Martin's Brandon, located (1617) 28
    burgesses from, in first Assembly ....30, n.
    location of 31
Martin's Hundred, located (1618) 29
    burgesses from, in first Assembly ....30, n.
    location of 31
Mason (1789), 60, 108, 149, C. 9 d, 185, 252
Mason (1804), 60, 113, 152, C. 9 b, 185, 252
    two counties by name of..... 14
Masonic flag, Brunswick records saved by 6, 76
Massacre (1622) 33
Mathews, 60, 111, 130 C. 3, 185, 253
Matoax, Indian name of Pocahontas 28
Maycock's Plantation, located (1618) 29
Mecklenburg, 60, 100, 135, C. 2, 185, 253
Mercer (1786), 60, 107, 147, C. 9 d, 185, 254
Mercer (1837), 60, 117, 156, C. 9 b, 185, 254
    two counties by name of..... 14
Middlesex, 60, 93, 128 (M), C. 9, 185, 254
    proceedings of first court of, 5, 84
    efforts to save records of, 14, 85
Monocans, enemies of Powhatan.. 24
    country of, explored by Newport 26
Monongalia, 60, 102, 144, C. 9 a & 9 c, 186, 254
Monroe, 61, 112, 151, C. 9 b, 186, 255
Montgomery, 61, 103, 141, C. 9 b, 186, 255
Morgan, 62, 115, 155, C. 9, 186, 255
Mortality, see "Population".

Index 281

N.

Nemattenow, death of, ignored by governor 33
Nansemond, 62, 91, 127 (M), C. 4, 186, 256
   bounds of (1643) 198
Nansemond River, Dale "views".. 27
Nelson (1785), 62, 106, 147, C. 9 d, 186, 256
Nelson (1808), 62, 114, 137, C. 5, 186, 256
   two counties by name of.... 14
New Kent, 62, 93, 128 (M), C. 3, 186, 256
New Norfolk, 62, 91, 126 (M), C. 4, 186, 257
Newport, Capt. Christopher, commanded fleet of 1607 23
   explores Powhatan River to Falls and erects cross 24
   returns to England 25
   arrived with second supply.. 25
   explores Monacan country.... 26
   arrives and explores Potomack 28
Newport News, concentration at, 33, n.
Nicholas, 62, 115, 154, C. 9 b, 187, 257
Norfolk, 63, 93, 129 (M), C. 4, 187, 257
   records of 85
Northampton, 63, 92, 127 (M), C. 1, 187, 258
Northumberland, 63, 92, 127 (M), C. 9, 187, 258
Nottoway, 63, 109, 136, C. 2, 187, 259
Notes, assembled in series at end of Alphabetical Arrangement, Part I 73

O.

Ohio .... 63, 102, 145, C. 9 a, 187, 259
Orange, 64, 96, 132 (M), C. 9, 188, 259
Origin of county names 18, 175
Opechancanough, attempt of, to poison colony, ignored by governor 33

P.

Page .... 64, 117, 143, C. 9 a, 188, 260
Paspehay, concentration at ...... 33, n.
Patomack River (Potomac), Smith explores 25
   Newport explores 28
Patrick, 64, 110, 137, C. 2, 188, 260
Patuxent River, Smith explores.. 25
Pendleton, 64, 108, 149, C. 9 a, 188, 260
Piedmont Plateau, number of counties in 15
Pittsylvania, 64, 100, 135, C. 2, 188, 260
Plantations, status of .... 28, n.
Pleasants, 64, 121, 158, C. 9 c, 188, 261

Pocahontas, 65, 116, 155, C. 9 a, 188, 261
Pocahontas (Indian), marries Rolfe 28
   baptized 28
   dies at Gravesend 28
Point Comfort, settlement at 26
Population, (1607), 23,—(1608), 25, —(1609), 26,—(1610), 26, 27,—(1617), 28,—(1618), 29,—(1619), 29,—(1620), 32,—(1621), 33, n.,— to 1622, 32, n., 33, 34,—to 1625, 32, n.,—(1625), 32, n., 34,—(1628), 35,—(1629), 32, n.,—(1634), 32, n., — (1640), 37,— (1648), 37,—(1649), 32, n.,—(1659), 37,—1665), 32, n., — (1671), 37, —(1675), 37,—(1681), 32, n.,—(1700), 37,—(1715), 32, n.,—(1717), 38,—(1754), 38,—(1755), 32, n.,—(1775), 38,—(1776), 32, n., —(1860), 38
Potomack, see "Patomack".
Powhatan, 65, 104, 136, C. 5, 188, 261
Powhatan (Indian), Newport defers to wishes of 24
   dies 29
Powhatan River, see "James River".
Preface, alphabetical section 14
   chronological section 14
   general section 6-14
   "genealogical" section 16-18
   geographical section 15-16
   origin of county names 18
   texts of acts 18-19
   bibliography 19
Preston, 65, 115, 154, C. 9 c, 188, 261
Prince Edward, 65, 99, 134, C. 2, 189, 262
Prince George, 65, 94, 129 (M), C. 2, 189, 262
   Act of Assembly forming.... 199
Prince William, 65, 95, 131 (M), C. 9, 189, 263
Princess Anne, 65, 94, 129 (M), C. 4, 189, 263
Proctor, Mrs., Indians fought off by .... 33, n.
Pulaski, 65, 118, 143, C. 9 b, 189, 264
Putnam, 65, 120, 158, C. 9 b, 189, 264

Q.

"Quarantine" station .... 27, n.
Quarter courts, established 35

R.

Raleigh, 66, 120, 158, C. 9 b, 189, 264
Raleigh (Sir Walter), Sickelmore sent to seek lost colony of 26
   dies 29
Randolph, 66, 108, 148, C. 9 c, 189, 264
Rappahannock (1656), 66, 93, 128 (M), C. 9, 189, 264

Rappahannock (1833), 66, 117, 137, C. 9, 189, 265
  two counties by name of...... 14
Rappahannock River, Smith explores 25
Ratcliffe, Capt. John, of the "Discovery" of 1707................ 23
Religious services, from time of landing...................... 23
Revolutionary military records, director of publication of........ 6
Richmond, 66, 94, 129 (M), C. 9, 190, 265
Richmond (City), first visit of white men to site of.......... 24
Ritchie, 66, 118, 157, C. 9 c, 190, 265
Roane, 67, 121, 159, C. 9 b, 190, 265
Roanoke, 67, 118, 143, C. 9 b, 190, 265
Rochdale Hundred, located (1612) 28
Rockbridge, 67, 104, 141, C. 9 a, 190, 265
Rockingham, 67, 105, 142, C. 9 a, 190, 266
Rolfe, John, marries Pocahontas.. 28
  tobacco culture introduced by. 28
Russell, 67, 107, 148, C. 9 b, 190, 266

S.

Sail-cloth, used as church........ 23
Salt-works on Smith's Island, located (1614) 28
Sandys, Sir Edwin, liberal ideas of 26
  controls affairs 29
"Sarah Constant" (ship), arrives (1607) 23
Savage's Neck, located (1619).... 30
Scott, 68, 114, 153, C. 9 b, 190, 266
Second Charter, issued........... 26
Shenandoah, 68, 105, 142, C. 9, 191, 266
Shires 36
  use of word................36, n.
Shirley Hundred, located (1612).. 28
  concentration at............33, n.
Sicklemore, sent to look for Raleigh's lost colony............... 26
Smith, Capt. John, explores King's and Chickahominy Rivers...... 25
  explores Patuxent River...... 25
  explores Patomack River to Falls 25
  explores Rappahannock River to Falls 25
  explores Appomattox River... 25
  disapproves explorations west of Falls and charged with jealousy 26
Smith, Sir Thomas, resigns as treasurer 29
  accomplishments of administration of 29
Smith's Hundred, located (1617).. 28
  burgesses for, in first Assembly ....30, n.
  location of 31

Smith's Island, discovered and named 25
  salt-works located on (1614).. 28
Smyth, 68, 117, 143, C. 9 b, 191, 267
Southampton, 68, 99, 130 (M), C. 7, 191, 267
  Act of Assembly forming.... 206
Southampton, Earl of, controls affairs 29
Southampton Hundred, formerly Smith's Hundred 28
  concentration at............33, n.
South Sea, eager quest for....25, 26
"Southside", classification of..... 15
"Southwest", classification of..... 15
Spaniards, attack by, guarded against 26
Spotsylvania, 68, 95, 131 (M), C. 9, 191, 268
Spotswood, Governor, visits the Valley 37
Stafford, 68, 93, 131 (M), C. 9, 191, 269
  proceedings of first court of, 5, 87
"Starvation Time" (1610) 26
Surry, 68, 92, 128 (M), C. 6, 191, 269
Sussex.........69, 99, 130, C. 6, 191, 269

T.

Taylor, 69, 119, 157, C. 9 c, 191, 270
Tazewell, 69, 112, 151, C. 9 b, 191, 270
Tassautessus (or Englishmen), Chickahominies become 28
Texts of Acts of Assembly, not in Hening 6, 197
"Tidewater", number of counties in 15
Tobacco, excitement over, saves colony 28
  Dale and Gates try to suppress culture of 28
  Yeardley encourages culture of 28
  culture of, at expense of necessities 29
  influence of cultivation of.... 35
"Trans - Alleghany", number of counties in 15
Trials by jury.................... 25
Tucker....69, 121, 159, C. 9 c, 192, 270
Tyler....69, 114, 153, C. 9 a, 192, 270
Tyler, Lyon G., unpublished maps by 6

U.

"Unmasked Face", ... 34
Upper Norfolk, 70, 91, 126 (M), C. 4, 192, 270
  bounds of 197
Upshur, 70, 120, 158, C. 9 c, 192, 271
"Upper parts", courts to be kept for 35

V.

"Valley", number of counties in.. 15
Vessels arriving in 1607.......... 23

W.

War Department, permission of,
   to use report to............... 6
Warde's Plantation, located (1619) 30
   burgesses from, in first Assembly ....30, n.
   location of 31
Warren, 70, 117, 143 (M), C. 9, 192, 271
Warrosquyoake, 70, 91, 126 (M),
                              C. 7, 192, 271
   Smith visits 26
   courts to be kept for......... 35
   bounds and population of.... 36
Warwick, 70, 92, 127 (M), C. 8, 192, 271
Warwick River, 70, 91, 126 (M),
                                C. 8, 192, 272
   bounds and population of..... 36
Washington, 70, 103, 141, C. 9 b,
                                 192, 272
Wayne, 71, 118, 156, C. 9 b, 192, 272
Webster, 71, 121, 159, C. 9 b, 193, 273

West, Capt. Francis, becomes governor 35
West Augusta District.........9, 74
Westmoreland, 71, 93, 128 (M), C.
                                 9, 193, 273
Westover, located (1619)......... 30
West Virginia, counties now in... 8, 9
Wetzel, 71, 119, 157, C. 9 a, 193, 274
Weyanoke, located (1617)........ 28
Wirt....71, 120, 158, C. 9 c, 193, 274
Wise....71, 121, 159, C. 9 b, 193, 274
Wood, 71, 111, 150, C. 9 c, 193, 274
Woodford, 71, 108, 149, C. 9 b, 193, 275
Wyatt, active against Indians.... 35
Wythe, 72, 110, 143, C. 9 b, 193, 275
Wyoming, 72, 120, 158, C. 9 b, 193, 275

Y.

Yeardley, Sir George, tobacco culture encouraged by 28
   "only Sir Thomas Dale's Man" 28
   deputy-governor 28, 29
   arrives as governor.......... 29
   dies 35
Yohogania, 72, 102, 145, C. 9 a, 193, 275
York, 72, 92, 127 (M), C. 3, 193, 276
   changes in name of........... 36

www.ingramcontent.com/pod-product-compliance
Lightning Source LLC
Chambersburg PA
CBHW032002220426
43664CB00005B/112